The Citizen's Guide To
STATE-BY-STATE
MARIJUANA
LAWS

PAUL ARMENTANO

reset.me

The Citizen's Guide to State-By-State Marijuana Laws

reset.me

© 2015 Reset.me
3101 Clairmont Road • Suite C • Atlanta, GA 30329

This book is authorized and approved by the National Organization for the Reform of Marijuana Laws (NORML).

Correspondence concerning this book may be directed to Reset.me, Attn: The Citizen's Guide to State-By-State Marijuana Laws, at the address above.

ISBN: 0794843719
Printed in the United States of America

Please visit our website at Reset.me.

CONTENTS

THIS BOOK IS A NECESSARY COMPANION FOR CANNABIS CONSUMERS

It has been state and federal policy since 1937 to prohibit cannabis cultivation, sales and use — with the underpinning notion that these prohibitions are supposed to be a deterrent to crime. Yet, oddly, state and federal governments do *not* historically broadcast cannabis-related laws and their penalties to the general public. Therefore, it is with a degree of high irony that the National Organization for the Reform of Marijuana Laws (NORML) has, since its founding in 1970, been the primary public source in America for up-to-date and accurate information specific to state and federal pot penalties.

Ask 50 cannabis consumers in America what their state's marijuana laws and penalties are, and you will likely receive 50 different replies. That is because no state's cannabis laws are exactly alike. With our 50 states come 50 totally different cannabis laws, penalties and enforcement priorities.

A cannabis consumer embarking upon a cross-country automobile journey from Portland, Maine, westerly to Portland, Oregon, will witness marijuana's legal status fluctuate wildly over the course of their journey. In many states, possessing cannabis is still strictly illegal, resulting in arrest, potential jail time and a criminal record. On other jurisdictions, pot possession may be a ticketable offense only. And in others, the retail sale of marijuana is entirely legal under state law. As of summer 2015, Alaska, Colorado, Oregon and Washington are the four states at the vanguard of

legalizing cannabis in America, with these historic changes in law being instigated not by elected officials, but rather by voters' passage of binding ballot initiatives.

In short, in 2015, cannabis prohibition and its law enforcement is almost entirely a *function of geography*. The very ground one stands upon when interfacing with police largely instructs what the legal outcome will be, and the map of America's cannabis laws today can only be described as a remarkable patchwork of both prohibition and legalization.

Therefore, *The Citizen's Guide to State-By-State Marijuana Laws* is still the unfortunate but necessary companion for the millions of American cannabis consumers and medical patients greatly looking forward to an end to the national prohibition of the noble herb and its concoctions.*

Many thanks to Paul Armentano, Laura Judy and Rick Steves from NORML for their contributions, and to Whitman Publishing for its groundbreaking cannabis-related series.

*Save this book! Why? Because post-prohibition, it will become a collector's item and memorial to the *Reefer Madness* epoch in America!

Allen St. Pierre
NORML Executive Director
Washington, D.C.

THE CITIZEN'S GUIDE TO STATE-BY-STATE MARIJUANA LAWS

By Paul Armentano

In the time it takes you to read the first page of this book, two more people will be arrested for violating marijuana laws. They could be your friends; they could be your neighbors. But they will not be alone. Since the late 1960s, U.S. law enforcement has made an estimated 25 million marijuana arrests. This total is nearly equal to the entire population of Texas.

In the last year for which federal data is available, police made over 700,000 marijuana-related arrests.[1] That's more than 1,900 pot arrests per day. More than 88 percent of those arrested for marijuana violations are charged with minor possession only. These are not people involved in marijuana trafficking, growing, or sales. They are ordinary citizens who decided to consume a substance that is safer than alcohol and that is less toxic than most conventional medications.

It's time to say enough.

MAKING THE CASE FOR MARIJUANA LAW REFORM

"Penalties against drug use should not be more damaging to an individual than the use of the drug itself. Nowhere is this more clear than in the laws against the possession of marijuana in private for personal use."[2]

— *President Jimmy Carter, 1977*

---

1   Federal Bureau of Investigation, The Uniform Crime Reporting Program. Washington, D.C.
2   Presidential message to Congress, Aug. 2, 1977.

"I don't think it (marijuana) is more dangerous than alcohol."[3]
— *President Barack Obama, 2014*

The National Organization for the Reform of Marijuana Laws was founded in 1970 under the guiding principle that the private, responsible use of marijuana by adults should not be subject to criminal or civil sanction. Forty-five years later, it is painfully apparent that the enforcement of cannabis criminalization burdens taxpayers, encroaches upon civil liberties, engenders disrespect for the law, disproportionately impacts youth and communities of color, and impedes scientists from investigating the plant's therapeutic properties.

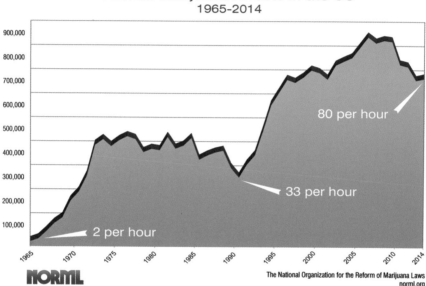

Annual Marijuana Arrests in the US 1965-2014

The National Organization for the Reform of Marijuana Laws
norml.org

Pot prohibition is expensive

Nearly half of all drug arrests in America are marijuana possession violations. Those arrested for violating marijuana laws face a litany of punishments. Penalties stemming from a pot-related arrest, even for a first-time offense, include the possibility of jail and a lifelong criminal record; probation and mandatory drug testing; loss of employment; loss of child custody; removal from subsidized housing; loss of student aid; loss of voting privileges; loss of adoption rights; and the loss of certain federal welfare benefits, such as food stamps. Prosecuting these offenses imposes a significant financial burden upon governments and taxpayers. A 2005 Harvard report calculated that state and federal governments spend nearly $8 billion per year to arrest, prosecute, and jail marijuana offenders.[4] Another analysis places this total at

3   David Remnick, "Going the distance: On and off the road with Barack Obama," *The New Yorker*, Jan. 27, 2014.
4   Jeffrey Miron, *Budgetary Implications for Marijuana Prohibition in the United States*, 2005. http://www. prohibitioncosts.org/mironreport/ Accessed April 9, 2015.

upwards of $10 billion per year.[5] Conversely, a recent Congressional Research Service report estimates that taxing the retail sales of cannabis nationwide would yield nearly $7 billion in new annual revenue.[6]

Tens of thousands of those arrested are also serving prison time for pot convictions. An estimated 13 percent of state inmates and just over 12 percent of federal inmates are incarcerated for marijuana-related drug violations.[7] That's upwards of 50,000 Americans behind bars for violating marijuana laws. In fiscal terms, this means U.S. taxpayers are spending more than $1 billion annually to imprison pot offenders.[8]

Prohibition violates civil liberties and engenders disrespect for the law
Stop-and-frisk, random workplace drug tests, drug dog searches, and suspicionless student drug testing are among the constitutionally questionable tactics routinely engaged in by members of law enforcement and others to enforce the war on weed. These practices create frequent tensions between citizens and their government by convincing young people and other targeted populations that the police and civic leaders are instruments of their oppression rather than their protection. They also make a mockery of America's longstanding principles of limited state intrusion into citizens' daily lives.

Moreover, these heavy-handed tactics are often imposed selectively upon particular populations, specifically those that are young, black, or poor. Nearly half of America's adult population, including the last three presidents, admit to having consumed cannabis. Yet far fewer have ever personally experienced the adverse consequences of a marijuana arrest or prosecution. This disparity in regard to who often bears the brunt of marijuana law enforcement promotes disrespect to the rule of law and alienates millions of otherwise law-abiding citizens. "[I]t's important for society not to have a situation in which a large portion of people have at one time or another broken the law and only a select few get punished," President Barack Obama acknowledged in a 2014 interview with *The New Yorker*. "[W]e should not be locking up kids or individual users for long stretches of jail time."[9]

---

5   Jon Gettman, *Lost Taxes and Other Costs of Marijuana Laws*, 2007. http://www.drugscience.org/Archive/bcr4/bcr4_index.html Accessed April 9, 2015.

6   Congressional Research Service, *Federal Proposals to Tax Marijuana: An Economic Analysis*, 2014. http://www.drugscience.org/Archive/bcr4/bcr4_index.html Accessed April 10, 2015.

7   NORML, "Nearly one in eight US drug prisoners is behind bars for pot," Oct. 12, 2006.

8   Paul Armentano, "Pot prisoners cost Americans $1 billion a year," *Alternet.org*, Feb. 9, 2007.

9   David Remnick, "Going the distance: On and off the road with Barack Obama," *The New Yorker*, Jan. 27, 2014.

BLACK/WHITE ARREST RATIO IS GROWING			
State	2001	2010	% Change in Disparity
Alaska	0.3	1.6	+384%
Minnesota	2.4	7.8	+231%
Wisconsin	2.4	6.0	+153%
Michigan	1.3	3.3	+149%
Kentucky	2.4	6.0	+146%
Tennessee	1.8	4.0	+122%
Ohio	1.9	4.1	+118%

Data courtesy of the ACLU

Prohibition disproportionately targets ethnic minorities and young people

Blacks and Latinos are far more likely to be arrested for possessing marijuana than are whites, even though both ethnic groups use cannabis at rates similar to Caucasians. A 2013 American Civil Liberties Union analysis of marijuana arrest data from 945 counties nationwide determined that blacks, on average, are four times more likely than whites to be arrested for violating marijuana possession laws. Authors reported racial disparities in arrest rates have grown significantly over the past decade. In some states, such as Alaska, Minnesota, and Wisconsin, African-Americans are nearly eight times as likely as Caucasians to be arrested for cannabis possession.[10]

The ACLU's findings are reinforced by analyses of pot possession arrests from major metropolitan areas. For example, a 2014 review of minor marijuana possession arrests in New York City found that blacks are arrested at seven times the rate of whites while Latinos are arrested four times more than Caucasians. Overall, 86 percent of those arrested for violating pot possession laws in the city were either African-Americans or Latino.[11] A separate review of criminal arrest data in Washington, D.C., revealed that 91 percent of all persons busted for possessing pot are black.[12] In Chicago, blacks and Hispanics make up 95 percent of those arrested for marijuana possession.[13]

Similarly troubling is the disproportionate enforcement of marijuana laws upon young people. According to an analysis commissioned by NORML, nearly 75 percent of all people arrested for breaking pot laws are under the age of 30, and one in four is age 18 or younger.[14] That's almost a quarter of a million teenagers busted

10 American Civil Liberties Union, *The War on Marijuana in Black and White*, June 2013. https://www.aclu.org/report/war-marijuana-black-and-white Accessed June 1, 2015.
11 Drug Policy Alliance, *Race, Class & Marijuana Arrests in Mayor DeBlasio's Two New Yorks*, Oct. 20, 2014. http://www.drugpolicy.org/sites/default/files/Race-Class-NYPD-Marijuana-Arrests-Oct-2014.pdf Accessed June 1, 2015.
12 Rend Smith, "Crime stats show D.C. leads nation in per capita marijuana arrests: the majority of people arrested on pot charges are black. Why?" *The Washington, D.C., City Paper*, Aug. 13, 2010.
13 Mick Dumke and Ben Joravsky, "The grass gap: People all over Chicago smoke pot – but almost everyone busted for it is black," *The Chicago Reader*, July 7, 2011.
14 Jon Gettman, *Crimes of Indiscretion: Marijuana Arrests in the United States*, NORML Foundation, 2005.

for weed each year. Branding these minor offenders, many of them still in high school or college, with a criminal record and the lifelong penalties and stigma associated with it that serves no legitimate societal purpose. By any assessment, the continued criminalization of cannabis is a disproportionate public policy response to behavior that is, at worst, a public health concern. But it should not be a criminal justice matter.

Prohibition limits clinical investigating of the plant's therapeutic benefits
Although tens of millions of Americans can obtain cannabis if they so desire it, virtually none of the nation's top scientists can readily get their hands on the herb. That's because federal regulations mandate that all clinical trials assessing the effects of cannabis in human subjects must first gain approval from an alphabet soup of government agencies, including the Food and Drug Administration, the Drug Enforcement Administration, and the National Institute on Drug Abuse. Additional government regulations mandate that all clinical protocols must utilize government-grown weed provided by the U.S. National Institute on Drug Abuse. (The University of Mississippi has possessed the sole federal license to grow legal marijuana in the United States since 1974.) Yet, historically, NIDA has been reticent to approve large-scale clinical studies (known as Phase III confirmation trials) exploring the plant's potential benefits. Speaking to *The New York Times* in 2010, a NIDA spokesperson acknowledged: "As the National Institute on Drug Abuse, our focus is primarily on the negative consequences of marijuana use. We generally do not fund research focused on the potential beneficial medical effects of marijuana."[15]

THE ORIGINS OF POT PROHIBITION
Pot prohibition is a relatively modern phenomenon. Mankind's use of the herb is not.

Humans have cultivated and consumed the cannabis plant since virtually the beginning of recorded history. Cannabis-based textiles dating to 7,000 B.C. have been recovered in northern China, and the plant's use as a medicinal and euphoric agent date back nearly as far. Modern cultures continue to use cannabis for these same purposes, despite a present-day, virtual worldwide ban on its cultivation and use.

Americans lived in harmony with the marijuana plant from the colonial era until just after the turn of the 20th century. Some historians believe that settlers harvested America's first hemp crop in 1611 near Jamestown, Virginia.[16] Shortly thereafter, the British Crown ordered colonialists to engage in wide-scale hemp cultivation[17] – a practice that farmers continued in earnest for the next 300 years.

---

15 Gardner Harris, "Researchers find study of medical marijuana discouraged," *The New York Times*, Jan. 18, 2010.
16 Ernest Abel. *Marijuana: The First Twelve Thousand Years*. Springer Press. 1980.
17 Lester Grinspoon. *Marijuana Reconsidered* (2nd edition). Quick American Archives. 1994.

William O'Shaughnessy

Physician William O'Shaughnessy introduced Americans to the herb's medicinal value in mid-1800s. While practicing in India, O'Shaughnessy began documenting the medical uses of cannabis, which he introduced into Western medicine in 1839. By the 1850s, the preparation of oral cannabis extracts became available in U.S. pharmacies, where they remained a staple for the next 60 years. Despite the drug's widespread availability as an herbal remedy, reports of recreational abuses of cannabis were virtually nonexistent in the literature of that time. In fact, during Congressional hearings leading up to the passage of the Harrison Narcotics Act of 1914 – the nation's first federal anti-drug act – witnesses argued against prohibiting cannabis, stating that "as a habit forming drug its use is almost nil."[18] Congress heeded their advice and wisely excluded cannabis from the statute.

But what was once reefer sanity quickly gave way to reefer madness. Over the following years, legislatures in several U.S. states, including California, Colorado, Maine, and Massachusetts, outlawed the plant's possession – often citing lurid, unsubstantiated claims about the weed's adverse effects among predominantly poor and ethnic populations. By the late 1920s, newspaper headlines and editorials sensationalizing the alleged dangers of pot began sweeping the nation. Well respected publications like *The New York Times* proclaimed that marijuana intoxication caused incurable insanity, while law enforcement personnel alleged that pot use triggered

18 David Musto. 1972. History of the Marijuana Tax Act. *Archives of General Psychiatry* 26: 101-108.

wanton sexual desires, and irreparably destroyed the brain. "If continued, the inevitable result is insanity, which those familiar with it describe as absolutely incurable, and, without exception ending in death," declared a 1933 editorial in *The Journal of Law and Criminology*.[19] Few in the public, and even fewer elected officials, disputed these claims.

By 1937, members of Congress – who had resisted efforts to clamp down on the drug some two decades earlier – were poised to take action. Following the lead of the states, most of which had now banned the plant's possession and use, federal politicians readied to enact their own pot prohibition.

On April 14, 1937, Rep. Robert L. Doughton of North Carolina introduced House Bill 6385. The measure sought to stamp out the recreational use of marijuana by imposing a prohibitive federal tax on activities involving the plant's cultivation and possession. Members of Congress held only two hearings to debate the merits of the bill. The federal government's chief witness during the hearings was Harry Anslinger, a law and order evangelist who directed the Federal Bureau of Narcotics. Anslinger's anti-pot zealotry was legendary. Under oath, Anslinger told members of Congress, "This drug is entirely the monster Hyde, the harmful effect of which cannot be measured"[20] and called for its blanket criminalization. Over objections from the American Medical Association, which testified vociferously against the proposed federal ban, members of the House and Senate overwhelmingly approved the measure. That August, President Franklin Roosevelt promptly signed the legislation into law. On Oct. 1, 1937, the Marihuana Tax Act officially took effect, thus setting in motion the federal prohibition that continues unabated today.

THE SHAFER COMMISSION & THE ADVENT OF DECRIMINALIZATION

While federal pot prohibition began with the passage of the Marijuana Tax Act, the plant's present-day illicit status is a consequence of its classification under the U.S. Controlled Substances Act. (The 1937 law was ultimately ruled unconstitutional by the U.S. Supreme Court in 1969.) Of the five drug categories established by the CSA, politicians placed cannabis in the most prohibitive category: Schedule I. But this decision was intended only to be temporary. That's because the Act called for the creation of a federally appointed commission to study all aspects of the cannabis plant, its use, and its consumers. The presumption was that lawmakers would revisit pot's restrictive status once this blue-ribbon commission completed its work and reported its findings back to Congress.

But things didn't work out as planned.

After nearly two years of scientific study, Congress' marijuana commission – known as the National Commission on Marijuana and Drug Abuse (aka the Shafer

---

19 MH Hayes and LE Bowery. 1933. Marihuana. *The Journal of Law and Criminology* 23: 1086-1098.
20 Larry Sloman. *Reefer Madness: A History of Marijuana* (Second Edition). St. Martin's Press. 1998.

Commission, named after its chairperson, Pennsylvania Gov. Raymond P. Shafer) – completed its investigation. The multi-million dollar fact-finding mission, titled *Marijuana: A Signal of Misunderstanding*, was trumpeted upon its completion as "the most comprehensive study of marijuana ever made in the United States."[21]

The Commission issued its report to Congress and to President Richard Nixon on March 22, 1972. In unambiguous language, it rebutted virtually every negative claim made about the herb's alleged dangers. Specifically, the Commission concluded that pot was not a so-called

President Richard M. Nixon

"gateway drug," that its use was not associated with violence or aggressive activity, and that its consumption was not physiologically or psychologically detrimental to health.[22]

"Neither the marijuana user nor the drug itself can be said to constitute a danger to public safety," it concluded. "Therefore, the Commission recommends ... [the] possession of marijuana for personal use no longer be an offense, [and that the] casual distribution of small amounts of marijuana for no remuneration, or insignificant remuneration no longer be an offense." This public policy recommendation, known as decriminalization, stipulates that those who possess or dispense personal use quantities of the herb no longer face arrest or jail time. Instead, minor pot violations are punishable by the payment of a small fine. By contrast, large-scale dealers and traffickers continue to face criminal sanctions and the plant itself remains contraband.

The Commission's findings and recommendations should have triggered a serious review of federal marijuana policy and penalties. That didn't happen. Instead, President Nixon vehemently rejected the Commission's conclusions and the federal government doubled down on demonizing pot. As had been the case more than three decades earlier, science and reason held little sway with federal policymakers, who instead chose to embrace cultural and racial stereotypes over facts and evidence.

---

21 *Marijuana: A Signal of Misunderstanding: The Official Report of the National Commissions on Marijuana and Drug Abuse.* Signet Books, 1972.
22 Advisory commissions in Great Britain (*The Wooten Report*, 1968) and Canada (*The Le Dain Commission*, 1973) reached similar conclusions.

Flexing the muscle of the newly formed anti-crime super-agency, the U.S. Drug Enforcement Administration, Nixon declared that his administration was launching the first official "war" on drugs. Public enemy No. 1 in this battle was marijuana.

Although federal officials ignored the Shafer Commission's call to decriminalize pot, state politicians took notice. In 1973, Oregon became the first U.S. state to amend its marijuana laws in a manner that mimicked the Commission's recommendations. Over the following years, 10 additional states – Alaska, California, Colorado, Maine, Minnesota, Mississippi, Nebraska, New York, North Carolina and Ohio – decriminalized marijuana possession offenses. In each of these states, minor marijuana offenders face fines, but no longer risk prison time (and, in most cases, they also no longer face a criminal record). These policy changes allow states to free up judicial and prosecutorial resources to focus on more serious crimes and have not resulted in increased marijuana use among young people or the general public. In fact, no less than the federal government's own review of statewide decriminalization policies concluded: "[D]ecriminalization has had virtually no effect either on the marijuana use or on related attitudes and beliefs about marijuana use among American young people. The data show no evidence of any increase, relative to the control states, in the proportion of the age group who ever tried marijuana. In fact, both groups of experimental states showed a small, cumulative net decline in annual prevalence after decriminalization."[23]

The popularity of decriminalization waned in the 1980s – a decade that marked the zenith of drug war fervor. Predictably, no additional states passed cannabis decriminalization laws during this time period. Yet, despite the advent of "Just Say No," advocates managed to hold the line. Throughout the Reagan/Bush era, no state legislature repealed their decriminalization laws.

By the late 1990s state politicians began once again to consider the benefits of decriminalizing pot. In 2001, Nevada became the first state in over two decades to reduce marijuana possession penalties to a fine-only offense. In recent years, several additional states have enacted similar changes in law, reducing minor pot possession offenses from criminal misdemeanors to civil infractions punishable by a fine only – no arrest, no jail, and no criminal record.

23 Lloyd Johnston, *Marijuana Decriminalization: The Impact on Youth 1976-1980*, Monitoring the Future Occasional Paper Series, University of Michigan: Institute for Social Research, 1981.

Shutterstock/William Casey

THE RISE OF MEDICAL MARIJUANA

It has long been said, "As goes California, so goes the nation." Nowhere have these words proven more prophetic than in the case of medical marijuana.

California voters didn't just make history on Nov. 3, 1996; they jump-started a nationwide revolution. Fifty-four percent of California voters decided in favor of Proposition 215, the Compassionate Use Act – the nation's first modern medical marijuana legalization law. The statute ensures that patients possessing a doctor's written or oral recommendation "have the right to obtain and use marijuana for medical purposes where that medical use is deemed appropriate." In the nearly two-decades since the law's enactment, Californians support for this right has not wavered. Five percent of California adults are estimated to either have used or are using cannabis therapeutically.[24] Of these, approximately one-third report using pot for pain relief and 92 percent acknowledge a high-degree of satisfaction with cannabis therapy.

California's historic vote was the first of many modern legislative victories. As of this writing, 23 states and the District of Columbia have enacted laws, either by

24 Ryan Ibarra et al., 2015. Prevalence of medical marijuana use in California, 2012. *Drug and Alcohol Review* 34: 141-146.

voter initiative or by the passage of legislation, providing for the physician-authorized use of cannabis therapy. In these states, patients diagnosed with a qualifying illness[25] who obtain a physician's written authorization may legally possess and/or cultivate limited quantities of cannabis. Many states also permit qualified patients to obtain cannabis from licensed dispensaries – facilities authorized by the state to produce and distribute medical marijuana. In more restrictive jurisdictions, patients are prohibited from growing their own pot and may only access it from dispensaries. Two states, New York and Minnesota, restrict patients from legally possessing herbal preparations of cannabis, instead mandating the plant be formulated into oils or pills.

The enactment of these therapeutic use laws has yet to persuade the federal government to revisit marijuana's federal classification. Federal law still classifies the plant (as well as all of its organic constituents) as a Schedule I controlled substance – meaning, by definition, that pot is one of the most dangerous drugs in the United States and that it possesses "no currently accepted medical use." In April 2015, a federal judge upheld the constitutionality of this classification, arguing that the federal law ought to remain in place as long as there remains any dispute among experts as to pot's safety and efficacy.[26]

THE SCIENCE BEHIND CANNABIS

Cannabis has been consumed for spiritual, medicinal, and recreational purposes for thousands of years, thus providing society with ample empirical evidence of the plant's relative safety and utility. Despite the U.S. government's nearly century-long prohibition of the herb, marijuana is nonetheless among the most studied biologically active substances of modern times. A search on PubMed, the repository for all peer-reviewed scientific papers, using the term "marijuana" yields more than 22,000 citations to scientific studies referencing the plant and/or its unique constituents (known as cannabinoids), nearly half of which have been published since 2005. This sum is greater than the total number of scientific papers available for ibuprofen, Ritalin, hydrocodone, Adderall, and Oxycodone combined.

This scientific record conflicts with the federal government's stance that cannabis is a highly dangerous substance that lacks medical utility and must be harshly criminalized. In fact, pot's active constituents are uniquely safe and effective therapeutic compounds. Unlike most prescription or over-the-counter medications, cannabinoids are incapable of causing the user to experience a fatal overdose, and they are

---

25 In all but two jurisdictions, California and Washington, D.C., physicians only may recommend medical cannabis to patients who are diagnosed with a qualifying medical condition. These conditions vary from state to state, but typically include conditions such as AIDS/HIV, cancer, and multiple sclerosis, among others. In California and Washington, D.C., physicians may legally recommend cannabis therapy to any patient for whom they believe might benefit from it.

26 Don Thompson and Sudhin Thanawala, "Judge keeps marijuana on list of most dangerous drugs," *The Associated Press*, April 15, 2015.

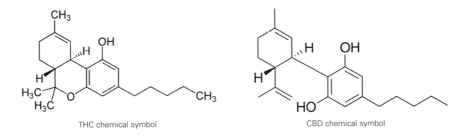

THC chemical symbol   CBD chemical symbol

relatively nontoxic to healthy cells or organs.[27] The same can hardly be said for most other therapeutics. For instance, annual deaths from opioid analgesics total some 16,000-plus per year (a 400 percent increase since the late 1990s)[28], while complications induced from the use of nonsteroidal anti-inflammatory drugs cause more than 100,000 hospitalizations and an estimated 16,500 deaths annually.[29]

To date, researchers have identified some 100 distinct cannabinoids. The most recognized cannabinoid is the plant's primary psychoactive (mood-altering) component, THC (delta-9-tetrahydrocannabinol). Other constituents in the plant include THCV (delta-9-tetrahydrocannabivarin), CBD (cannabidiol), CBC (cannabichromene), and CBG (cannabigerol). Many of these cannabinoids possess acknowledged therapeutic properties in animals and/or human subjects, including anti-diabetic activity, anti-cancer activity, anti-inflammatory activity, anti-convulsant activity, anti-spasticity activity, bone-stimulating activity, neuroprotective activity, and analgesic activity.[30] (A synthetic form of THC, marketed under the trade name Marinol, has been FDA-approved since the mid-1980s).

A review of the available literature identifies over 100 controlled studies worldwide, involving thousands of subjects, evaluating the safety and efficacy of cannabis or individual cannabinoids.[31] (By contrast, most FDA-approved pharmaceuticals are approved based on only two pivotal trials.[32]) These human studies provide consistent evidence that the plant and its variety of components offer effective relief for the treatment of a wide range of conditions, such as painful neuropathy, Crohn's and other gastrointestinal disorders, severe nausea and cachexia, loss of appetite,

27 Mitch Earleywine. *Understanding Marijuana: A New Look at the Scientific Evidence*. Oxford University Press, 2002.

28 Center for Disease Control and Prevention, "Opioids drive continued increase in drug overdose deaths," Feb. 20, 2013.

29 James Graumlich. 2001. Preventing gastrointestinal complications of NSAIDS. *Postgraduate Medicine* 109: 117-120.

30 Izzo et al., 2009. Non-psychotropic plant cannabinoids: new therapeutic opportunities from an ancient herb. *Trends in Pharmacological Sciences* 30: 515-527.

31 Arno Hazekamp and Franjo Grotenhermen, 2010. Review of clinical studies with cannabis and cannabinoids 2005-2009. *Cannabinoids* 5: 1-21.

32 Downing et al., 2013. Clinical trial evidence supporting FDA approval of novel therapeutics, 2005-2012. *Journal of the American Medical Association* 311: 368-377.

multiple sclerosis, and seizure disorders such as epilepsy.[33] Over the past decade, the Center for Medicinal Cannabis Research at the University of California has conducted numerous FDA-approved clinical trials assessing pot's medicinal efficacy. In every study conducted by the Center, subjects using whole-plant cannabis showed a statistically significant medical benefit. "I kind of expected, well, we're going to have a few studies that say yes and a few that will say no, and then at the end of the day we'll still be arguing," said the program's director, Dr. Igor Grant. "But in fact every single study showed benefit."[34] A recent review of these studies, published in the medical journal *Open Neurology*, concluded, "Based on evidence currently available the Schedule I classification (for cannabis) is not tenable; it is not accurate that cannabis has no medical value, or that information on safety is lacking."[35]

THE FUTURE IS NOW

The passage of medical marijuana laws has played a pivotal role in influencing the way Americans think about pot and pot policy. In the early 1990s, prior to the emergence of medical marijuana legalization, only 16 percent of U.S. adults supported making the herb legal for adult use.[36] Eighty-one percent of Americans opposed the idea. By the mid-1990s, support began to slowly rise – with roughly one-quarter of the public saying cannabis should be made legal for those over the age of 21.[37]

A decade later, public opinion had dramatically begun to shift. By 2005, more than one-third of the country (36 percent) told Gallup pollsters, "The use of cannabis should be made legal." By 2009, Gallup reported that public support had spiked to 44 percent. Changes in law were soon to follow.

In 2010, Richard Lee – founder of Oaksterdam University in Oakland, California – set his sights on making marijuana legal for all adults, not just for those possessing a doctor's note. The ballot campaign, known as California's Proposition 19, sought to permit those age 21 and older to possess and grow personal use quantities of pot while also establishing local licensing laws governing the plant's retail production and sale. While the largely grassroots effort – the bulk of the campaign was funded primarily by Richard Lee's own savings – gained both national and even international attention, it ultimately failed at the ballot box, gaining just over 46 percent of the vote. Nationwide, however, momentum in favor of legalizing pot continued to grow. In October 2011, Gallup reported for the first time that one-half of all Americans believed that cannabis should be legal.

33 Paul Armentano. *Emerging Clinical Applications For Cannabis and Cannabinoids: A Review of the Recent Scientific Literature* (Sixth edition). NORML Foundation. 2015. http://norml.org/library/recent-research-on-medical-marijuana

34 David Wagner, "San Diego scientist: Every medical pot study showed a benefit to the patient," KPBS News, March 3, 2015.

35 Grant et al., 2012. Medical marijuana: clearing away the smoke. *The Open Neurology Journal* 6: 18-25.

36 Pew Research Center, "Opinion on Legalizing Marijuana: 1969-2015," April 14, 2015.

37 Gallup. Historical Trends: Illegal Drugs. http://www.gallup.com/poll/1657/illegal-drugs.aspx Accessed April 9, 2015.

GALLUP POLL: Americans' Views on Legalizing Marijuana

"Do you think the use of marijuana should be legal, or not?"

Yes, legal ●
No, not legal ●

90% 81%
80%   73%
70%
60%   66%   64%   58%
50%
40%
30% 28%   34%   39%
20% 12%   25%
10%

1969 1973 1977 1981 1985 1989 1993 1997 2001 2005 2009 2013

NORML
norml.org

Having learned some hard lessons from California's unsuccessful 2010 effort, advocates in 2012 targeted Colorado and Washington for a pair of well-financed statewide legalization campaigns. The two initiatives (Amendment 64 in Colorado and Initiative 502 in Washington) were far from identical. For instance, A-64 permitted adults to legally grow up to six marijuana plants for their own personal use while Washington's plan kept home cultivation criminalized. I 502 also placed a cap on the number of allowable state-licensed retail cannabis producers and sellers, while Colorado's proposal placed no such limits. The two measures also differed in the percentage of tax placed upon retail sales of pot.

Advocates' campaign strategies also differed. While Colorado's talking points emphasized pot's safety relative to alcohol and stressed the potential of marijuana tax revenue to help pay for school construction, I-502 campaign organizers explicitly targeted women voters age 30 to 50 – a demographic that in past efforts had been initially supportive of legalization but had ultimately switch their vote to "no." They did so by arguing that the law's passage would tightly control marijuana access and create safer communities.

Ultimately, both efforts bore fruit at the ballot box. In Colorado, 55 percent of voters – a greater percentage of those who chose in favor of either President Barack Obama or Republican candidate Mitt Romney – decided in favor of Amendment 64. A similar percentage of Washington state voters approved I-502. Just like that, for the first time since 1937, the social use and sale of cannabis was legal in two jurisdictions of the United States.

These statewide victories only furthered Americans' appetite for legal marijuana. In 2013, Gallup reported that 58 percent of the public believed that the herb should be legal while only 39 percent opposed the idea. In November of 2014, voters in

Alaska and Oregon similarly approved marijuana legalization initiatives (by 52 and 56 percent, respectively). The Alaska measure, which took effect on Feb. 24, 2015, permits the adult possession of up to one ounce of cannabis and up to six plants, while establishing regulations for pot's retail production and sale. The Oregon law, which took effect on July 1, 2015, permits adults to possess up to eight ounces of herb and grow as many as four plants, while also regulating its commercial cultivation and retail sale. Retail cannabis sales began in Oregon on Oct. 1, 2015.

Voters in the District of Columbia also joined the party on election night. A stunning 70 percent of voters in the nation's capitol approved I-71, a municipal measure removing all criminal and civil penalties for activity involving the possession of up to two ounces of pot and/or the cultivation of six plants.[38] Despite threats from various members of Congress, District officials enacted the depenalization measure without incident in early 2015. In perhaps the most dramatic example of how seismically public opinion had shifted over the past 25 years, D.C. Police Chief Cathy Lanier unequivocally expressed her support for the law change. "We've embraced it," she announced. "All those arrests do is make people hate us. … Marijuana smokers are not going to attack and kill a cop. They just want to get a bag of chips and relax. Alcohol is a much bigger problem."[39]

STATE MARIJUANA LAWS

Decriminalization   Hemp   Legalization   Medical   Medical CBD

NORML

---

38 Unlike legalization laws in other states, the D.C. measure does not allow for the retail production or sale of cannabis.

39 Eleanor Clift, "D.C. police chief stands up to Congress over pot," *The Daily Beast*, Feb. 28, 2015.

WHAT IS OLD IS NEW AGAIN: THE RE-EMERGENCE OF HEMP

Hemp is a distinct variety of the cannabis plant species. It is tall and fibrous and contains minimal (less than one percent) amounts of THC. Various parts of the plant can be utilized in the making of textiles, paper, paints, clothing, plastics, cosmetics, foodstuffs, insulation, animal feed, and other products. A 1938 edition of the magazine *Popular Mechanics* trumpeted hemp as the "new billion dollar crop" – boasting that the plant "can be used to produce more than 25,000 products, ranging from dynamite to Cellophane."[40]

The passage of the 1937 Marihuana Tax Act marked the death knell to what had once been a thriving commercial industry. (Hemp re-emerged as a legal, government-subsidized crop during World War II when the USDA demanded the crop's production to assist with the war effort, but this legal exemption was short-lived.) Yet, despite nearly a century of prohibition, hemp products continue to be sought after in the U.S. marketplace. States a 2015 Congressional Research Report, "[T]he U.S. market for hemp-based products has a highly dedicated and growing demand base. ... [A] commercial hemp industry in the United States could provide opportunities as an economically viable alternative crop for some U.S. growers."[41] Nevertheless, the United States remains the only developed nation in which industrial hemp is not an established commercial crop. But that reality is quickly changing.

In February 2014, members of Congress included a new provision in the federal farm reauthorization act permitting certain states to grow hemp absent federal reclassification of the plant. Specifically, Section 7606 of the law states: "[A]n institution of higher education ... or a state department of agriculture may grow or cultivate industrial hemp ... for purposes of research" in states that permit it. Within months, several states – including Indiana, New York, and Tennessee – had approved laws explicitly authorizing such activity, and in the fall of 2014, Kentucky farmers became the first to engage in state-sanctioned hemp production since the 1940s.[42]

As of this writing, 25 states have enacted legislation recognizing hemp as an agricultural crop rather than as a controlled substance.

---

40 "The new billion dollar crop," *Popular Mechanics*, February 1938
41 Congressional Research Service, *Hemp as an agricultural commodity*, Feb. 2, 2015.
42 Janet Patton, "University of Kentucky harvests first legal hemp crop," *Lexington Herald-Leader*, Sept. 23, 2014.

This is a field of hemp, a distinct variety of the cannabis plant species. Photo courtesy of Shutterstock/Ten03.

WHAT ABOUT CBD?

The mainstreaming of marijuana as a medicine has renewed interest in cannabinoids other than THC. In particular, investigators are now taking a closer look at CBD.

Scientists first isolated cannabidiol in 1940, some two and a half decades prior to the discovery of pot's most popular cannabinoid, THC. But until recently, little attention was paid to it.

Unlike THC, cannabidiol does not induce euphoria. Rather, scientists believe that the compound actually tempers THC's psychoactivity. As a result, domestic cannabis strains destined for the recreational market seldom contain high

CBD oil shows great promise in helping control seizures in children. Shutterstock/Lusie Lia

percentages of CBD.[43] However, medical patients seeking the therapeutic qualities of cannabis without the plant's mood-altering effects have begun to gravitate toward selectively bred CBD-dominant plant strains.

A review of the scientific literature identifies several therapeutic properties associated with CBD, including anti-psychotic activity, anti-tremor activity, anti-inflammatory activity, anti-oxidative activity, anti-diabetic activity, and cardio protection.[44] Human trials also find the compound to be safe and well tolerated.[45] In recent years,

43 Burgdorf et al., 2011. Heterogenity in the composition of marijuana seized in California. *Drug and Alcohol Dependence* 117: 59-61.
44 Antonio Zuardi. 2008. Cannabidiol: from an inactive cannabinoid to a drug with a wide spectrum of action. *Revista Brasileira de Psiquiatria* 30: 271-280.
45 Bergamaschi et al., 2011. Safety and side effects of cannabidiol, a Cannabis sativa constituent. *Current Drug Safety* 6: 237-249.

the majority of attention paid to CBD revolves around its potential to mitigate symptoms in children with rare forms of intractable and sometimes life-threatening seizure disorders, such as Dravet syndome and Lennox-Gastaut syndrome.

According to one recent study, about one-third of children taking plant-derived extracts possessing CBD experience a 50 percent reduction in seizures[46] and randomized clinical studies assessing CBD's effects versus placebo are ongoing in a number of teaching hospitals around the country. But it is not only doctors' attitudes about CBD that are changing. State laws are also changing – and changing rapidly.

In 2014, lawmakers in Alabama, Florida, Iowa, Kentucky, Mississippi, Missouri, North Carolina, South Carolina, Utah, and Wisconsin passed measures permitting the use of CBD for pediatric epilepsy or other debilitating conditions. Georgia, Oklahoma, Tennessee, Texas, Virginia, and Wyoming passed similar laws in the spring and summer of 2015. Unfortunately for patients, only three states – Florida, Missouri, and Texas – provide regulations for the in-state production of high CBD cannabis and, to date, none of these programs are up and running. Consequently, patients who reside in CBD-only states must procure the substance in a state where the plant is legal (e.g., Colorado) and then return home with the product – behavior that is not only impractical but that also places them at risk of federal charges of interstate drug trafficking.[47]

PROHIBITION IS CRUMBLING AND THE SKY ISN'T FALLING

Pot prohibition is collapsing: four states and Washington, D.C., have legalized the plant's use by adults; 23 states permit its use medicinally; over a dozen states recognize the medical utility of CBD; and half of all U.S. states recognize hemp as an agricultural commodity. As more states successfully replace criminalization with regulation, it is becoming self-evident that anti-legalization advocates lack any sound evidence to support their flat-Earth position.

Marijuana liberalization has not increased rates of teen pot use

State-specific studies consistently report that legalizing pot for adults doesn't inspire greater use by teens. Investigators at Columbia University in New York and the University of Michigan assessed the relationship between state medical marijuana laws and rates of adolescent marijuana use over a 24-year period in a sampling of over one million adolescents in 48 states. Researchers reported no increase in teens' overall use of the plant that could be attributable to changes in law, and acknowledged a "robust" decrease in use among eighth graders.[48] Separate data published

---

46 Press et al., 2015. Parental reporting of response to oral cannabis extracts for treatment of refractory epilepsy. *Epilepsy & Behavior* 45: 49-52.

47 As of this writing, five separate bills to legalize the therapeutic use of CBD have been introduced in the United States Congress.

48 Hasin et al., 2015. Medical marijuana laws and adolescent marijuana use in the USA from 1991 to 2014: results from annual, repeated cross-sectional surveys. *Lancet Psychiatry*, posted online ahead of print on June 16, 2015.

by the Colorado Department of Public Health & Environment similarly report that fewer high school students are consuming cannabis since voters decided in 2012 to legalize its possession, production, and sale.[49] Adolescents' use of cannabis in Washington has also declined since the state began legally regulating the plant, according to a report by Washington State University for Public Policy.

Americans' use of other illicit drugs has not risen following the enactment of statewide marijuana liberalization laws. For instance, cocaine consumption has fallen remarkably in recent years.[50] Even more notably, two recent studies report far fewer deaths from heroin and/or prescription opiates in states that have legalized medical cannabis compared to those states that haven't.[51 and 52]

Organized crime has not infiltrated the legal marijuana market

There is no tangible evidence indicating that states' allowances of the production of cannabis for either medicinal or recreational purposes have provided enhanced opportunities for criminal drug traffickers. In fact, just the opposite appears to be true. According to a recent National Public Radio report, the advent of legal pot in the U.S. is significantly reducing market demand for Mexican-grown weed. "Two or three years ago, a kilogram [2.2 pounds] of marijuana was worth $60 to $90," NPR reported. "But now they're paying us $30 to $40 a kilo. It's a big difference. If the U.S. continues to legalize pot, they'll run us [Mexican drug rings] into the ground...The day we get $20 a kilo, it will get to the point that we just won't plant marijuana anymore."[53] Separate reporting by *The Washington Post* tells a similar tale. Pot's wholesale price in Mexico has "collapsed" over the past five years, the *Post* reported. "It's not worth it anymore," a lifelong Mexican cannabis farmer told reporters. "I wish the Americans would stop with this legalization."[54]

Pot legalization has not caused carnage on the roads

There is little evidence that drivers who test positive for THC alone possess significantly elevated risks of motor vehicle accidents compared to drug-free drivers. A 2015 study published by the United States National Highway Traffic Safety Administration reported that THC-positive drivers possessed no increased accident risk, once investigators controlled for age and gender.[55] The NHTSA study is the largest ever conducted to assess the role of drugs and alcohol in car accidents. By

49 Jacob Sullum, "Despite legalization, Colorado teenagers stubbornly refuse to smoke more pot," *Reason.com*, Aug. 8, 2014.
50 Nosyk et al. 2015. The rise of marijuana and the fall of cocaine in the United States. *Addiction* 110: 737.
51 Bachhuber et al., 2014. Medical cannabis laws and opioid analgesic overdose mortality in the United States, 1999-2010. *JAMA Internal Medicine* 174: 1668-1673.
52 National Bureau of Economic Research, *Do Medical Marijuana Laws Reduce Addictions and Deaths Related to Pain Killers?* June 2015. http:/www.nber.org/papers/w21345.
53 John Burnett, "Legal pot in the U.S. may be undercutting Mexican marijuana," National Public Radio, Dec. 1, 2014.
54 Nick Miroff, "Tracing the U.S. heroin surge back to the border as Mexican cannabis output falls," *The Washington Post*, April 6, 2014.
55 NHTSA, *Drug and Alcohol Crash Risk*, U.S. Department of Transportation, Feb. 2015.

contrast, authors found that drivers with legal blood alcohol levels possessed nearly a four-fold risk of accident.

Nonetheless, legalization critics have warned that liberalizing cannabis laws will lead to an increase in pot-related traffic accidents. So far, these fears have not come to fruition. Despite significant changes in states' marijuana laws, traffic fatalities have declined steadily over the past decades and now stand at near historic lows.[56] Further, states that have amended their pot laws and penalties have not experienced an increase in traffic fatalities. A 2013 study published in the *Journal of Law and Economics* reported that marijuana legalization is associated with up to an 11 percent decrease in traffic deaths – a finding that authors theorized was likely due to the public's reduced consumption of alcohol.[57]

Marijuana liberalization is associated with decreased crime

Allegations that pot legalization laws and/or the establishment of retail pot facilities will increase crime have proven false. A 2014 study by researchers at the University of Texas Department of Criminology tracked crime rates across all 50 states in the years between 1990 and 2006, during which time 11 states legalized medical cannabis access. They concluded, "The central finding gleaned from the present study was that MML (medical marijuana legalization) is not predictive of higher crime rates and may be related to reductions in rates of homicide and assault. … [T]hese findings run counter to arguments suggesting the legalization of marijuana for medical purposes poses a danger to public health in terms of exposure to violent crime and property crimes."[58]

Similarly, a 2012 federally commissioned study reported that the establishment of pot dispensaries is not associated with elevated rates of either violent crimes or property crimes. It concluded, "There were no observed cross-sectional associations between the density of medical marijuana dispensaries and either violent or property crime rates in this study. These results suggest that the density of medical marijuana dispensaries may not be associated with crime rates."[59]

Incidences of violent crime in Denver, the epicenter for Colorado's marijuana retail industry, fell significantly following the opening of retail marijuana business in 2014. Between Jan. 1 and April 30, 2014, violent crime and property crime dropped 10.6 percent compared to that same span one year earlier.[60] Homicides fell to less than half of the previous year's levels, and motor vehicle theft decreased by over one-third.

56 Colin Bird, "U.S. traffic deaths drop to historic low," *Cars.com*, Sept. 8, 2010.

57 Anderson et al., 2013. Medical marijuana laws, traffic fatalities, and alcohol consumption. *Journal of Law and Economics* 56: 333-369.

58 Morris et al., 2014. Medical marijuana laws on crime: Evidence from state panel data, 1999-2000. *PLoS One* 9: e92816.

59 Kepple et al., 2012. Exploring the ecological association between crime and medical marijuana dispensaries. *Journal of Studies on Alcohol and Drugs* 73: 523-530.

60 *RT USA*, "Crime down and revenue up in Colorado since start of marijuana legalization," June 5, 2014.

SO WHAT'S NEXT?

Prospects for cannabis legalization – or, perhaps more accurately, re-legalization – have never been brighter.

As of this writing, over a dozen state legislatures are considering measures to legalize the plant's adult use and sale, and several others are debating legislative proposals to either reduce criminal penalties or expand medical access. At the federal level, members of Congress in 2014 for the first time voted to limit the Justice Department's ability to take action against state-licensed operations that are in full compliance with the medical marijuana laws of their states. Presently, several pieces of legislation that seek to reschedule marijuana are before the U.S. House and Senate.

National polls continue to show record high support for allowing adults to possess and buy pot, while super-majorities endorse allowing physicians to authorize cannabis therapy. Health leaders like CNN's Dr. Sanjay Gupta continue to publicly espouse support for marijuana law reform[61], and federal agencies like the DEA and NIDA appear to be more open to allowing clinical research than ever before. (In the spring of 2015, the DEA demanded the University of Mississippi pot farm increase its supply of research-grade marijuana production three-fold.[62]) Nationwide, pot arrests are down almost 20 percent from their all-time highs nearly a decade ago, no doubt in part because of the implementation of marijuana liberalization laws in Colorado, Washington, and elsewhere.

Which state will be next to legalize the adult use of cannabis? In 2016, voters in at least half a dozen states, including Arizona, California, Maine, Massachusetts, and Nevada, are expected to have the opportunity to decide on marijuana policy – and to make history.

The genie is out of the bottle. And he's not going back in.

HOW TO USE THIS BOOK

The information contained in this book is no substitute for legal advice. If you have been arrested or are facing the threat of arrest for a marijuana-related offense, you should consult with legal counsel. NORML provides a committee of criminal defense attorneys specializing in marijuana law defense. To contact an attorney in your local area, please visit: http://lawyers.norml.org/.

A WORD OF CAUTION

State lawmakers frequently revisit and amend marijuana penalties. Therefore it is possible, even likely, that some of the penalties in place at the time of this writing may be amended by the time this book is published. To confirm the very latest information pertaining to state-specific marijuana laws and penalties, please see

---

61 Sanjay Gupta, "I am doubling down on marijuana," CNN, March 6, 2014.
62 Jonah Bennett, "DEA says federal government needs to grow way more weed," *The Daily Caller*, April 7, 2015.

NORML's website at http://norml.org/laws or inquire with your local NORML-affiliated attorney at: http://lawyers.norml.org/.

About NORML

NORML was founded in 1970 as a non-profit legal, advocacy, and educational organization. NORML's mission is to move public opinion sufficiently to legalize the responsible use of marijuana by adults and to serve as an advocate for responsible cannabis consumers. To learn more about NORML or to become a dues-paying member, please visit http://www.norml.org. To locate your local NORML affiliate, please visit: http://norml.org/chapters.

STATE RECREATIONAL
MARIJUANA
LAWS

ALABAMA
LAWS & PENALTIES

Offense	Penalty	Incarceration	Max. Fine
POSSESSION			
Personal Use			
Any amount	Misdemeanor	1 year	$ 6,000
Other Than Personal Use			
Any amount	Felony	1 year and 1 day* - 10 years	$ 15,000
* Mandatory minimum sentence and fine			
SALE			
Any amount	Felony	2* - 20 years	$ 30,000
By a person over 18 to a minor	Felony	10 years - life	$ 60,000
Within 3 mile radius of a school or a public housing project	Felony	5 years	$ 0
* Mandatory minimum sentence and fine			
TRAFFICKING			
In excess of 2.2 lbs - less than 100 lbs	Felony	3 years*	$ 25,000
100 lbs - less than 500 lbs	Felony	5 years*	$ 50,000
500 lbs - less than 1,000 lbs	Felony	15 years*	$ 200,000
* Mandatory minimum sentence and fine			
CULTIVATION			
Manufacture 2nd Degree	Felony	2* - 20 years	$ 30,000
Manufacture 1st Degree	Felony	10 years - life	$ 60,000
* Mandatory minimum sentence and fine			
HASH & CONCENTRATES			
Possession	Felony	1 year and 1 day - 10 years	$ 15,000
Manufacture 2nd Degree	Felony	2 - 20 years	$ 30,000
Manufacture 1st Degree	Felony	10 years - life	$ 60,000
* Mandatory minimum sentence and fine			
PARAPHERNALIA			
Use or possession of paraphernalia with intent to use	Misdemeanor	1 year	$ 6,000
Delivery or sale	Misdemeanor	1 year	$ 6,000
Use, deliver, or sell, possess with intent to deliver or sell, or manufacture with intent to deliver or sell, or to possess with intent to use, drug paraphernalia to manufacture a controlled substance	Felony	1 year and 1 day - 10 years	$ 15,000
Subsequent violation of delivery or sale	Felony	1 year and 1 day - 10 years	$ 15,000
Delivery or sale to a minor	Felony	2 - 20 years	$ 30,000
MISCELLANEOUS			

A marijuana conviction will result in a 6 month driver's license suspension.

Carly's Law is an affirmative and complete defense for the parent or caretaker of an individual who has a prescription for the possession and use of cannabidiol (CBD).

Penalty Details

Possession for Personal Use

In Alabama, marijuana for "personal use only" is a Class A Misdemeanor, punishable by a maximum sentence of 1 year and a maximum fine of $6,000.

Marijuana possessed for reasons other than "personal use," or if the offender has been previously convicted of marijuana possession for "personal use" only, is unlawful possession of marijuana in the first degree and is a Class C felony, punishable by a prison sentence of a minimum of one year in prison and a maximum sentence of 10 years in prison, along with a maximum fine of $15,000.

See
* Code of Alabama §13A-5-6
* Code of Alabama §13A-5-7
* Code of Alabama §13A-5-11
* Code of Alabama §13A-5-12
* Code of Alabama §13A-12-213
* Code of Alabama §13A-12-214
* Code of Alabama §13A-12-214.2
* Code of Alabama Section §20-2-23

Sale

Sale of a controlled substance in Alabama is a Class B felony punishable with a minimum sentence of 2 years and a maximum sentence of 20 years, along with a maximum fine of $30,000.

The sale to a minor is a felony which is punishable by a sentence of 10 years-life imprisonment and a maximum fine of $60,000.

Sale within 3 miles of a school or a public housing project is an additional felony punishable by an additional sentence of 5 years imprisonment.

* The imposition of the sentence will not be suspended and probation will not be granted.

See
* Code of Alabama §13A-5-6
* Code of Alabama §13A-5-11
* Code of Alabama §13A-12-211
* Code of Alabama §13A-12-215
* Code of Alabama §13A-12-250
* Code of Alabama §13A-12-270

Cultivation

Cultivation in Alabama is punished as either simple possession or as possession with intent to distribute, depending on the amount of marijuana being produced and other factors that may lead to the conclusion that the marijuana was being grown for reasons other than strict personal use. See the "Possession for Personal Use" section for further penalty details.

Unlawful manufacture of a controlled substance in the 2nd degree. The manufacturing of a controlled substance under Schedules I. Unlawful manufacture of a controlled substance in the second degree is a Class B felony.

See
* Code of Alabama §13A-12-217

Unlawful manufacture of a controlled substance in the 1st Degree. Unlawful manufacture in the 2nd Degree AND any of the following two:

* Possession of a firearm.
* Use of a booby trap.
* Illegal possession, transportation, or disposal of hazardous or dangerous materials or while transporting or causing to be transported materials in furtherance of a clandestine laboratory operation, there was created a substantial risk to human health or safety or a danger to the environment.
* A clandestine laboratory operation was to take place or did take place within 500 feet of a residence, place of business, church, or school.
* A clandestine laboratory operation actually produced any amount of a specified controlled substance.

See
* Code of Alabama §13A-12-218

Trafficking

The sale, cultivation, or manufacture of 2.2 lbs- 100 pounds is considered trafficking and is a felony punishable by a mandatory minimum sentence of 3 years imprisonment and a possible sentence of 10-99 years, as well as a maximum fine of $25,000.

The sale, cultivation, or manufacture of 100 pounds- 500 pounds is a felony punishable by a mandatory minimum sentence of 5 years and a maximum fine of $50,000.

The sale, cultivation, or manufacture of 500 pounds-1,000 pounds is a felony punishable by a mandatory minimum sentence of 15 years and a maximum fine of $200,000.

See
* Code of Alabama § 13A-12-231

Hash & Concentrates

In Alabama, hashish and THC concentrates are Schedule 1 substances.

Possession of a Schedule I substance is a Class C felony. A conviction for a Class C felony results in a sentence of 1year and one day to 10 years. This differs from Alabama's treatment of marijuana because with hashish there is no lesser penalty for personal use. Possession of hashish or concentrates in Alabama will be a Class C felony even if the compound would have been for personal use.

Manufacture of hashish and THC concentrates are considered manufacture of a controlled substance in the second degree which is punishable as a Class B felony. A Class B felony conviction is punishable by a term of imprisonment between 2 - 20 years and a fine no greater than $30,000. The possession of equipment or materials with the intent to manufacture a controlled substance is included under the charge of manufacture.

Manufacture of a Schedule I substance is a Class A felony if two or more of these factors are met:

* The manufacture occurred within 500 feet of a school, church, place of business, or home;
* During the manufacture a person 17 years old or young was present;
* The manufacture produced any amount of a Schedule I substance;
* A firearm was present;
* There was the use of a booby trap.
* A danger was created during the transportation or delivery of dangerous materials necessary for the manufacture that posed a risk to human health or safety.

Class A felonies conviction is punishable by a term of imprisonment between 10 - 99 years and a fine no greater than $60,000 or twice the value of manufacturing materials and products.

See
* Code of Alabama §13A-5-6
* Code of Alabama §13A-5-11
* Code of Alabama §13A-12-212
* Code of Alabama §13A-12-217
* Code of Alabama §13A-12-218
* Code of Alabama §20-2-23

Sale, furnishing, or giving a Schedule I substance by a person over 18 to a person under 18 is a Class A felony, punishable by a term of imprisonment between 10-99 years and a fine no greater than 60,000 or twice the value of the concentrate involved.

See
* Code of Alabama §13A-12-215

Paraphernalia

Sale or possession of paraphernalia is a Class A misdemeanor punishable by a maximum sentence of 1 year imprisonment and a maximum fine of $6,000.

Sale of paraphernalia to a minor 3 or more years younger than the seller is a Class B felony punishable by 2-20 years imprisonment and a maximum fine of $30,000.

See
* Code of Alabama §13A-5-6
* Code of Alabama §13A-5-7
* Code of Alabama §13A-5-11
* Code of Alabama §13A-5-12
* Code of Alabama §13A-12-260

Miscellaneous

A marijuana conviction will result in a 6 month driver's license suspension.

See
* Code of Alabama §13A-12-290
* Code of Alabama §13A-12-291

ALASKA
LAWS & PENALTIES

Offense	Penalty	Incarceration	Max. Fine
POSSESSION			
Personal Use			
1 oz or less	None	None	$ 0
1 - 4 oz in your residence*	Not classified	N/A	$ 0
1 - less than 4 oz	Misdemeanor	1 year	$ 10,000
4 oz or more	Felony	5 years	$ 50,000
Any amount within 500 feet of school grounds or rec. center**	Felony	5 years	$ 50,000
Public consumption	Violation	None	$ 100
With Intent to Distribute			
Less than 1 oz***	Misdemeanor	1 year	$ 10,000
1 oz or more	Felony	5 years	$ 50,000

* Based on an Alaskan Supreme Court decision, possession in the home for Personal Use is protected conduct by the right-to-privacy provision in their state constitution.

** If charged with possession of marijuana in a school zone, an affirmative defense may be raised in court that the conduct took place entirely within a private residence.

*** State regulators are anticipated to begin issuing permits in February 2016 for retailers wishing to engage in cannabis sales. Currently, a person may convey up to one ounce to anyone 21 years old or older without compensation.

Offense	Penalty	Incarceration	Max. Fine
SALE OR DELIVERY			
Less than 1 oz	Misdemeanor	1 year	$ 10,000
1 oz or more	Felony	5 years	$ 50,000
To a person under 19 who is 3 years or more younger than the seller.	Felony	10 years	$ 100,000
CULTIVATION			
Up to 6 plants (no more than 3 mature)	None	None	$ 0
6 - 25 plants in your residence*	Not classified	N/A	$ 0
25 plants or more	Felony	5 years	$ 1,000
To a person under 19 who is 3 years or more younger than the seller.	Felony	10 years	$ 100,000

* Based on an Alaskan Supreme Court decision, possession in the home for Personal Use is protected conduct by the right-to-privacy provision in their state constitution.

Offense	Penalty	Incarceration	Max. Fine
HASH & CONCENTRATES			
Possession of 3g or less	Misdemeanor	0 - 1 year	$ 10,000
Possession of more than 3g	Felony	0 - 2 years	$ 50,000
Delivery, manufacture, or possessing With Intent to Distribute any amount	Felony	1 - 3 years	$ 100,000
CIVIL ASSET FORFEITURE			
Vehicles and other assets can be seized in a civil proceeding, regardless of whether criminal charges are brought.			
MISCELLANEOUS			
If under 1 ounce of marijuana is gifted	No Liability	None	$ 0
Offense within owned structure	Felony	5 years	$ 500,000
Administrative revocation of license to drive for consumption or possession			

Penalty Details

Marijuana is a Schedule VIA substance under the Controlled Substances chapter of Alaskan criminal law. However, tetrahydrocannabinols, hash, and hash oil are Schedule IIIA substances.

See
- Alaska Stat. § 11.71.160
- Alaska Stat. § 11.71.190

Possession for Personal Use

Adults may possess up to one ounce of marijuana and/or to grow up to six marijuana plants (no more than three mature) for non-commercial purposes. Sharing or gifting 1 ounce or less, or 6 plants or less for personal use to persons at least 21 years of age quantities of marijuana is also permitted under the new law; however the consumption of cannabis in public remains an offense and is punishable by a fine of up to $100.

See
- Alaska Stat. § 17.38.020
- Alaska Stat. § 17.38.040

Possession of 1 to less than 4 ounces is a Class A misdemeanor punishable by up to 1 year imprisonment and/or a fine up to $10,000. However, if the use, display, or possession was for personal use and occurred in the confines of the offender's private residence, there is no penalty and this act is protected under the Alaskan constitutional right to privacy.

Possession of 4 or more ounces of marijuana is a class C felony punishable by up to 5 years imprisonment and/or a fine up to $50,000.

See
- Alaska Stat. § 11.71.040
- Alaska Stat. § 11.71.050
- Alaska Stat. § 11.71.060
- Alaska Stat. § 12.55.035
- Alaska Stat. § 12.55.125(d), (e)
- Alaska Stat. § 12.55.135
- Ravin v. State, 537 P.2d 494 (Alaska 1975)
- Noy v. State, 83 P.3d 545 (Alaska Ct. App. 2003)

Possession within 500 feet of school grounds, a recreation or youth center, or on a school bus is a class C felony punishable by up to 5 years imprisonment and/or a fine up to $50,000. It is an affirmative defense to this charge that the violation occurred entirely within the confines of a personal residence.

See
- Alaska Stat. § 11.71.040
- Alaska Stat. § 12.55.035
- Alaska Stat. § 12.55.125(d), (e)

Possession with Intent to Distribute

It is a class A misdemeanor punishable by up to 1 year imprisonment and/or a fine up to $10,000 to possess with intent to distribute less than 1 ounce of marijuana. Possession with intent to distribute an ounce or more of marijuana is a class C felony punishable by up to 5 years imprisonment and/or a fine up to $50,000.

See
- Alaska Stat. § 11.71.040
- Alaska Stat. § 11.71.050
- Alaska Stat. § 12.55.035
- Alaska Stat. § 12.55.125
- Alaska Stat. § 12.55.135

Sale/Delivery

Retail sales of cannabis by state-licensed entities to those over the age of 21 are regulated in this state. Marijuana sales by unlicensed entities remain subject to criminal penalties.

It is a class A misdemeanor punishable by up to 1 year imprisonment and/or a fine up to $10,000 to deliver with or without compensation less than 1 ounce of marijuana. Delivery with or without compensation of an ounce or more of marijuana is a class C felony punishable by up to 5 years imprisonment and/or a fine up to $50,000.

See
- Alaska Stat. § 11.71.040
- Alaska Stat. § 11.71.050
- Alaska Stat. § 12.55.035
- Alaska Stat. § 12.55.125
- Alaska Stat. § 12.55.135

Delivery to a person under the age of 19 by a person at least 3 years his senior is a class B felony punishable by up to 10 years imprisonment and/or a fine up to $100,000.

See
- Alaska Stat. § 11.71.030
- Alaska Stat. § 12.55.035

Cultivation

Adults may possess up to one ounce of marijuana and/or to grow up to six marijuana plants (no more than three mature) for non-commercial purposes. Cultivation shall be in a location where plants are not visible to public view without use of binoculars, aircraft, or other optical aids. One must take reasonable precautions to ensure the plants are secure from unauthorized access. Cultivation may only occur on property lawfully possessed by the cultivator or with consent from the person in lawful possession. Violation of these rules while otherwise in compliance with AS § 17.38.020 is punishable by a fine of up to $750.

See
- Alaska Stat. § 17.38.030

Cultivation of less than 25 plants of marijuana for personal use in a private residence is protected under the right to privacy of the Alaska constitution. Cultivation of 25 plants or more is a class C felony punishable by up to 5 years imprisonment and/or a fine up to $50,000.

See
- Alaska Stat. § 11.71.040
- Alaska Stat. § 12.55.035
- Alaska Stat. § 12.55.125
- Ravin v. State, 537 P.2d 494 (Alaska 1975)
- Noy v. State, 83 P.3d 545 (Alaska Ct. App. 2003)

Hash & Concentrates

Hashish, hashish oil, and any other compound, mixture, or preparation containing THC is a Schedule IIIA substance.

See
- Alaska Stat. §11.71.160(f)
- Alaska Stat. §11.71.900

Possessing less than 3 grams of hashish or concentrate is considered misconduct involving a controlled substance in the fifth degree. Misconduct involving a controlled substance in the fifth degree is a Class A misdemeanor. A Class A misdemeanor conviction is punishable by a fine of up to $10,000 and a sentence of up to 1 year.

See
- Alaska Stat. §11.71.050
- Alaska Stat. §12.55.035(b)(5)
- Alaska Stat. §12.55.135(a)

Possessing more than three grams or more of hashish or concentrate is considered misconduct involving a controlled substance in the fourth degree. Possessing hashish or concentrates on a school bus or within 500 feet of a school or youth center is also misconduct involving a controlled substance in the fourth degree. Misconduct involving a controlled substance in the fourth degree is a Class C felony. A Class C felony conviction is punishable by a fine of up to $50,000 and a sentence of 0 -2 years, but previous felony convictions will increase the sentence up to 5 years total.

See
- Alaska Stat. §11.71.040
- Alaska Stat. §12.55.125(e)
- Alaska Stat. §12.55.035(b)(4)

Delivering any amount of a hashish or concentrate to an individual less than 19 years in age and who is at least three years younger than the person delivering the substance is misconduct involving a controlled substance in the first degree. Misconduct involving a controlled substance in the first degree is an unclassified felony which is punishable by a fine of up to $500,000 and a sentence of 5 - 99 years.

See
- Alaska Stat. §11.71.010
- Alaska Stat. §12.55.125(b)
- Alaska Stat. §12.55.035(b)(1)

Delivering, manufacturing, or possessing hashish or THC concentrates with the intent to deliver is considered misconduct involving a controlled substance in the third degree, which is a Class B felony. A Class B felony conviction is punishable by a fine of up to $100,000 and a sentence of 1 - 3 years, but previous felony convictions will increase the sentence up to 10 years total.

See
- Alaska Stat. §11.71.030
- Alaska Stat. §12.55.125(d)
- Alaska Stat. §12.55.035(b)(3)

If charged with misconduct involving a controlled substance in the fourth degree due to the crime occurring within 500 feet of a school or youth center then the defendant may raise the affirmative defense that all the activity took place within a private residence. This defense does not prevent a lesser charge from being brought.

See
- Alaska Stat. §12.71.040(h)

While Alaska does recognize medical affirmative defenses for possession of marijuana, those defenses do not apply to hashish or concentrates.

See
- Alaska Stat. §12.71.090

Paraphernalia

Alaska does not have any laws punishing the possession, sale, or manufacture of paraphernalia.

Sentencing

The court, after rendering judgment or within 60 days of doing so, may suspend imposition of a sentence or part of a sentence and place the offender on probation. For first time offenders, the court may suspend imposition of a sentence for up to 1 year or for the maximum duration of the sentence that may be imposed, whichever is greater, if it determines that it would be in the interest of justice.

See
- Alaska Stat. § 12.55.080
- Alaska Stat. § 12.55.085

For violations of the controlled substances chapter of Alaskan criminal law which involve the person's own use of the substance, they may be committed to the Department of Corrections for treatment for up to 1 year. This may be in place of fine or imprisonment, but only if the imprisonment would not have exceeded 1 year.

See
- Alaska Stat. § 11.71.305

Presumptive terms of imprisonment increase for subsequent felony convictions.

See
- Alaska Stat. § 12.55.085(d)(3)-(4)

Forfeiture

Vehicles and other property may be seized for controlled substance violations. Within 20 days of seizure of the property, the commissioner of public safety must notify all persons with an interest in the property. A person has 30 days to respond to this notice with a claim to the property.

See
- Alaska Stat. § 17.30.110
- Alaska Stat. § 17.30.112
- Alaska Stat. § 17.30.116

Miscellaneous

Administrative revocation of license to drive for consumption or possession of alcohol or drugs

The department shall revoke the driver's license or permit, privilege to drive, or privilege to obtain a license of a person not yet 18 years of age for six months when notified of an informal adjustment and shall revoke the person's driver's license or permit... for an additional six months if informed of unsuccessful adjustment.

See
- Alaska Stat. § 28.15.176
- Alaska Stat. § 47.12.060(b)(4)

Knowingly maintaining a structure used for drug offenses

It is a class C felony punishable by up to 5 years imprisonment and/or a fine up to $50,000 to maintain a structure (including vehicles and houses) that the owner knows is used for selling, storing, or using marijuana.

See
- Alaska Stat. § 11.71.040
- Alaska Stat. § 12.55.035

Civil damages

When a person engages in action that causes civil damages while under the influence of a controlled substance and the intoxication contributed significantly to the damages, the person who sold or gave them the substance is strictly liable to him for the damages.

See
- Alaska Stat. § 09.65.205

ARIZONA
LAWS & PENALTIES

Offense	Penalty	Incarceration	Max. Fine
POSSESSION			
Less than 2 lbs	Felony	4 months - 2 years	$ 150,000
2 - less than 4 lbs	Felony	6 months - 2.5 years	$ 150,000
4 lbs or more	Felony	1 - 3.75 years	$ 150,000
SALE			
Less than 2 lbs	Felony	1 - 3.75 years	$ 150,000
2 - 4 lbs	Felony	2 - 8.75 years	$ 150,000
More than 4 lbs	Felony	3 - 12.5 years	$ 150,000
MANUFACTURE/CULTIVATION			
Less than 2 lbs	Felony	6 months - 2.5 years	$ 150,000
2 - 4 lbs	Felony	1 - 3.75 years	$ 150,000
More than 4 lbs	Felony	2 - 8.75 years	$ 150,000
TRAFFICKING			
Less than 2 lbs	Felony	2 - 8.75 years	$ 150,000
2 lbs or more	Felony	3 - 12.5 years	$ 150,000
HASH & CONCENTRATES			
Possession or Use	Felony	1 - 3.75 years	$ 150,000
Manufacture, Sale, or Trafficking	Felony	3 - 12.5 years	$ 150,000
PARAPHERNALIA			
Possession or advertising of paraphernalia	Felony	4 months - 2 years	$ 150,000

MISCELLANEOUS

Employing a minor in the commission of a drug offense, being convicted of a prior felony, or committing a drug offense in a school zone, lead to an increased sentence.

Penalty Details

Possession

Possession for personal use of less than 2 pounds of marijuana is a Class 6 felony, punishable by a minimum sentence of 4 months, a maximum sentence of 2 years, and a minimum fine of $1000 or a fine to exhaust the proceeds of the drug offense. If probation is granted after conviction for this offense, the offender will face a mandatory sentence of 24 hours of community service.

Possession for personal use of 2-4 pounds of marijuana is a Class 5 felony, punishable by a minimum sentence of 6 months, a maximum sentence of 2.5 years, and a minimum fine of $1000 or a fine to exhaust the proceeds of the drug offense. If probation is granted after conviction for this offense, the offender will face a mandatory sentence of 24 hours of community service.

Possession for personal use of more than 4 pounds of marijuana is a Class 4 felony, punishable by a minimum sentence of 1 year, a maximum sentence of 3.75 years, and a minimum fine of $1000 or a fine to exhaust the proceeds of the drug offense. If probation is granted after conviction for this offense, the offender will face a mandatory sentence of 24 hours of community service.

See
- Arizona REV. STAT. § 13-3401
- Arizona REV. STAT. § 13-3405
- Arizona REV. STAT. § 13-702
- Arizona REV. STAT. § 13-801
- Arizona REV. STAT. § 13-821

Sale

The sale, or possessing for sale, of less than 2 pounds of marijuana is a Class 4 felony, punishable by a minimum sentence of 1 year, a maximum sentence of 3.75 years, and a minimum fine of $1000 or a fine to exhaust the proceeds of the drug offense. If probation is granted after conviction for this offense, the offender will face a mandatory sentence of 240 hours of community service.

The sale, or possessing for sale, of between 2-4 pounds of marijuana is a Class 3 felony, punishable by a minimum sentence of 2 years, a maximum sentence of 8.75 years, and a minimum fine of $1000 or a fine to exhaust the proceeds of the drug offense.

The sale, or possessing for sale, of more than 4 pounds of marijuana is a Class 2 felony, punishable by a minimum sentence of 2 years, a maximum sentence of 12.5 years, and a minimum fine of $1000 or a fine to exhaust the proceeds of the drug offense.

See
- Arizona REV. STAT. § 13-3405
- Arizona REV. STAT § 13-702
- Arizona REV. STAT. § 13-801
- Arizona REV. STAT § 13-821

Manufacture/Cultivation

Producing less than 2 pounds of marijuana is a Class 5 felony, punishable by a minimum sentence of 6 months, a maximum sentence of 2.5 years, and a minimum fine of $1000 or a fine to exhaust the proceeds of the drug offense. If probation is granted after conviction for this offense, the offender will face a mandatory sentence of 240 hours of community service.

Producing between 2-4 pounds of marijuana is a Class 4 felony, punishable by a minimum sentence of 1 year, a maximum sentence of 3.75 years, and a minimum fine of $1000 or a fine to exhaust the proceeds of the drug offense.

Producing more than 4 pounds of marijuana is a Class 3 felony, punishable by a minimum sentence of 2 years, a maximum sentence of 8.75 years, and a minimum fine of $1000 or a fine to exhaust the proceeds of the drug offense.

See
- Arizona REV. STAT. § 13-3405
- Arizona REV. STAT. § 13-702
- Arizona REV. STAT. § 13-801
- Arizona REV. STAT § 13-821

Trafficking

Bringing less than 2 pounds of marijuana into AZ is a Class 3 felony, punishable by a minimum sentence of 2 years, a maximum sentence of 8.75 years, and a minimum fine of $1000 or a fine to exhaust the proceeds of the drug offense. If probation is granted after conviction for this offense, the offender will face a mandatory sentence of 24 hours of community service.

Bringing 2 pounds or more of marijuana into AZ is a Class 2 felony, punishable by a minimum sentence of 2 years, a maximum sentence of 12.5 years, and a minimum fine of $1000 or a fine to exhaust the proceeds of the drug offense.

See
- Arizona REV. STAT. § 13-3405
- Arizona REV. STAT. § 13-702
- Arizona REV. STAT. § 13-801
- Arizona REV. STAT § 13-821

Hash & Concentrates

In AZ, hashish and concentrates are Schedule I narcotic drugs listed as "Cannabis." "Cannabis" is classified in Arizona as "The resin extracted from any part of a plant of the genus cannabis, and every compound, manufacture, salt, derivative, mixture or preparation of such plant, its seeds or its resin ... and every compound, manufacture, salt, derivative, mixture or preparation of such resin or tetrahydrocannabinol."

See
- Arizona REV. STAT. § 13-3401(20)(w)
- Arizona REV. STAT. § 13-3401(4)(a)-(b)

Knowingly possessing or using a narcotic drug is a class 4 felony, punishable by a minimum of 1 year imprisonment, a maximum of 3 years in prison, and a maximum fine of not less than two thousand dollars or three times the value as determined by the court of the narcotic drugs involved in or giving rise to the charge, whichever is greater.

Knowingly possessing a narcotic drug for sale is a class 2 felony, punishable by a minimum of 3 years imprisonment, a maximum of 10 years imprisonment, and a maximum fine of not less than two thousand dollars or three times the value as determined by the court of the narcotic drugs involved in or giving rise to the charge, whichever is greater.

Knowingly possessing the equipment or chemicals, or both, for the purpose of manufacturing a narcotic drug is a class 3 felony, punishable by a minimum of 2 years imprisonment, a maximum of 7 years imprisonment, and a maximum fine of not less than two thousand dollars or three times the value as determined by the court of the narcotic drugs involved in or giving rise to the charge, whichever is greater.

Manufacturing a narcotic drug is a class 2 felony, punishable by a minimum of 3 years imprisonment, a maximum of 10 years imprisonment, and a maximum fine of not less than two thousand dollars or three times the value as determined by the court of the narcotic drugs involved in or giving rise to the charge, whichever is greater.

Transporting a narcotic drug into the state is a class 2 felony, punishable by a minimum of 3 years imprisonment, a maximum of 10 years imprisonment, and a maximum fine of not less than two thousand dollars or three times the value as determined by the court of the narcotic drugs involved in or giving rise to the charge, whichever is greater.

See
- Arizona REV. STAT. § 13-3408
- Arizona REV. STAT. § 13-702
- Arizona REV. STAT. § 13-801
- Arizona REV. STAT § 13-821

Paraphernalia

Any possession of drug paraphernalia, as well as advertising for the sale of drug paraphernalia, is a Class 6 felony, punishable by a minimum sentence of 4 months, a maximum sentence of 2 years, and a minimum fine of $1000 or a fine to exhaust the proceeds of the drug offense.

See
- Arizona REV. STAT. § 13-3415
- Arizona REV. STAT. § 13-702
- Arizona REV. STAT. § 13-801
- Arizona REV. STAT § 13-821

Miscellaneous

Employing a minor in the commission of a drug offense, being convicted of a prior felony, or committing a drug offense in a school zone, lead to an increased sentence.

See
- Arizona REV. STAT. § 13-3409
- Arizona REV. STAT. § 13-3410
- Arizona REV. STAT. § 13-3411
- Arizona REV. STAT. § 13-703

Class 6 Felony; Designation

If convicted of any Class 6 felony not involving a dangerous offense and if the court is of the opinion that it would be unduly harsh to sentence the defendant for a felony, the court may enter judgment of conviction for a Class 1 misdemeanor, or may place the defendant on probation in accordance with chapter 9 of this title. This does not apply to any person who stands convicted of a Class 6 felony and who has previously been convicted of two or more felonies.

See
- Arizona Rev. Stat. § 13-604

Fines

A class 1 misdemeanor fine shall be not more than $2500. The minimum fine for a first time drug offense is $1000. For a second or subsequent offense there shall be a fine of at least $2000.

See
- Arizona REV. STAT. § 13-802
- Arizona REV. STAT. § 13-821

ARKANSAS
LAWS & PENALTIES

Offense	Penalty	Incarceration	Max. Fine
POSSESSION			
Less than 4 oz (first offense)	Misdemeanor	1 year or less	$ 2,500
1 - less than 4 oz (subsequent offense)	Felony	6 years or less	$ 10,000
4 oz - less than 10 lbs	Felony	6 years or less	$ 10,000
10 - less than 25 lbs	Felony	3* - 10 years	$ 10,000
25 - less than 100 lbs	Felony	5* - 20 years	$ 15,000
100 - less than 500 lbs	Felony	6* - 30 years	$ 15,000
* Mandatory minimum sentence			
DELIVERY			
14 g or less	Misdemeanor	1 year or less	$ 2,500
14 g - 4 oz	Felony	6 years or less	$ 10,000
4 oz - 25 lbs	Felony	3* - 10 years	$ 10,000
25 - 100 lbs	Felony	5* - 20 years	$ 15,000
100 - 500 lbs	Felony	6* - 30 years	$ 15,000
* Mandatory minimum sentence			
Includes possession with intent to deliver			
Includes manufacture			
TRAFFICKING			
500 lbs or more	Felony	10* - 40 years	$ 15,000
* Mandatory minimum sentence			
HASH & CONCENTRATES			
Penalties for hashish are the same as for marijuana. Please see the marijuana penalties section for further details.			
PARAPHERNALIA			
Possession with purpose to use	Misdemeanor	1 year or less	$ 2,500
Possession with purpose to grow	Felony	6 years or less	$ 10,000
Delivery of smoking paraphernalia to a minor at least 3 years younger	Misdemeanor	1 year or less	$ 2,500
Delivery of growing paraphernalia to a minor at least 3 years younger	Felony	5* - 20 years	$ 15,000
* Mandatory minimum sentence			

Penalty Details

Simple Possession:

Possession of less than 4 ounces of marijuana is a Class A Misdemeanor, punishable by up to 1 year in jail and a fine of up to $2,500.

Possession of between 1 ounce and less than 4 ounces by an offender who has had 2 or more previous drug convictions is a Class D Felony, punishable by up to 6 years in prison and a fine of up to $10,000.

Possession of between 4 ounces and less than 10 pounds is a Class D Felony, punishable by up to 6 years in prison and a fine of up to $10,000.

Possession of between 10 pounds and less than 25 pounds is a Class C Felony, punishable by a mandatory 3 year minimum sentence, up to 10 years, and a fine not to exceed $10,000.

Possession of between 25 pounds and less than 100 pounds is a Class B Felony, punishable by a mandatory 5 year minimum sentence, up to 20 years, and a fine not to exceed $15,000.

Possession of 100 pounds and less than 500 pounds is a Class A Felony, punishable by a mandatory 6 year minimum sentence, up to 30 years, and a fine not to exceed $15,000.

See
• Arkansas Code 5-64-419(b)(5)
First time possession offenders may be sentenced to parole for a period of not less than one year, in lieu of jail time.

See
• Arkansas Code 5-64-413
A second or subsequent conviction will result in a doubled penalty.

See
• Arkansas Code 5-64-408

Possession with Intent to Deliver

Possession of up to 14 g (1/2 Oz) of marijuana with the intent to deliver it to an another individual is a Class A misdemeanor, punishable by up to 1 year in jail and a fine of up to $2,500.

Possession of between 14 g (1/2 Oz) and less than 4 ounces of marijuana with the intent to deliver it to an another individual is a Class D Felony, punishable by up to 6 years in prison and a fine of up to $10,000.

Possession of between 4 ounces and less than 25 pounds of marijuana with the intent to deliver it to an another individual is a Class C Felony, punishable by a mandatory 3 year minimum sentence, up to 10 years, and a fine not to exceed $10,000.

Possession of between 25 pounds and less than 100 pounds of marijuana with the intent to deliver it to an another individual is a Class B Felony, punishable by a mandatory 5 year minimum sentence, up to 20 years, and a fine not to exceed $15,000.

Possession of between 100 pounds and less than 500 pounds of marijuana with the intent to deliver it to an another individual is a Class A Felony, punishable by a mandatory 6 year minimum sentence, up to 30 years, and a fine not to exceed $15,000.

Possession with Intent to Distribute can be shown if the:

1. Person possesses means to weigh and separate marijuana
2. Person possesses a written record of drug transactions
3. Marijuana is bagged separately to facilitate delivery
4. Person possesses a firearm on their person
5. Person possesses at least 2 other controlled substances in addition to the marijuana
6. Any other proof that the individual was intending to deliver the marijuana can be shown

See
• Arkansas Code 5-64-436
A second or subsequent conviction will result in a doubled penalty.

See
• Arkansas Code 5-64-408

Delivery

Delivering 14g or less of marijuana to another individual, with or without remuneration, is a Class A Misdemeanor, punishable by up to 1 year in jail and a fine of up to $2,500.

Delivering between 14g and less than 4 ounces of marijuana to another individual, with or without remuneration, is a Class D Felony, punishable by up to 6 years in prison and a fine of up to $10,000.

Delivering between 4 ounces and less than 25 pounds of marijuana to another individual, with or without remuneration, is a Class C Felony, punishable by a mandatory 3 year minimum sentence, up to 10 years, and a fine not to exceed $10,000.

Delivering between 25 pounds and less than 100 pounds of marijuana to another individual, with or without remuneration, is a Class B Felony, punishable by a mandatory 5 year minimum sentence, up to 20 years, and a fine not to exceed $15,000.

Delivering between 100 pounds and less than 500 pounds of marijuana to another individual, with or without remuneration, is a Class A Felony, punishable by a mandatory 6 year minimum sentence, up to 30 years, and a fine not to exceed $15,000.

See
• Arkansas Code 5-64-438
Delivering marijuana to a minor at least 3 years younger than the deliverer will result in a doubled penalty

See
• Arkansas Code 5-64-406 (b)
A second or subsequent conviction will result in a doubled penalty.

See
• Arkansas Code 5-64-408

Cultivation

Cultivation in Arkansas is punished as either simple possession or as possession with intent to deliver, depending on the amount of marijuana being produced and other factors that may lead to the conclusion that the marijuana was being grown for reasons other than strict personal use. See the "Simple Possession" and "Possession with Intent to Deliver" sections for further penalty details.

Manufacture

Manufacturing 14 g or less of marijuana is a Class A Misdemeanor, punishable by up to 1 year in jail and a fine of up to $2,500.

Manufacturing between 14 g and 4 ounces of marijuana is a Class D Felony, punishable by up to 6 years in prison and a fine of up to $10,000.

Manufacturing between 4 ounces and 25 pounds of marijuana is a Class C Felony, punishable by a mandatory 3 year minimum sentence, up to 10 years, and a fine not to exceed $10,000.

Manufacturing between 25 pounds and 100 pounds of marijuana is a Class B Felony, punishable by a mandatory 5 year minimum sentence, up to 20 years, and a fine not to exceed $15,000.

Manufacturing 100 pounds or more of marijuana is a Class A Felony, punishable by a mandatory 6 year minimum sentence, up to 30 years, and a fine not to exceed $15,000.

See
• Arkansas Code 5-64-439
A second or subsequent conviction will result in a doubled penalty.

See
• Arkansas Code 5-64-408

Trafficking

Possessing 500 pounds or more of marijuana is classified as trafficking and is a Class Y Felony, punishable by a mandatory minimum sentence of 10 years and a maximum of 40 years imprisonment.

See
• Arkansas Code 5-64-440

Hash & Concentrates

Penalties for hashish are the same as for marijuana. Please see the marijuana penalties section for further details.

See
• Arkansas Code § 5-64-101(17)   • Arkansas Code § 5-64-215

Paraphernalia

Possession with purpose to use paraphernalia is a Class A misdemeanor, punishable by up to 1 year in jail and a fine of up to $2,500.

Possession of growing paraphernalia is a Class D Felony, punishable by up to 6 years in prison and a fine of up to $10,000.

See
• Arkansas Code 5-64-443
Delivering of drug paraphernalia to a minor at least 3 years younger than the deliver is a Class A Misdemeanor, punishable by up to 1 year in jail and a fine of up to $2,500.

Delivery during the course and in furtherance of a felony violation is a Class B Felony and punishable by a mandatory 5 year minimum sentence, up to 20 years, and a fine not to exceed $15,000.

Delivering of growing paraphernalia to a minor at least 3 years younger than the deliver is a Class B Felony, punishable by a mandatory 5 year minimum sentence, up to 20 years, and a fine not to exceed $15,000.

See
• Arkansas Code 5-64-444
A second or subsequent conviction will result in a doubled penalty.

See
• Arkansas Code 5-64-408

Miscellaneous

Whenever a person pleads guilty, nolo contendere, or is found guilty of any criminal offense involving the illegal possession or use of controlled substances, or of any drug offense, in this state or any other state, the court having jurisdiction of such matter... shall prepare... an order to suspend the driving privileges of the person for six (6) months.

See
• Arkansas Code 27-16-915

CALIFORNIA
LAWS & PENALTIES

Offense	Penalty	Incarceration	Max. Fine
POSSESSION			
Personal Use			
28.5 grams or less	Infraction	N/A	$ 100
28.5 grams or less, over 18 years, and occurred on school grounds	Misdemeanor	10 days	$ 500
28.5 grams or less, under 18 years	Misdemeanor	10 days*	$ 250
More than 28.5 grams	Misdemeanor	6 months	$ 500
With Intent to Distribute			
Any amount	Felony	16 months - 3 years	$ 0

*Detention center

Offense	Penalty	Incarceration	Max. Fine
SALE OR DELIVERY			
Any amount	Felony	2 - 4 years	$ 0
Gift of 28.5 grams or less	Misdemeanor	N/A	$ 100
Over 18 years to an individual 14-17 years	Felony	3 - 5 years	$ 0
Over 18 years to an individual under 14 years	Felony	3 - 7 years	$ 0
CULTIVATION			
Any amount	Felony	16 months - 3 years	$ 0
HASH & CONCENTRATES			
Possession	N/A	1 year	$ 500
Unauthorized manufacture	N/A	16 months - 3 years	$ 500
Chemical manufacture	N/A	3 - 7 years	$ 50,000
PARAPHERNALIA			
Sale, delivery, possession with intent, and manufacture with intent	Misdemeanor	15 days - 6 months	$ 500
Involving a minor at least 3 years junior	Misdemeanor	1 year	$ 1,000

FORFEITURE

Vehicles and other property may be seized for controlled substance violations.

MISCELLANEOUS

Using a minor in the unlawful sale or transport of marijuana is a Felony punishable by 3-7 years imprisonment. Inducing a minor to use marijuana is also a Felony punishable by 3-7 years imprisonment.

Any violation of the California Uniform Controlled Substances Act results in a fine up to $150.

A person who participates in the illegal marketing of marijuana is liable for civil damages.

It is a Misdemeanor to loiter in a public place with the intent to commit certain controlled substances offenses.

A controlled substance conviction can result in suspension of driving privileges.

Penalty Details

Marijuana is a Schedule I hallucinogenic substance under the California Uniform Controlled Substances Act.

See
- California Health & Safety Code § 11054(d)(13)

Possession for Personal Use

Possession of up to and including 28.5 grams of marijuana is an infraction punishable by a fine of $100. Possession of more than 28.5 grams is a misdemeanor punishable by up to 6 months imprisonment and/or a fine up to $500. If the amount possessed is 28.5 grams or less but the person is 18 years of age or older and the possession occurred on school grounds, the person is guilty of a misdemeanor punishable by up to 10 days imprisonment and/or a fine up to $500. If the offender was younger than 18 years of age, then the offense is a misdemeanor punishable by a fine up to $250 for the first offense and a fine up to $500 or commitment to a detention center for up to 10 days.

See
- California Health & Safety Code § 11357

Possession with Intent to Distribute

Possession with intent to distribute any amount of marijuana is a felony punishable by 16-36 months imprisonment.

See
- California Health & Safety Code § 11359
- California Penal Code § 1170(h)

Sale/Delivery

Sale or delivery of any amount of marijuana is a felony punishable by 2-4 years imprisonment. However, a gift or mere transportation of 28.5 grams or less of marijuana is a misdemeanor punishable by fine up to $100. If a person is arrested for this misdemeanor, they shall be released upon presentation of sufficient identification and signing of a written promise to appear in court.

See
- California Health & Safety Code § 11360

Delivery or attempted delivery without compensation of any amount of marijuana by an individual aged 18 years or older to an individual who is 14-17 years old is a felony punishable by 3-5 years imprisonment. Delivery or attempted delivery without compensation of any amount of marijuana by an individual aged 18 years or older to an individual who is under the age of 14 is a felony punishable by 3-7 years imprisonment. Sale or attempted sale of any amount of marijuana by an individual aged 18 years or older to an individual under 18 years of age is a felony punishable by 3-7 years imprisonment.

See
- California Health & Safety Code § 11361

Cultivation

Cultivation of any amount of marijuana is a felony punishable by 16-36 months imprisonment.

See
- California Health & Safety Code § 11358
- California Penal Code § 1170(h)

Hash & Concentrates

In California, hashish or concentrates are referred to as "concentrated cannabis". Possession of concentrated cannabis is punishable by a fine of $500 and a term of imprisonment no longer than 1 year.

See
- California Health & Safety Code §11006.5
- California Health & Safety Code §11357(a)

The penalties associated with the manufacture of hashish or concentrates depends on what method was used during the manufacture. If the manufacturing process involved extraction chemicals, such as butane, then it is considered manufacture by means of chemical synthesis of a controlled substance. Manufacture by means of chemical synthesis of a controlled substance carries a fine no greater than $50,000 and a term of imprisonment of 3, 5, or 7 years as determined by the court. If the manufacturing process utilized screens, presses, or any other means not involving a chemical synthesis, then the offense is considered unauthorized processing of marijuana. Unauthorized processing of marijuana carries a term of imprisonment 16 months, 2 years, or three years as determined by the court.

See
- California Health & Safety Code §11379.6(a)
- California Health & Safety Code §11358
- California Penal Code §1170(h)
- People v. Bergen, 166 Cal.App.4th 161 (2008)

Apart from the provisions mentioned, concentrated cannabis is included within the definition of marijuana for all other offenses, such as intent to sell, providing to a minor, etc. For information concerning those offenses, check the California marijuana laws section of this website.

See
- California Health & Safety Code §11018

Paraphernalia

There is no penalty for the simple possession of marijuana paraphernalia. Sale, delivery, possession with intent to sell or deliver, and manufacture with intent to sell or deliver marijuana paraphernalia is a misdemeanor punishable by 15-180 days imprisonment and/or a fine of $30-$500. Delivery of marijuana paraphernalia by an individual aged 18 years or older to a minor at least 3 years his junior is a misdemeanor punishable by up to 1 year imprisonment and/or a fine up to $1,000.

See
- California Health & Safety Code § 11364.7
- California Health & Safety Code § 11374

Sentencing

Possession for personal use, using or being under the influence of marijuana, presence in a room where a marijuana violation occurs, or cultivation if the amount is for personal use are offenses that are eligible for deferred entry of judgment if certain conditions are met. These include: no prior convictions for controlled substances violations; the offense charged did not involve violence; there is no evidence that narcotics or restricted dangerous drugs were involved; the offender has never had probation or parole revoked; the offender has not completed this deferred entry within 5 years of the time of the charged offense; and the offender has no felony convictions within 5 years of the time of the charged offense.

See
- California Penal Code § 1000

Probation may be available for marijuana offenses. As a condition of probation for controlled substances violations, offenders must participate in education or treatment if the court determines that it will benefit the offender. Sentences for many violations may not be eligible for probation or suspension if the offender has been previously convicted of a felony offense involving a controlled substance.

See
- California Health & Safety Code § 11370
- Cal. Health & Safety Code § 11373
- California Penal Code § 1203.1

Forfeiture

Vehicles and other property may be seized for controlled substance violations. Upon conviction for sale, possession with intent to distribute, or cultivation of marijuana, the seized property becomes the property of the state. If law enforcement seizes property which it does not intend to use as evidence and the seizing agency does not refer the case to the Attorney General for forfeiture proceedings within 15 days, the property must be returned. If the Attorney General intends to pursue a forfeiture proceeding, then a person claiming interest in the property has 30 days from actual notice or publication of notice of the proceedings to respond.

See
- California Health & Safety Code §§ 11469-11495

Miscellaneous

Involvement of a minor in a drug offense

Using a minor in the unlawful sale or transport of marijuana is a felony punishable by 3-7 years imprisonment. Inducing a minor to use marijuana is also a felony punishable by 3-7 years imprisonment.

See
- California Health & Safety Code § 11361

Drug program fee

Any violation of the California Uniform Controlled Substances Act results in a fine up to $150 in addition to the authorized fine for the offense.

See
- California Health & Safety Code § 11372.7

Drug Dealer Liability Act

A person who participates in the illegal marketing of marijuana is liable for civil damages caused by these actions.

See
- California Health & Safety Code §§ 11700-11717

Loitering for drug activities

It is a misdemeanor to loiter in a public place with the intent to commit certain controlled substances offenses.

See
- California Health & Safety Code §§ 11530-11538

Suspension of Driving Privileges

A controlled substance conviction can result in suspension of driving privileges for up to 3 years if the use of a motor vehicle was used in or incidental to the offense. For each drug-related conviction that a person 13-20 years old may receive, their driving privileges are suspended for 1 year, but if the person does not yet have the privilege to drive, suspension will begin at the time the person becomes legally eligible to drive.

See
- California Vehicle. Code § 13202
- California Vehicle. Code § 13202.5

COLORADO
LAWS & PENALTIES

Offense	Penalty	Incarceration	Max. Fine
POSSESSION			
Personal Use			
1 oz or less*	No Penalty	None	$ 0
Transfer of 1 oz or less for no remuneration*	No Penalty	None	$ 0
More than 1 - 2 oz	Petty Offense	None	$ 100
Open and public displays or uses of 2 oz or less	Petty Offense	None	$ 100
More than 2 - 6 oz	Misdemeanor	0 - 12 months	$ 700
More than 6 - 12 oz	Misdemeanor	6 - 18 months	$ 5,000
More than 12 oz	Felony	1 - 2 years	$ 100,000

* By persons 21 years of age or older.

With Intent to Distribute

Possession of 8 oz or more is considered possession with the intent to distribute will enhance the sentence.

SALE OR DISTRIBUTION			
4 oz or less	Misdemeanor	6 - 18 months	$ 5,000
More than 4 oz – 12 oz	Felony	6 months - 2 years	$ 100,000
More than 12 oz – 5 lbs	Felony	2 - 6 years	$ 500,000
More than 5 lbs – 50 lbs	Felony	4 - 16 years	$ 750,000
More than 50 lbs	Felony	8 - 32 years	$ 1,000,000

Sale to a minor has a greater penalty. See details for information.

CULTIVATION			
6 plants or fewer*	No Penalty	None	$ 0
6 - 30 plants	Felony	6 months - 2 years	$ 100,000
More than 30 plants	Felony	2 - 6 years	$ 500,000

* By persons 21 years of age or older.

HASH & CONCENTRATES			
Possession			
1 oz or less*	No Penalty	None	$ 0
1 - 3 oz	Misdemeanor	6 - 18 months	$ 5,000
More than 3 oz	Felony	6 months - 2 years	$ 100,000
Distribute, Transfer, or Possess with Intent			
2 oz or less	Misdemeanor	6 - 18 months	$ 5,000
More than 2 oz – 6 oz	Felony	6 months - 2 years	$ 100,000
More than 6 oz – 2.5 lbs	Felony	2 - 6 years	$ 500,000
More than 2.5 lbs – 25 lbs	Felony	4 - 16 years	$ 750,000
More than 25 lbs	Felony	8 - 32 years	$ 1,000,000

* By persons 21 years of age or older.

Sale, Transfer or Dispense to a minor has a greater penalty. See details for information.

PARAPHERNALIA			
Possession of paraphernalia	Petty Offense	N/A	$ 100

Penalty Details

Possession for Personal Use

Private possession by persons 21 years of age or older of up to one ounce is no penalty. Private cultivation of up to six marijuana plants, with no more than three being mature is no penalty. Transfer of one ounce or less for no remuneration is no penalty.

See

Colo. Const. Art. XVIII, Section 16(3)

Possession of more than 1 - 2 ounces is a drug petty offense that is punishable by a maximum fine of $100. The offender will be summoned and a court appearance is mandatory. Failure to appear in court is a Class 3 misdemeanor, which is punishable by up to 6 months in jail and a fine of up to $750.

Possession of more than 2 to 6 ounces of marijuana is a level 2 drug misdemeanor, punishable by up to 1-year imprisonment and a fine not to exceed $700.

Possession of more than 6 ounces to 12 ounces is a level 1 drug misdemeanor, which is punishable by up to eighteen months of imprisonment and a fine of $500 - $5000.

Possession of more than 12 ounces is a level 4 drug felony which is punishable by 6 months - 2 years of imprisonment, as well as a fine between $1,000-$100,000.

One who openly and publicly displays, uses, or consumes 2 ounces of marijuana or less is guilty of a drug petty offense and may be subject to24 hours of community service as well as a maximum fine of $100.

See
- § 18-1.3-401.5
- § 18-1.3-501
- §§ 18-18-406(4), (5)

Possession with Intent to Distribute

Possession of 8 ounces of marijuana or more is a lesser-included offense of possession with the intent to distribute. Each element of the possession offense is included except the quantity, which is a sentence enhancer, not an essential element of the offense.

See
- People v. Garcia, 251 P.3d 1152 (Colo. App. 2010).

Sale or Distribution

Transfer of one ounce or less for no remuneration by persons 21 years of age or older is no penalty.

See
- Colo. Const. Art. XVIII, Section 16

Retail sales of cannabis by state licensed entities to those over the age of 21 are regulated in this state. Marijuana sales by unlicensed entities remain subject to criminal penalties.

The sale of 4 ounces or less of marijuana is a level 1 drug misdemeanor punishable by 6-18 months imprisonment as well as a fine between $500-$5,000.

The sale of more than 4 ounces, but not more than 12 ounces of marijuana is a level 4 drug felony and punishable by a sentence of 6 months - 2 years and a fine of $ 1,000 - $ 100,000.

The sale of more than 12 ounces but not more than 5 pounds of marijuana is a level 3 drug felony punishable by a sentence of 2 - 6 years and a fine of $ 2,000 - $ 500,000.

The sale of more than 5 pounds but not more than 50 pounds of marijuana is a level 2 drug felony punishable by a sentence of 4 - 16 years and a fine of $ 3,000 - $ 750,000.

The sale of more than 50 pounds of marijuana is a level 1 drug felony and punishable by a sentence of 8 - 32 years and a fine of $ 5,000 - $ 1,000,000.

See
- § 18-1.3-401.5
- § 18-1.3-501
- § 18-18-406(2)(b)

To a Minor:

The sale, transfer, or dispensing of not more than 1 ounce of marijuana to a minor if the person is an adult and two years older than the minor is a level 4 drug felony punishable by a sentence of 6 months - 2 years and a fine of $ 1,000 - $ 100,000.

The sale, transfer, or dispensing of more than one ounce, but not more than six ounces of marijuana to a minor if the person is an adult and two years older than the minor is a level 3 drug felony punishable by a sentence of 2 - 6 years and a fine of $ 2,000 - $ 500,000.

The sale, transfer, or dispensing of more than 6 ounces, but not more than 2.5 pounds of marijuana to a minor if the person is an adult and two years older than the minor is a level 2 drug felony punishable by a sentence of 4 - 16 years and a fine of $ 3,000 - $ 750,000.

The sale, transfer, or dispensing of more than 2.5 pounds of marijuana to a minor if the person is an adult and two years older than the minor is a level 1 drug felony punishable by a sentence of 8 - 32 years and a fine of $ 5,000 - $ 1,000,000.

See
- § 18-1.3-401.5
- § 18-1.3-501
- § 18-18-406(1)

Cultivation

There is no penalty in Colorado for persons who privately cultivate up to 6 marijuana plants, with no more than 3 being mature.

See

Colo. Const. Art. XVIII, Section 16(3)

The cultivation of 6 plants or fewer is a level 1 drug misdemeanor punishable by 6-18 months imprisonment as well as a fine between $500-$5,000, if not at least 21 years of age.

The cultivation of more than 6 but not more than 30 plants is a level 4 drug felony punishable by 6 months - 2 imprisonment as well as a fine between $1,000-$100,000.

The cultivation of more than 30 plants is a level 3 drug felony punishable by 2-6 years imprisonment as well as a fine between $2,000-$500,000.

See
- § 18-1.3-401.5
- § 18-1.3-501

18-18-406(3) of the Colorado Revised Statutes

Hash & Concentrates

Private possession by persons 21 years of age or older of up to one ounce is no penalty.

See

Colo. Const. Art. XVIII, Section 16

Possession of more than 1 - 3 ounces of hashish or extracts is a level 1 misdemeanor punishable by a fine between $500 and $5,000 dollars and/or a term of imprisonment between 6 and 18 months.

Possession of more than 3 ounces of marijuana concentrate commits a level 4 drug felony punishable by 6 months - 2 years imprisonment as well as a fine between $1,000-$100,000.

See
- § 18-1.3-401.5
- § 18-1.3-501
- § 10-18-406(4)

Sale:

The sale of 2 ounces or less of marijuana concentrate is a level 1 drug misdemeanor punishable by 6 -18 months imprisonment as well as a fine between $500-$5,000.

The sale of more than 2 ounces - 6 ounces of marijuana concentrate is a level 4 drug felony punishable by 6 months -2 years imprisonment as well as a fine between $1,000-$100,000.

The sale of more than 6 ounces - 2.5 pounds of marijuana concentrate is a level 3 drug felony punishable by 2 - 6 years imprisonment as well as a fine between $5,000-$500,000.

The sale of more than 2.5 - 25 pounds is a level 2 drug felony punishable by a sentence of 4 - 16 years and a fine of $ 3,000 - $ 750,000.

The sale of more than 25 pounds is a level 1 drug felony punishable by a sentence of 8 - 32 years and a fine of $ 5,000 - $ 1,000,000.

See
- § 18-1.3-401.5
- § 18-1.3-501
- § 18-18-406(2)(b)

Sale to a Minor:

The sale, transfer, or dispensing of more than 1 pound of marijuana concentrate to a minor if the person is an adult and two years older than the minor is a level 1 drug felony punishable by a sentence of 8 - 32 years and a fine of $ 5,000 - $ 1,000,000.

The sale, transfer, or dispensing of more than 3 ounces, but not more than 1 pound of marijuana concentrate to a minor if the person is an adult and two years older than the minor is a level 2 drug felony punishable by 4 - 16 years and a fine of $ 5,000 - $ 750,000.

The sale, transfer, or dispensing of more than .5 ounces, but not more than 3 ounces, of marijuana concentrate to a minor if the person is an adult and two years older than the minor is a level 3 drug felony punishable by a sentence of 2 - 6 years and a fine of $ 2,000 - $ 500,000.

The sale, transfer, or dispensing of not more than .5 ounces of marijuana concentrate to a minor if the person is an adult and two years older than the minor is a level 4 drug felony punishable by a sentence of 6 months - 2 years and a fine of $ 1,000 - $ 100,000.

See
- § 18-1.3-401.5
- § 18-1.3-501
- § 18-18-406(1)

Paraphernalia

Possession of paraphernalia is a drug petty offense that is punishable by a fine of up to $100.

See
- § 18-18-428 of the Colorado Revised Statutes

CONNECTICUT
LAWS & PENALTIES

Offense	Penalty	Incarceration	Max. Fine
POSSESSION			
Personal Use			
Less than 1/2 oz (first offense)	Civil Penalty	N/A	$ 150
Less than 1/2 oz (subsequent offense)	Civil Penalty	N/A	$ 500
1/2 - less than 4 oz (first offense)	Civil Penalty	1 year	$ 1,000
1/2 - less than 4 oz (subsequent offense)	Felony	5 years	$ 3,000
4 oz or more (first offense)	Felony	5 years	$ 2,000
4 oz or more (subsequent offense)	Felony	10 years	$ 5,000
DISTRIBUTION OR CULTIVATION			
Less than 1 kilogram (first offense)	Felony	7 years	$ 25,000
Less than 1 kilogram (subsequent offense)	Felony	15 years	$ 100,000
1 kilogram or more (first offense)	Felony	5* - 20 years	$ 25,000
1 kilogram or more (subsequent offense)	Felony	10* - 25 years	$ 100,000

Within 1,500 feet of an elementary/middle school, public housing project, or daycare center is punishable by an additional 3 years imprisonment.

By a person 18 years or older to a person under 18 is punishable by an additional 2 years imprisonment.

Distribution or cultivation includes possession With Intent to Distribute or cultivate marijuana.

* Mandatory minimum sentence

HASH & CONCENTRATES

Penalties for hashish are the same as for marijuana. Please see the marijuana penalties section for further details.

PARAPHERNALIA

Offense	Penalty	Incarceration	Max. Fine
With the intent to use it to cultivate, distribute or inhale/ingest less than 1/2 oz	Civil Infraction	N/A	$ 300
With the intent to use it to cultivate, distribute or inhale/ingest more than 1/2 oz	Misdemeanor	3 months	$ 500
Distributing paraphernalia or possessing with the intent to distribute	Misdemeanor	1 year	$ 2,000

Distributing or possessing paraphernalia within 1500 feet of an elementary/middle school is punishable by an additional 1 year of imprisonment.

FORFEITURE

Any item used for the Cultivation or distribution of marijuana is subject to forfeiture.

Penalty Details

Possession for Personal Use

Possession of less than one-half ounce of marijuana by a first time offender carries a civil penalty of $150.

Possession of less than one-half ounce for subsequent offenses carries a penalty of a civil fine between $200 and $500.

Possession of more than one-half ounce of marijuana but less than four ounces of marijuana by a first time offender can be punished with a prison term not to exceed one year and a $1,000 fine.

Possession of more than one-half ounce of marijuana but less than four ounces of marijuana after a first offense is a class D felony and carries a penalty of imprisonment for a term not to exceed five years and a fine not to exceed $3,000.

For first offenders, possession of 4 ounces or more of marijuana is a class D felony punishable by a fine of up to $2,000 and/or up to 5 years of imprisonment. Subsequent offenses are a class C felony punishable by a fine of up to $5,000 and/or up to 10 years of imprisonment.

See
- Connecticut Gen. Stat. §21a-279
- Connecticut Gen. Stat. §21a-279a

Distribution or Cultivation

Distribution or cultivation includes possession with intent to distribute or cultivate marijuana.

For first offenders distribution or cultivation of less than 1 kilogram of marijuana is punishable by a fine of up to $25,000 and/or up to 7 years of imprisonment. Subsequent offenses are punishable by a fine of up to $100,000 and/or up to 15 years of imprisonment.

The court may prescribe an alternative sentence of up to 3 years imprisonment. The offender may then be released at any time during those 3 years and placed on probation for the remainder of their term.

See
- Connecticut Gen. Stat. §21a-277(b)
- Connecticut Gen. Stat. §21a-277(d)

For first offenders distribution or cultivation of 1 kilogram or more of marijuana is punishable by 5-20 years of imprisonment. Subsequent offenses are punishable by up 10-25 years of imprisonment. The court cannot reduce a sentence below the minimum years of prison time required by the statute, this means that first offenders face a minimum of 5 years imprisonment and subsequent offenders a minimum of 10 years imprisonment. The court may make exceptions to these mandatory minimum sentences if the defendant is under 18 or is/was mentally impaired.

For non-violent first offenders, the court may depart from the mandatory minimum sentence if a particular reason is stated.

See
- Connecticut Gen. Stat. §21a-200(a)
- Connecticut Gen. Stat. §21a-278(b)

Distribution or cultivation of marijuana within 1,500 feet of an elementary/middle school, public housing project, or daycare center is punishable by an additional 3 years imprisonment on top of any other sentence imposed.

See
- Connecticut Gen. Stat. §21a-278(a)

Distribution of marijuana by a person 18 years or older to a person under 18 is punishable by an additional 2 years imprisonment, on top of any other sentence imposed. There is an exception to this rule if the distributor is less than 2 years older than the minor.

See
- Connecticut Gen. Stat. §21a-278(b)

Using a person under 18 years of age to assist in the sale of marijuana is punishable by 3 years imprisonment, on top of any other sentence already imposed.

See
- Connecticut Gen. Stat. §21a-278(c)

Hash & Concentrates

The Connecticut statute uses the terms "Marijuana" and "Cannabis-type substance" to refer to plant Cannabis or any substance made from or with Cannabis, including hashish or concentrates. The terms are given the exact same definition in the statute. The term "Marijuana" is used to distinguish "Marijuana" from other hallucinogenic substances, whereas the term "Cannabis-type substance" is used to define penalties for possession of said substances. The penalties for all infractions involving hashish or marijuana concentrates are therefore the same as the penalties for all infractions involving plant marijuana.

See
- Connecticut Gen. Stat. §21a-240(7), (29)

Paraphernalia

Possession of paraphernalia with the intent to use it to cultivate, distribute or inhale/ingest more than one-half ounce of marijuana is a class C misdemeanor and is punishable by up to 3 months imprisonment and a fine of up to $500.

Distributing paraphernalia or possessing it with the intent to distribute it is a class A misdemeanor, punishable by up to one year in prison and/or a $2,000 civil fine. In order to be guilty of this crime the defendant must know or should have known that the item would be used to cultivate, distribute, or inhale/ingest more than one-half ounce of marijuana.

Paraphernalia possession or distribution intended to manufacture or ingest less than one-half ounce of marijuana is a civil infraction, which will result in a fine of between $100-$300 (including administrative costs).

Distributing or possessing paraphernalia within 1,500 feet of an elementary/middle school is punishable by an additional 1 year of imprisonment.

See
- Connecticut Gen. Stat. 21a-267
- Connecticut Gen. Stat. 53a-42

Forfeiture

Any item used for the cultivation or distribution of marijuana is subject to forfeiture. This includes vehicles or aircraft that are used to transport marijuana for the purpose of distributing it.

See
- Connecticut Gen. Stat. 21a-246

DELAWARE
LAWS & PENALTIES

Offense	Penalty	Incarceration	Max. Fine
POSSESSION			
Less than 175 grams	Misdemeanor	3 months	$ 575
175 – less than 1500 grams	Felony	3 years	N/A**
1500 – less than 3000 grams	Felony	5 years	N/A**
3000 – less than 4000 grams	Felony	8 years	N/A**
4000 – less than 5000 grams	Felony	15 years	N/A**
5000 grams or more	Felony	2* - 25 years	N/A**

Aggravating factors add increased incarceration

* Mandatory minimum sentence

** Maximum fines are at the discretion of the court for felony charges at sentencing.

DISTRIBUTION, SALE, OR MANUFACTURE			
Less than 1500 grams	Felony	8 years	N/A**
1500 – less than 4000 grams	Felony	15 years	N/A**
4000 grams or more	Felony	2* - 25 years	N/A**

Aggravating factors add increased incarceration

* Mandatory minimum sentence

** Maximum fines are at the discretion of the court for felony charges at sentencing.

HASH & CONCENTRATES

Penalties for hashish are the same as for marijuana. Please see the marijuana penalties section for further details.

PARAPHERNALIA			
Use or possesses with the intent to use	Misdemeanor	6 months	$ 1,000
Deliver or possesses with the intent to deliver	Felony	2 years	N/A**
Deliver to a minor who is under 18 years	Felony	3 years	N/A**

** Maximum fines are at the discretion of the court for felony charges at sentencing.

FORFEITURE

All substances, raw materials, products, equipment, property, vehicles, research products, paraphernalia, money and other assets can be seized.

MISCELLANEOUS

First time offenders may be placed on probation instead of sent to prison or fined.

Penalty Details

Under Delaware law marijuana is a schedule I drug. Legislation was approved in 2015 amending penalties for the possession of up to one ounce (28.35 grams) to a civil penalty, punishable by no more than a $100 fine. The use of marijuana by minors, in public, or in a moving vehicle will remain a criminal offense. The changes in Delaware's criminal code go into effect on December 18, 2015.

Possession for Personal Use

Sentencing penalties are provided in the chart above or listed under the miscellaneous section below.

Personal use quantity of marijuana is one ounce or less.

Possession of less than 175 grams of marijuana is an unclassified misdemeanor. If there are one or more aggravating factors involved, possession is a class B misdemeanor.

Possession of 175 – less than 1,500 grams is a class F felony, with one prior conviction a class D felony, with two or more prior convictions a class C felony. If one aggravating factor is involved possession is a class D felony, with one or more prior convictions a class C felony. If two or more aggravating factors are involved possession is a class C felony.

Possession of 1,500 – less than 3,000 grams is a class E felony, with one prior conviction a class C felony, with two or more prior convictions a class B felony. If one aggravating factor is involved possession is a class C felony, with one or more prior convictions a class B felony. If two or more aggravating factors are involved possession is a class B felony.

Possession of 3,000 – less than 4,000 grams is a class D felony, with one or more prior convictions a class B felony. If at least one aggravating factor is involved possession is a class B felony.

Possession of 4,000 – less than 5,000 grams is a class C felony. If at least one aggravating factor is involved possession is a class B felony.

Possession of 5,000 grams or more, with or without an aggravating factor is a class B felony.

See
- Delaware CODE ANN. tit. 16, § 4714
- Delaware CODE ANN. tit. 16, §§ 4755 & 4756
- Delaware CODE ANN. tit. 16, § 4764
- Delaware CODE ANN. tit. 16, §§ 4751B - 4752
- Delaware CODE ANN. tit. 16, § 4753

Distribution, Sale, or Manufacture

Distribution, Sale, or Manufacture of less than 1,500 grams is a class D felony, with one prior conviction a class C felony, with two or more prior convictions a class B felony. If one or more aggravating factors are involved the offense is a class C felony.

Distribution, Sale, or Manufacture of 1,500 – less than 4,000 grams is a class C felony, with one or more prior convictions a class B felony. If one or more aggravating factors are involved the offense is a class B felony.

Distribution, Sale, or Manufacture of more than 4,000 grams is a class B felony.

See
- Delaware CODE ANN. tit. 16, §§ 4751B - 4752
- Delaware CODE ANN. tit. 16, § 4753
- Delaware CODE ANN. tit. 16, § 4754

Hash & Concentrates

The Delaware statute uses the general term "Marijuana" to refer to plant Cannabis and "every compound, manufacture, salt, derivative, mixture or preparation of the plant, its seeds or resin." Nowhere does the statute differentiate penalties for Marijuana and Hashish or Concentrates. Both substances are classified under Schedule I of the Delaware Controlled Substances schedule.

See
- Delaware CODE ANN. tit. 16 § 4701(26)
- Delaware CODE ANN. tit. 16 Del.C. § 4714(d)(19)

Paraphernalia

Any person who uses or possesses with the intent to use drug paraphernalia is guilty of a class B misdemeanor, punishable with confinement for up to 6 months and a fine of no more than $1,000.

Any person who delivers drug paraphernalia or possesses drug paraphernalia with the intent to deliver, is guilty of a class G felony, punishable by up to 2 years incarceration.

Any person who delivers drug paraphernalia to another person who is under 18 yeas old is guilty of a class E felony, punishable by up to 3 years incarceration.

See
- Delaware CODE ANN. tit. 16, §§ 4771 through 4774

Forfeitures

All controlled substances, which have been manufactured, distributed, possessed, dispensed or acquired including any property, which is used, or intended for use, as a container for property

All raw materials, products and equipment of any kind, which are used, or intended for use, in manufacturing, delivering, importing or exporting any controlled substance including any property, which is used, or intended for use, as a container for property.

Any conveyances, including aircraft, vehicles, or vessels which are used, or are intended for use, to transport, or in any manner to facilitate the transportation, sale, trafficking in or possession with intent to deliver marijuana; all books, records, and research products and materials including formulas, microfilm, tapes and data which are used or intended for use in violation of this chapter; all drug paraphernalia; all moneys, negotiable instruments, securities or any other thing of value furnished, or intended to be furnished, in exchange for a controlled substance or drug paraphernalia; all profits or proceeds traceable to securities, assets or interest used, or intended to be used, to facilitate any drug crime.

See
- Delaware CODE ANN. tit. 16, §4784

Miscellaneous

Sentencing

- An unclassified misdemeanor is punishable by up to 30 days imprisonment and a fine not to exceed $575, unless otherwise specified.
- A class B misdemeanor is punishable by up to 6 months imprisonment and a fine not to exceed $1,000.
- A class A misdemeanor is punishable by up to 1 year imprisonment and a fine not to exceed $2,300.
- A class G felony is punishable by up to 2 years imprisonment.
- A class F felony is punishable by up to 3 years imprisonment.
- A class E felony is punishable by up to 5 years imprisonment.
- A class D felony is punishable by up to 8 years imprisonment.
- A class C felony is punishable by up to 15 years imprisonment.
- A class B felony is punishable by 2 – 25 years imprisonment.
- Felony penalty fines do not have a cap. All drug crimes require additional 15% surcharge for the rehabilitation fund.
- Also a 6 month license suspension may be added in addition to the sentences provided above.

Super Weights

Marijuana weighing 15,000 grams (33 pounds) or less is punishable by 4 – 10 years imprisonment. More than 15,000 - 37,500 grams (83 pounds) is punishable by 6 – 12 years imprisonment. More than 37,500 – 75,000 grams (165 pounds) is punishable by 8 – 15 years imprisonment.

See
- Delaware CODE ANN. tit.16 § 4701(14)

Aggravating Factors

The offense was committed within a protected school zone or park or place of worship or occurred in a protected school zone and protected park or place of worship are present, then both may be alleged and proven, but together they count only as one.

The Defendant was an adult and the offense involved a minor (at least 4 years younger than the defendant) as a co-conspirator, accomplice, or the intended/actual recipient.

The Defendant, by use of violence or force, during or immediately following the offense, intentionally prevented or attempted to prevent the officer from making an arrest; or fled from an officer in a vehicle from, thereby creating a substantial risk of physical injury to other persons.

See
- Delaware CODE ANN. tit. 16 § 4751A

First time offenders may be placed on probation instead of sent to prison or fined. Probation includes state sponsored drug treatment, drug testing, suspension of offender's driver's license, and community service. Successful completion of the program results in the charges against the individual being dropped and a conviction not appearing on the offender's record. If the offender does commit another drug crime, however, this adjudication does count as a conviction.

See
- Delaware CODE ANN. tit. 16, §4767

DISTRICT OF COLUMBIA
LAWS & PENALTIES

Offense	Penalty	Incarceration	Max. Fine
POSSESSION			
2 oz or less*	None	None	$ 0
6 plants or less*	None	None	$ 0
More than 2 oz	Misdemeanor	6 months	$ 1,000

*Initiative 71, which took effect on 2/26/15, permits adults 21 years of age or older to possess up to two ounces of marijuana in one's primary residence without penalty. Transfer without payment (but not sell) up to one ounce of marijuana to another person 21 years of age or older is also permitted. Provided that all persons residing within a single house or single rental unit may not grow more than twelve cannabis plants, with six or fewer being mature, flowering plants.

SALE, DISTRIBUTION, INTENT TO DISTRIBUTE, AND CULTIVATION			
6 plants or less*	None	None	$ 0
1/2 lb or less(first offense)	Not Classified	6 months	$ 1,000
Subsequent offense	Not Classified	2 years	$ 5,000
Any amount	Not Classified	5 years	$ 50,000

*Initiative 71, which took effect on 2/26/15, permits adults 21 years of age or older to cultivate no more than six plants (with three or fewer mature at any one time) in one's primary residence without penalty. Provided that all persons residing within a single house or single rental unit may not grow more than twelve cannabis plants, with six or fewer being mature, flowering plants.

Involving a minor by a person over 21 brings additional penalty and/or fine.

Within 1000 feet of an appropriately identified public or private day care center, elementary school, vocational school, secondary school, junior college, college, or university, or any public swimming pool, playground, video arcade, youth center, or public library, or in and around public housing may bring a doubled penalty.

HASH & CONCENTRATES			
Possession	N/A	180 days	$ 1,000
Manufacture	N/A	5 years	$ 50,000
PARAPHERNALIA			
Possession or sale of paraphernalia 21 years and up	None	None	$ 0
Possession of paraphernalia under 21 years	None	30 days	$ 100
Sale of paraphernalia	None	6 months	$ 1,000
Sale of paraphernalia subsequent offense	None	2 years	$ 5,000
FORFEITURE			

All substances, raw materials, products, equipment, property, vehicles, research products, paraphernalia, money and other assets can be seized.

Penalty Details

Possession

Adults 21 years of age or older may possess up to two ounces of marijuana and cultivate no more than six plants (with three or fewer mature at any one time) in their primary residence without penalty. Transfer without payment (but not sell) up to one ounce of marijuana to another person 21 years of age or older is also permitted.

See
• Ballot Initiative 71

Unless marijuana was obtained through a doctor's recommendation, intentional or knowing possession of more than two ounces of marijuana is a misdemeanor with a penalty of incarceration of up to 6 months and a fine of not more than $1,000.

For a first offense: the court may, without entering a judgment of guilty and with the consent of such person, defer further proceedings and place him or her on probation upon such reasonable conditions as it may require and for such period, not to exceed one year, as the court may prescribe. This action does not qualify as a conviction.

See
• D.C. Code § 48-904.01

Sale, Distribution, Intent to Distribute, and Cultivation

Adults 21 and older may cultivate up to six marijuana plants (no more than three mature at any one time) in their primary residence without penalty. Not-for-profit transactions involving small amounts of the substance are also permitted.

See
• Ballot Initiative 71

An offender who been convicted of distribution, manufacture, or possession with intent to distribute may be imprisoned for not more than 5 years, fined not more than $50,000, or both. For a first conviction, and offender with no prior convictions for distribution, manufacture, or possession with intent to distribute, and who was caught with ½ pounds or less of marijuana, may be imprisoned for not more than 6 months or fined not more than $1000 or both.

For a first offense: the court may, without entering a judgment of guilty and with the consent of such person, defer further proceedings and place him or her on probation upon such reasonable conditions as it may require and for such period, not to exceed one year, as the court may prescribe.

See
• D.C. Code § 48-904.01

Distribution to a minor by a person over 21 brings a doubled penalty.

See
• § 40-904.06 (b)

The enlistment of a minor to distribute a controlled substance by one who is over 21 can be punished with up to 10 years in prison and a $10,000 fine. For a second offense, an offender can be imprisoned for no longer than 20 years and fined not more than $20,000.

See
• D.C. Code §48-904.07 (b)

Distributing or possessing with the intent to distribute within 1000 feet of an appropriately identified public or private day care center, elementary school, vocational school, secondary school, junior college, college, or university, or any public swimming pool, playground, video arcade, youth center, or public library, or in and around public housing may bring a doubled penalty.

See
• D.C. Code §48-904.07a

If a violation occurs after the person has been convicted the person shall be imprisoned for not more than 2 years, or fined not more than $5,000, or both.

See
• Ballot Initiative 71

Hash & Concentrates

Hashish is a Schedule II drug in Washington D.C.

See
• D.C. Code § 48-902.06(F)

Possession of hashish is punishable upon conviction with imprisonment for not more than 180 days and a fine of not more than $1,000.

See
• D.C. Code § 48-904.01(d)(1)

Manufacturing or selling hashish is punishable, upon conviction, with imprisonment for not more than 5 years and a fine of not more than $50,000.

See
• D.C. Code § 48-904.01(a)

Conditional Release for 1st time offenders is available, and record expungement occurs, by request, after successful completion of the program.

See
• D.C. Code § 48-904.01(e)(1)

Hash pipes, sifters, and bubble bags are paraphernalia in Washington D.C., and conviction for possession of such will lead to imprisonment for not more than 30 days and a fine for not more than $100.

See
• D.C. Code § 48-1101(3)   • D.C. Code § 48-1103(a)

Paraphernalia

Paraphernalia possession or sale, for any person 21 years of age or older, is permitted for the use, growing, or processing of marijuana or cannabis. Any person in violation of possession laws shall be imprisoned for not more than 30 days or fined for not more than $100, or both. Any person in violation of selling laws shall be imprisoned for not more than 6 months or fined for not more than $1,000, or both. For a subsequent violation a person shall be imprisoned for not more than 2 years, or fined not more than $5,000, or both.

See
• Ballot Initiative 71

Forfeiture

The following are subject to forfeiture:

1. All controlled substances which have been manufactured, distributed, dispensed, or acquired in violation of this chapter;
2. All raw materials, products, and equipment of any kind which are used, or intended for use, in manufacturing, compounding, processing or delivering any controlled substance in violation of this chapter;
3. All property which is used, or intended for use, as a container for said controlled substances;
4. All conveyances, including aircraft, vehicles or vessels, which are used, or intended for use, to transport, or in any manner to facilitate the transportation, for the purpose of sale or receipt of said controlled substances;
5. All books, records, and research products and materials, including formulas, microfilm, tapes, and data, which are used, or intended for use, in violation of drug laws;
6. All cash or currency which has been used, or intended for use, in violation of drug laws;
7. Everything of value furnished or intended to be furnished in exchange for a controlled substance ; and
8. Any real property that is used or intended to be used in any manner to commit or facilitate the commission of a violation of drug laws.

See
• D.C. Code §48-905.02

FLORIDA
LAWS & PENALTIES

Offense	Penalty	Incarceration	Max. Fine
POSSESSION			
20 grams or less	Misdemeanor	1 year	$ 1,000
More than 20 grams - 25 lbs	Felony	5 years	$ 5,000
More than 25 – less than 2000 lbs	Felony	3* - 15 years	$ 25,000
2000 – less than 10,000 lbs	Felony	7* - 30 years	$ 50,000
10,000 lbs or more	Felony	15* - 30 years	$ 200,000
Less than 25 plants	Felony	5 years	$ 5,000
25 - 300 plants	Felony	15 years	$ 10,000
300 - 2,000 plants	Felony	3* - 15 years	$ 25,000
2000 - 10,000 plants	Felony	7* - 30 years	$ 50,000
Within 1000 feet of a school, college, park, or other specified areas	Felony	15 years	$ 10,000
* Mandatory minimum sentence			
SALE			
20 grams or less without remuneration	Misdemeanor	1 year	$ 1,000
25 lbs or less	Felony	5 years	$ 5,000
More than 25 – less than 2000 lbs (or 300 - 2,000 plants)	Felony	3* - 15 years	$ 25,000
2000 – less than 10,000 lbs (or 2000 - 10,000 plants)	Felony	7* - 30 years	$ 50,000
10,000 lbs or more	Felony	15* - 30 years	$ 200,000
Within 1000 feet of a school, college, park, or other specified areas	Felony	15 years	$ 10,000
* Mandatory minimum sentence			
HASH & CONCENTRATES			
Possession of hashish or concentrates	Felony	5 years	$ 5,000
Selling, manufacturing or delivering	Felony	5 years	$ 5,000
PARAPHERNALIA			
Possession of paraphernalia	Misdemeanor	1 year	$ 1,000
MISCELLANEOUS			
Conviction causes a driver's license suspension for a period of 1 year			

Penalty Details

Possession

Possession of 20 grams or less of cannabis is a misdemeanor punishable by a maximum sentence of 1 year imprisonment and a maximum fine of $1,000.

Possession of more than 20 grams of cannabis is a felony punishable by a maximum sentence of 5 years imprisonment and a maximum fine of $5,000.

Any person who is knowingly in active or constructive possession of 25 pounds or less of cannabis is a felony punishable by a maximum sentence of 5 years imprisonment and a maximum fine of $5,000.

Any person who is knowingly in active or constructive possession of more than 25 pounds - 2,000 pounds of cannabis (or 300-2,000 plants) is a felony punishable by a mandatory minimum sentence of 3 years imprisonment and a maximum sentence of 15 years imprisonment and a maximum fine of $25,000.

Any person who is knowingly in active or constructive possession of 2,000 pounds – less than 10,000 pounds of cannabis (or 2,000-10,000 plants) is a felony punishable by a mandatory minimum sentence of 7 years and a maximum sentence of 30 years imprisonment as well as a maximum fine of $50,000.

Any person who is knowingly in active or constructive possession of 10,000 pounds of cannabis or more is a felony punishable by a mandatory minimum sentence of 15 years imprisonment and a maximum sentence of 30 years imprisonment as well as a maximum fine of $200,000.

Sale or delivery within 1,000 feet of a school, college, park, or other specified areas is a felony punishable by a maximum sentence of 15 years imprisonment and a maximum fine of $10,000.

See
- Florida Criminal Code § 893.13(h) (3)
- Florida Criminal Code § 893.03(1) (c)(7)
- Florida Criminal Code § 893.135
- Florida Criminal Code § 775.082(a)

Sale/Delivery

The delivery of 20 grams or less without remuneration is a misdemeanor punishable by a maximum sentence of 1-year imprisonment and a maximum fine of $1,000.

The sale of 25 pounds or less of cannabis is a felony punishable by a maximum sentence of 5 years imprisonment and a maximum fine of $5,000.

The sale of more than 25 pounds- less than 2,000 pounds of cannabis (or 300-2,000 plants) is a felony punishable by a mandatory minimum sentence of 3 years imprisonment and a maximum sentence of 15 years imprisonment and a maximum fine of $25,000

The sale of 2,000 pounds – less than 10,000 pounds of cannabis (or 2,000-10,000 plants) is a felony punishable by a mandatory minimum sentence of 7 years and a maximum sentence of 30 years imprisonment as well as a maximum fine of $50,000.

The sale of 10,000 pounds or more of cannabis is a felony punishable by a mandatory minimum sentence of 15 years imprisonment and a maximum sentence of 30 years imprisonment as well as a maximum fine of $200,000.

Sale or delivery of cannabis within 1,000 feet of a school, college, park, or other specified areas is a felony punishable by a maximum sentence of 15 years imprisonment and a maximum fine of $10,000.

See
- Florida Criminal Code § 893.13
- Florida Criminal Code § 893.03(c) (35)
- Florida Criminal Code § 893.13
- Florida Criminal Code § 893.135
- Florida Criminal Code § 775.082(a)
- Florida Criminal Code § 775.083(1)

Hash & Concentrates

Hashish or concentrates are considered schedule I narcotics in Florida.

See
- Florida Criminal Code § 893.03(1) (c)

Possession of hashish or concentrates is a felony in the third degree. A felony of the third degree is punishable by a term of imprisonment no greater than 5 years and a fine no greater than $5,000.

See
- Florida Criminal Code § 893.13(6) (b)
- Florida Criminal Code § 775.083(1) (c), (d)
- Florida Criminal Code § 775.082(3) (d)
- Florida Criminal Code § 775.082(4) (a)

Possessing more than 3 grams of hash, selling, manufacturing, delivering, or possessing with intent to sell, manufacture or deliver, hashish or concentrates is a felony of the third degree. A felony of the third degree is punishable by a term of imprisonment no greater than 5 years and a fine no greater than $5,000.

The offense is charged as a felony of the second degree if the offense occurred:

- Within 1,000 feet of a child care facility between 6 A.M. and 12 midnight;
- Within 1,000 feet of a park or community center;
- Within 1,000 feet of a college, university or other postsecondary educational institute;
- Within 1,000 feet of any church or place of worship that conducts religious activities;
- Within 1,000 feet of any convenience business;
- Within 1,000 feet of public housing;
- Within 1,000 feet or an assisted living facility.

A felony of the second degree is punishable by a term of imprisonment no greater than 15 years and a fine no greater than $10,000.

See
- Florida Criminal Code § 893.13(1) (a)(2)
- Florida Criminal Code § 893.13
- Florida Criminal Code § 775.083(1) (b), (c)
- Florida Criminal Code § 775.082(3) (c), (d)
- *Rutherford v. State*, 386 So.2d 881 (Fla. 1980).

Florida defines any product, equipment, or device used to make hashish or concentrates as drug paraphernalia.

See
- Florida Criminal Code § 893.145

Paraphernalia

Possession of drug paraphernalia is a misdemeanor in the first degree, punishable by a maximum sentence of one 1-year imprisonment and a maximum fine of $1,000.

See
- Florida Criminal Code § 775.083
- Florida Criminal Code § 893.145
- Florida Criminal Code § 803.145
- Florida Criminal Code § 893.147

Miscellaneous

Conviction causes a driver's license suspension for a period of 1 year.

See
- Florida Criminal Code § 322.055
- Florida Criminal Code § 322.050

GEORGIA
LAWS & PENALTIES

Offense	Penalty	Incarceration	Max. Fine
POSSESSION			
Personal Use			
1 oz or less	Misdemeanor	1 year	$ 1,000
More than 1 oz	Felony	1* - 10 years	$ 5,000
With Intent to Distribute			
10 lbs or less	Felony	1* - 10 years	$ 5,000
10 - 2000 lbs	Felony	5* - 30 years	$ 100,000
2000 - 10,000 lbs	Felony	7* - 30 years	$ 250,000
More than 10,000 lbs	Felony	15* - 30 years	$ 1,000,000
Within 1,000 feet of school grounds, a park, or a housing project, or in a drug free zone	Felony	5* - 40 years	$ 40,000
*Mandatory Minimum Sentence			
SALE OR DELIVERY			
10 lbs or less	Felony	1* - 10 years	$ 5,000
10 - 2000 lbs	Felony	5* - 30 years	$ 100,000
2000 - 10,000 lbs	Felony	7* - 30 years	$ 250,000
More than 10,000 lbs	Felony	15* - 30 years	$ 1,000,000
Within 1,000 feet of school grounds, a park, or a housing project, or in a drug free zone	Felony	5* - 40 years	$ 40,000
*Mandatory Minimum Sentence			
CULTIVATION			
10 lbs or less	Felony	1* - 10 years	$ 5,000
10 - 2000 lbs	Felony	5* - 30 years	$ 100,000
2000 - 10,000 lbs	Felony	7* - 30 years	$ 250,000
More than 10,000 lbs	Felony	15* - 30 years	$ 1,000,000
Within 1,000 feet of school grounds, a park, or a housing project, or in a drug free zone	Felony	5* - 40 years	$ 40,000
*Mandatory Minimum Sentence			
HASH & CONCENTRATES			
Possession of less than 1 g (solid substance) or less than 1 ml (liquid substance)	Felony	1* - 3 years	$ 5,000
Possession of 1 g – less than 4 g (solid substance) or 1 ml - less than 4 ml (liquid substance)	Felony	1* - 8 years	$ 5,000
Possession	Felony	1* - 15 years	$ 5,000
Manufacturing, distributing, selling, or possessing with the intent to distribute	Felony	5* - 30 years	$ 5,000
*Mandatory Minimum Sentence			
Subsequent offenses carry stricter penalties.			
PARAPHERNALIA			
Possession or sale of paraphernalia	Misdemeanor	1 year	$ 1,000
Second and third offenses carry additional penalties and fines.			
FORFEITURE			
Vehicles and other property may be seized.			
MISCELLANEOUS			
Abandoning marijuana in a public place	Misdemeanor	1 year	$ 1,000
Involving a minor	Felony	5 - 20 years	$ 20,000
Distribution of marijuana flavored product	Misdemeanor	N/A	$ 500
Use of any communications facility	Felony	1 - 4 years	$ 30,000

Any conviction of a marijuana possession, sale, or cultivation offense results in suspension of driving license.

Penalty Details

Marijuana is not a scheduled substance, but is regulated under the Georgia Controlled Substances Act.

When a person is found guilty of a felony punishable by imprisonment for a maximum term of ten years or less, the judge may, impose punishment as for a misdemeanor. A misdemeanor is punishable by a fine not to exceed $1,000.00 or by confinement in the county or other jail, county correctional institution, not to exceed 12 months, or both. A person convicted of a misdemeanor of a high and aggravated nature shall be punished by a fine not to exceed $5,000.00

See
• Ga. Code Ann. §§ 16-13-25 - 30   • O.C.G.A. § 17-10-3, 4, & 5

Possession for Personal Use

Possession of 1 ounce or less of marijuana is a misdemeanor punishable by up to 12 months imprisonment and/or a fine up to $1,000, or public works for up to 12 months. Possession of over an ounce is a felony punishable by a minimum of 1 and maximum of 10 years imprisonment.

See
• O.C.G.A. § 16-13-2(b)   • O.C.G.A. § 16-13-30(j)

Possession with Intent to Distribute

Possession with intent to distribute 10 pounds or less of marijuana is a felony punishable by a minimum of 1 and maximum of 10 years imprisonment. Possession of over 10 pounds but less than 2,000 pounds is punishable by a minimum of 5 years and maximum of 30 years imprisonment and a fine of $100,000. Possession of 2,000 pounds or more but less than 10,000 pounds is punishable by a minimum of 7 years and maximum of 30 years imprisonment and a fine of $250,000. Possession of 10,000 pounds or more is punishable by a minimum of 15 years and maximum of 30 years imprisonment and a fine of $1,000,000.

See
• O.C.G.A. § 16-13-30(j)   • O.C.G.A. §§ 16-13-31(c), (h)

Possession with intent to distribute within 1,000 feet of school grounds, a park, or a housing project, or in a drug free zone is a felony punishable by up to 20 years imprisonment and/or a fine up to $20,000 for a first offense. A second or subsequent offense is punishable by a minimum of 5 years and maximum of 40 years imprisonment and/or a fine up to $40,000. It is an affirmative defense that the conduct took place entirely within a private residence, no one 17 years old or younger was present, and the conduct was not committed for financial gain.

See
• O.C.G.A. §§ 16-13-32.4 - 32.6

Sale/Delivery

Sale or delivery of 10 pounds or less of marijuana is a felony punishable by a minimum of 1 and maximum of 10 years imprisonment. Sale or delivery of over 10 pounds but less than 2,000 pounds is punishable by a minimum of 5 years and maximum of 30 years imprisonment and a fine of $100,000. Sale or delivery of 2,000 pounds or more but less than 10,000 pounds is punishable by a minimum of 7 years and maximum of 30 years imprisonment and a fine of $250,000. Sale or delivery of 10,000 pounds or more is punishable by a minimum of 15 years and maximum of 30 years imprisonment and a fine of $1,000,000.

See
• O.C.G.A. § 16-13-30(j)   • O.C.G.A. §§ 16-13-31(c), (h)

Sale or delivery within 1,000 feet of school grounds, a park, a housing project, or in a drug free zone is a felony punishable by up to 20 years imprisonment and/or a fine up to $20,000 for a first offense. A second or subsequent offense is punishable by a minimum of 5 years and maximum of 40 years imprisonment and/or a fine up to $40,000. It is an affirmative defense that the conduct took place entirely within a private residence, no one 17 years old or younger was present, and the conduct was not committed for financial gain.

See
• O.C.G.A. §§ 16-13-32.4 - 32.6

Cultivation

Cultivation of 10 pounds or less of marijuana is a felony punishable by a minimum of 1 and maximum of 10 years imprisonment. Cultivation of over 10 pounds but less than 2,000 pounds is punishable by a minimum of 5 years and maximum of 30 years imprisonment and a fine of $100,000. Cultivation of 2,000 pounds or more but less than 10,000 pounds is punishable by a minimum of 7 years and maximum of 30 years imprisonment and a fine of $250,000. Cultivation of 10,000 pounds or more is punishable by a minimum of 15 years and maximum of 30 years imprisonment and a fine of $1,000,000.

See
• O.C.G.A. § 16-13-30(j)   • O.C.G.A. §§ 16-13-31(c), (h)

Cultivation within 1,000 feet of school grounds, a park, or a housing project, or in a drug free zone is a felony punishable by up to 20 years imprisonment and/or a fine up to $20,000 for a first offense. A second or subsequent offense is punishable by a minimum of 5 years and maximum of 40 years imprisonment and/or a fine up to $40,000. It is an affirmative defense that the conduct took place entirely within a private residence, no one 17 years old or younger was present, and the conduct was not committed for financial gain.

See
• O.C.G.A. §§ 16-13-32.4 to 32.6

Hash & Concentrates

In Georgia, hashish and concentrates that contain more than 15% THC by volume are a Schedule I substance and are punished more harshly than natural-form marijuana.

See
• Ga. Code Ann. § 16-13-25(3)(P)   • Ga. Code Ann. § 16-13-21 (16)

Possessing less than 1 gram of a solid substance, less than 1 milliliter of a liquid substance or placed onto a secondary medium with a combined weight of less than 1 gram is a felony, punishable by imprisonment of not less than 1 year nor more than 3 years. Possessing 1 gram but less than 4 grams of a solid substance, 1 milliliter but less than 4 milliliters of a liquid substance or if placed onto a secondary medium with a combined weight of 1 gram but less than 4 grams is a felony, punishable by imprisonment of not less than 1 year but less than 28 grams. Possessing 4 grams but less than 28 grams of a solid substance, 4 milliliters but less than 28 milliliters of a liquid substance, or if placed onto a secondary medium with a combined weight of 4 grams but less than 28 grams is a felony punishable by imprisonment of not less than 1 year nor more than 15 years.

Manufacturing, distributing, selling, or possessing hashish or concentrates with the intent to distribute is a felony, which is punishable by imprisonment for not less than 5 years nor more than 30 years. Upon conviction of a second or subsequent offence, the violator shall be imprisoned for not less than 10 years nor more than 40 years or life imprisonment.

See
• O.C.G.A. § 16-13-30

Possession of paraphernalia with the intent to use said paraphernalia to ingest or produce hashish or concentrates is a misdemeanor, punishable by a maximum sentence of 1 year and prison and a maximum fine of $1,000.

See
• O.C.G.A. § 16-13-32.2.

Manufacturing, distributing, or possessing with intent to deliver hashish or concentrates within 1,000 ft. of a school, housing project, public park, or commercial drug-free zone is a felony, punishable by imprisonment for not more than 20 years or a fine of not more than $20,000.00, or both. Subsequent offenses bring enhanced penalties.

See
• O.C.G.A. § 16-13-32.4   • O.C.G.A. § 16-13-32.6
• O.C.G.A. § 16-13-32.5

Paraphernalia

Possession of paraphernalia is a misdemeanor punishable by up to 1 year imprisonment and/or a fine up to $1,000. Sale or possession with intent to distribute is a misdemeanor for the first offense punishable by up to 1 year imprisonment and/or a fine up to $1,000, a misdemeanor of a high and aggravated nature for a second offense punishable by up to 5 years imprisonment and/or a fine up to $5,000, and a felony for a third offense punishable by a minimum of 1 year and a maximum of 5 years imprisonment and a fine up to $5,000.

See
• O.C.G.A. §§ 16-13-32 to 32.2   • O.C.G.A. §§ 17-10-3 to 4

Sentencing

A person who has not previously been convicted of a drug charge in any US territory may, after being convicted of or pleading guilty to a marijuana possession charge, have the proceedings against them deferred and be put on probation for up to 5 years. The probation may include mandatory drug treatment for up to 3 years. Successful completion of the terms of probation will result in result in a dismissal of the proceedings against the person.

See
• O.C.G.A. §§ 16-13-2(a), (c)

When a person is found guilty of a felony punishable by imprisonment for a maximum term of 10 years or less, the judge may, in his discretion, sentence that person as if it were a misdemeanor.

See
• O.C.G.A. § 17-10-5

Repeat felony offenses are to be sentenced by the maximum term allowed for by the felony committed

See
• O.C.G.A. § 17-10-7

Forfeiture

Vehicles and other property may be seized for controlled substance violations. The seizing agency has 60 days after the seizure to initiate a forfeiture proceeding. The seizing agency must notify all those with an interest in the property. If the property value is $25,000 or less, then a person with an interest in the property has 30 days to make a claim to it, to which the district attorney has 30 days to respond.

See
• O.C.G.A. § 16-13-49

Miscellaneous

Abandoning dangerous drugs

Anyone who abandons a controlled substance, including marijuana, in a public place is guilty of a misdemeanor punishable by up to 12 months imprisonment and/or a fine up to $1,000.

See
• O.C.G.A. § 16-13-3   • O.C.G.A. § 17-10-3

Involvement of a minor in a marijuana offense

Involving a minor in the sale or cultivation of marijuana is a felony punishable by a minimum of 5 years and maximum of 20 years imprisonment and/or a fine up to $20,000.

See
• O.C.G.A. § 16-13-30(k)

Distribution of marijuana flavored product

The sale or delivery of a marijuana flavored product to a minor is a misdemeanor punishable by a $500 fine for each offense.

See
• O.C.G.A. § 16-13-30.6

Use of communications facility in a controlled substances felony

Use of any communications facility, including a computer, a telephone, or mail, in the commission or facilitation of a drug offense that is considered a felony is punishable by a minimum of 1 year and maximum of 4 years and/or a fine up to $30,000.

See
• O.C.G.A. § 16-13-32.3

Suspension of driver's license

Any conviction of a marijuana possession, sale, or cultivation offense results in suspension of that individual's driving license. For a first offense in 5 years, the period of suspension is at least 180 days and the restoration fee is up to $210, or $200 when reinstatement is processed by mail. A second offense in 5 years results in a suspension for at least 3 years, but after 1 year the individual may apply for reinstatement for a fee up to $310, or $300 when reinstatement is processed by mail. A third or subsequent offense in 5 years results in a suspension for at least 5 years, but after 2 years the individual may apply for reinstatement a 3 year driving permit if certain conditions are met and they pay a fee up to $410, or $400 when reinstatement is processed by mail.

See
• O.C.G.A. § 40-5-75(a)

HAWAII
LAWS & PENALTIES

Offense	Penalty	Incarceration	Max. Fine
POSSESSION			
Personal Use			
Less than 1 oz	Misdemeanor	30 days	$ 1,000
1 oz - 1 lb	Misdemeanor	1 year	$ 2,000
1 lb or more	Felony	5 years	$ 10,000
Commercial Promotion			
1 - 2 lbs	Felony	5 years	$ 10,000
2 - less than 25 lbs	Felony	10 years	$ 25,000
25 lbs or more	Felony	20 years	$ 50,000
Within 750 feet of school grounds or a park, or on or within 10 feet of a parked school vehicle	Felony	5 years	$ 10,000
SALE OR DELIVERY			
Less than 1 oz	Misdemeanor	1 year	$ 2,000
1 oz - 1 lb	Felony	5 years	$ 10,000
1 - less than 5 lbs	Felony	10 years	$ 25,000
5 lbs or more	Felony	20 years	$ 50,000
Within 750 feet of school grounds or a park, or on or within 10 feet of a parked school vehicle	Felony	5 years	$ 10,000
CULTIVATION			
25 - 50 plants	Felony	5 years	$ 10,000
50 - less than 100 plants	Felony	10 years	$ 25,000
100 plants or more	Felony	20 years	$ 50,000
Less than 25 plants on another's property	Felony	10 years	$ 25,000
25 plants or more on another's property	Felony	20 years	$ 50,000
In a structure where a minor under 16 years is present carries additional penalty			
PARAPHERNALIA			
Use, possession or sale of paraphernalia	Felony	5 years	$ 10,000
Delivery to a minor at least 3 years junior	Felony	10 years	$ 25,000
FORFEITURE			
Vehicles and other property may be seized.			
HASH & CONCENTRATES			
Possession			
Less than 1/8 oz	Misdemeanor	1 year	$ 2,000
1/8 - less than 1 oz	Felony	10 years	$ 25,000
1 oz or more	Felony	20 years	$ 50,000
Distribution			
Less than 1/8 oz	Felony	10 years	$ 25,000
1/8 oz or more	Felony	20 years	$ 50,000
MISCELLANEOUS			
Promoting through a minor	Felony	10 years	$ 25,000
Within school grounds, school vehicles, or a public park	Felony	20 years	$ 50,000

Discovery of marijuana in a vehicle may result in each occupant being charged with possession.

Penalty Details

Marijuana is a Schedule I hallucinogenic substance under the Hawaii Uniform Controlled Substances Act. It is also listed as a detrimental drug.

See
- Hawaii Rev. Stat. § 329-14(d)(20)
- Hawaii Rev. Stat. § 712-1240

Possession for Personal Use

Possession of less than 1 ounce of marijuana is a petty misdemeanor punishable by up to 30 days imprisonment and/or a fine of $1,000. Possession of 1 ounce or more but less than 1 pound is a misdemeanor punishable by up to 1 year imprisonment and/or a $2,000 fine. Possession of 1 pound or more, of marijuana is a Class C felony punishable by up to 5 years imprisonment and/or a fine of up to $10,000.

See
- Hawaii Rev. Stat. § 706-663
- Hawaii Rev. Stat. § 706-640
- Hawaii Rev. Stat. §§ 712-1247 to 1249

Discovery of marijuana in a vehicle may result in each occupant being charged with possession unless the marijuana was found on an occupant's person or was in a compartment accessible only by occupants of that seat.

See:
- Hawaii Rev. Stat. § 712-1251

Possession with Intent to Distribute

Possession of 1 pound or more but less than 2 pounds is a class C felony punishable by up to 5 years in prison and/or $10,000 fine. Possession of 2 pounds or more but less than 25 pounds is a class B felony punishable by up to 10 years in prison and/or $25,000 fine. Possession of 25 pounds or more is a class A felony punishable by 20 years in prison and/or $50,000 fine.

See
- Hawaii Rev. Stat. § 706-640
- Hawaii Rev. Stat. §§ 706-659 to 660
- Hawaii Rev. Stat. § 712-1247
- Hawaii Rev. Stat. §§ 712-1249.4 to 1249.5

Possession with intent to distribute any amount of marijuana within 750 feet of school grounds or a park, or on or within 10 feet of a parked school vehicle is a class C felony punishable by up to 5 years in prison and/or $10,000 fine.

See
- Hawaii Rev. Stat. § 706-640
- Hawaii Rev. Stat. § 706-660
- Hawaii Rev. Stat. § 712-1249.6

Sale/Delivery

Distribution of less than 1 ounce of marijuana is a misdemeanor punishable by up to 1 year imprisonment and/or a $2,000 fine. Distribution of 1 ounce or more but less than 1 pound is a class C felony punishable by up to 5 years in prison and/or $10,000 fine. Distribution of 1 pound or more but less than 5 pounds is a class B felony punishable by 10 years in prison and a $25,000 fine. Distribution of 5 pounds or more of marijuana is a class A felony punishable by 20 years in prison and a $50,000 fine.

See
- Hawaii Rev. Stat. § 706-640
- Hawaii Rev. Stat. §§ 706-659 to 660
- Hawaii Rev. Stat. §§ 712-1247 to 1248
- Hawaii Rev. Stat. §§ 712-1249.4 to 1249.5

Distribution any amount of marijuana within 750 feet of school grounds or a park, or on or within 10 feet of a parked school vehicle is a class C felony punishable by up to 5 years in prison and/or $10,000 fine.

See
- Hawaii Rev. Stat. § 706-640
- Hawaii Rev. Stat. § 706-660
- Hawaii Rev. Stat. § 712-1249.6

Cultivation

Cultivation of 25 or more but less than 50 marijuana plants is a class C felony punishable by up to 5 years in prison and/or $10,000 fine. Cultivation of 50 or more but less than 100 plants is a class B felony punishable by 10 years in prison and/or $25,000 fine. Cultivation of 100 or more marijuana plants is a class A felony punishable by 20 years in prison and/or $50,000 fine.

See
- Hawaii Rev. Stat. § 706-640
- Hawaii Rev. Stat. §§ 706-659 to 660
- Hawaii Rev. Stat. § 712-1247
- Hawaii Rev. Stat. §§ 712-1249.4 to 1249.5

Cultivation of less than 25 marijuana plants on another's property without their permission is a class B felony punishable by 10 years in prison and/or $25,000 fine. Cultivation of 25 or more plants on another's property without their permission is a class A felony punishable by 20 years in prison and/or $50,000 fine.

See
- Hawaii Rev. Stat. § 706-640
- Hawaii Rev. Stat. §§ 706-659 to 660
- Hawaii Rev. Stat. §§ 712-1249.4 to 1249.5

Cultivation in a structure where the individual knows a person under the age of 16 years old is present results in an additional 2 years imprisonment on top of the sentence for cultivation. However, if the cultivation occurred in a structure where an individual 18 years old or younger was present and the cultivation causes substantial bodily injury to the minor, then the additional imprisonment will be a term of 5 years.

See
- Hawaii Rev. Stat. § 712-1240.5

Hash & Concentrates

All Marijuana, including Marijuana Concentrates, is classified as Schedule I under Hawaii law. Marijuana Concentrates are classified as a "harmful drug". Under Hawaiian law, hashish, tetrahydrocannabinol, and any other salt, alkaloid, mixture, compound or derivative of marijuana qualifies as a Marijuana Concentrate. Cases applying this statute have determined that Marijuana Concentrates charges should only be brought when the compound in question contains THC but does not have the outward appearance of any part of the Marijuana plant. Case law has also confirmed that there is no minimum threshold of THC content required to classify a compound as a Concentrate, even if the THC content of the compound is less than the average for plant Marijuana.

Promoting a Harmful Drug 1st Degree
- Class A Felony, up to 20 years imprisonment and a fine not exceeding $50,000
- Possession of 1 ounce or more of Marijuana Concentrates or
- Distribution of 1/8 ounce or more of Marijuana Concentrates or
- Distribution of Marijuana Concentrates to a minor in any amount
- Promoting a Harmful Drug 2nd Degree
- Class B Felony, up to 10 years imprisonment and a fine not exceeding $25,000
- Possession of 1/8 ounce or more of Marijuana Concentrates or
- Distribution of any amount of Marijuana Concentrates

Promoting a Harmful Drug 4th Degree
- Misdemeanor, up to 1 year imprisonment and a fine not exceeding $2000
- Possession of any amount of Marijuana concentrates

See
- Hawaii Rev. Stat §§ 712-1240, 1244, 1245, & 1246.5
- Hawaii Rev. Stat. § 706-640
- Hawaii Rev. Stat. § 706-659
- Hawaii Rev. Stat § 706-660
- Hawaii Rev. Stat. § 706-663
- *State v. Choy*, 661 P.2d 1206 (Haw. Int. Ct. App. 1983).

Paraphernalia

Use or possession of paraphernalia is a class C felony punishable by up to 5 years in prison and/or a $10,000 fine. Sale or manufacture of paraphernalia is also a class C felony. Delivery of paraphernalia by a person 18 years or older to a minor at least 3 years their junior is a class B felony punishable by up to 10 years imprisonment and/or a $25,000 fine.

See
- Hawaii Rev. Stat. § 329-43.5

Sentencing

First time offenders who have plead or been found guilty of certain possession or distribution charges are eligible for suspended judgment and probation. Upon completion of the terms of the probation, the court shall discharge the offender and dismiss the proceedings against him. There may only be 1 discharge and dismissal for each person. Additionally, first time offenders for paraphernalia or possession charges are eligible for probation if they are non-violent, in need of substance abuse treatment, and have submitted a proposal to the court for treatment.

See
- Hawaii Rev. Stat. § 712-1255
- Hawaii Rev. Stat. § 706-622.5

Terms of imprisonment for felonies may increase if the offender has prior felony convictions or other conditions are met.

See
- Hawaii Rev. Stat. § 706-662

Forfeiture

Vehicles and other property may be seized for controlled substance violations. Seizures of property may be made on probable cause that they are subject to forfeiture or by the rules of civil procedure. The seizing agency has 20 days to give notice to all parties who have an interest in the property. They have 30 days to notify the prosecuting attorney, who has 45 days to initiate the forfeiture proceedings. A prosecuting attorney may instead file administrative forfeiture proceedings.

See
- Hawaii Rev. Stat. § 329-55
- Hawaii Rev. Stat. § 712A

Miscellaneous

Promoting a controlled substance through a minor

Any person who uses an individual under the age of 18 to facilitate the distribution of a controlled substance is guilty of a class B felony punishable by B felony in 10 years in prison and/or $25,000 fine, unless the offense occurred on or within school grounds, school vehicles, or a public park, in which case it is a class A felony punishable by 20 years in prison and/or $50,000 fine.

See
- Hawaii Rev. Stat. § 706-640
- Hawaii Rev. Stat. §§ 706-659 to 660
- Hawaii Rev. Stat. § 712-1249.7

Possession in a motor vehicle

Discovery of marijuana in a vehicle may result in each occupant being charged with possession unless the marijuana was found on an occupant person or was in a compartment accessible only by occupants of that seat.

See
- Hawaii Rev. Stat. § 712-1251

Driver's license of commercial driver

Shall revoke the license of a commercial driver if convicted of the unlawful transportation, possession, or use of a controlled substance while on duty.

See:
- Hawaii Rev. Stat. §286-240(6)

IDAHO
LAWS & PENALTIES

Offense	Penalty	Incarceration	Max. Fine
POSSESSION			
Personal Use			
3 oz or less	Misdemeanor	1 year	$ 1,000
3 oz - less than 1 lb	Felony	5 years	$ 10,000
With Intent to Distribute			
1 - less than 5 lbs or 25 - less than 50 plants	Felony	1 year*	$ 50,000
5 - less than 25 lbs or 50 - less than 100 plants	Felony	3 years*	$ 50,000
25 lbs or more or 100 plants or more	Felony	5 years*	$ 50,000
Where a person under the age of 18 is present	Felony	5 years	$ 5,000

* Mandatory minimum sentence

Possession of 1 lb or more, or 25 or more plants is considered Trafficking.

Offense	Penalty	Incarceration	Max. Fine
SALE OR DELIVERY			
1 - less than 5 lbs or 25 - less than 50 plants	Felony	1 year*	$ 50,000
5 - less than 25 lbs or 50 - less than 100 plants	Felony	3 years*	$ 50,000
25 lbs or more or 100 plants or more	Felony	5 years*	$ 50,000
Where a person under the age of 18 is present	Felony	5 years	$ 50,000

* Mandatory minimum sentence

Offense	Penalty	Incarceration	Max. Fine
CULTIVATION			
1 - less than 5 lbs or 25 - less than 50 plants	Felony	1 year*	$ 50,000
5 - less than 25 lbs or 50 - less than 100 plants	Felony	3 years*	$ 50,000
25 lbs or more or 100 plants or more	Felony	5 years*	$ 50,000
Where a person under the age of 18 is present	Felony	5 years	$ 50,000

* Mandatory minimum sentence

Possession of 1 lb or more, or 25 or more plants is considered Trafficking.

Offense	Penalty	Incarceration	Max. Fine
HASH & CONCENTRATES			

Penalties for hashish are the same as for marijuana. Please see the marijuana penalties section for further details.

Offense	Penalty	Incarceration	Max. Fine
PARAPHERNALIA			
Use or possession of paraphernalia	Misdemeanor	1 year	$ 1,000
Manufacture or sale of paraphernalia	Felony	9 years	$ 30,000
FORFEITURE			

Vehicles and other property may be seized.

Offense	Penalty	Incarceration	Max. Fine
MISCELLANEOUS			
Use or intoxication in public	Misdemeanor	6 months	$ 1,000
Presence at location where marijuana is cultivated or stored	Misdemeanor	3 months	$ 300
Maintaining a structure used for selling or storing marijuana	Misdemeanor	1 year	$ 25,000

Possession of marijuana and under the age of 18 will result in driver's license revocation for a period of not more than 1 year.

Penalty Details

Marijuana is a Schedule I hallucinogenic substance under the Idaho Uniform Controlled Substances Act.

See
- Idaho Code Ann. § 37-2705(d)(22)

Possession for Personal Use

Possession of 3 ounces or less of marijuana is a misdemeanor punishable by up to 1 year imprisonment and/or a fine up to $1,000. If the quantity possessed is more than 3 ounces but less than 1 pound, it is a felony punishable by up to 5 years imprisonment and/or a fine up to $10,000.

See
- Idaho Code Ann. §§ 37-2732(c)(3), (e)

Possession with Intent to Distribute

Possession with intent to distribute up to 1 pound or up to 24 plants of marijuana is a felony punishable by up to 5 years imprisonment and/or a fine up to $15,000. Possession of 1 pound or more, or 25 or more plants, is considered trafficking in marijuana, a felony punishable by up to 15 years imprisonment and a fine up to $50,000. If the amount possessed was 1 pound or more but less than 5 pounds, or 25 plants or more but less than 50 plants, the offender receives a mandatory minimum fixed term of 1 year imprisonment and a mandatory fine of at least $5,000. Possession of 5 pounds or more but less than 25 pounds, or 50 plants or more but less than 100 plants, of marijuana receives a mandatory minimum fixed term of 3 years imprisonment and a mandatory fine of at least $10,000. Possession of 25 pounds or more, or 100 plants or more, of marijuana receives a mandatory minimum fixed term of 5 years imprisonment and a mandatory fine of at least $15,000. The maximum number of years of imprisonment for trafficking shall be 15 years and the maximum fine shall be $50,000. Suspension and deferral are not available for trafficking in marijuana offenses, and parole may not be granted until the minimum sentences are completed. A second offense of trafficking in marijuana will receive a mandatory minimum term of imprisonment that is double that authorized for the offense.

See
- Idaho Code Ann. § 37-2732(a)(1)(B)
- Idaho Code Ann. §§ 37-2732B(a)(1), (7)-(8)

A conviction for possession with intent to deliver is punishable by a mandatory minimum of 3 years to life imprisonment if it is within 10 years of a conviction in any U.S. territory for an offense related to dealing, selling, or trafficking controlled substances that was punishable by imprisonment of more than 1 year.

See
- Idaho Code Ann. § 37-2739A

Possession with intent to distribute marijuana on premises where a person under the age of 18 is present is a felony punishable by up to 5 years imprisonment and/or a fine up to $5,000.

See
- Idaho Code Ann. § 37-2737A

Sale/Delivery

Delivery of up to 1 pound or up to 24 plants of marijuana is a felony punishable by up to 5 years imprisonment and/or a fine up to $15,000. Delivery or import into Idaho of 1 pound, or more or 25 plants or more, is considered trafficking in marijuana, a felony punishable by up to 15 years imprisonment and a fine up to $50,000. If the amount delivered or imported was 1 pound or more but less than 5 pounds, or 25 plants or more but less than 50 plants, the offender receives a mandatory minimum fixed term of 1 year imprisonment and a mandatory fine of at least $5,000. Delivery or import into Idaho of 5 pounds or more but less than 25 pounds, or 50 plants or more but less than 100 plants, of marijuana receives a mandatory minimum fixed term of 3 years imprisonment and a mandatory fine of at least $10,000. Delivery or import into Idaho of 25 pounds or more, or 100 plants or more, of marijuana receives a mandatory minimum fixed term of 5 years imprisonment and a mandatory fine of at least $15,000. The maximum number of years of imprisonment for trafficking shall be 15 years and the maximum fine shall be $50,000. Suspension and deferral are not available for trafficking in marijuana offenses, and parole may not be granted until the minimum sentences are completed. A second offense of trafficking in marijuana will receive a mandatory minimum term of imprisonment that is double that authorized for the offense.

See
- Idaho Code Ann. § 37-2732(a)(1)(B)
- Idaho Code Ann. §§ 37-2732B(a)(1), (7)-(8)

A conviction for delivery is punishable by a mandatory minimum of 3 years to life imprisonment if it is within 10 years of a conviction in any U.S. territory for an offense related to dealing, selling, or trafficking controlled substances that was punishable by imprisonment of more than 1 year.

See
- Idaho Code Ann. § 37-2739A

Delivery by a person aged 18 or older to a person aged 18 years or younger who is at least 3 years their junior is punishable by a term of imprisonment that is twice that authorized for delivery.

See
- Idaho Code Ann. § 37-2737

Delivery on premises where a person under the age of 18 is present is a felony punishable by up to 5 years imprisonment and/or a fine up to $5,000.

See
- Idaho Code Ann. § 37-2737A

Cultivation

Cultivation of up to 1 pound or up to 24 plants of marijuana is a felony punishable by up to 5 years imprisonment and/or a fine up to $15,000. Cultivation of 1 pound or more, or 25 plants or more, is considered trafficking in marijuana, a felony punishable by up to 15 years imprisonment and a fine up to $50,000. If the amount cultivated was 1 pound or more but less than 5 pounds, or 25 plants or more but less than 50 plants, the offender receives a mandatory minimum fixed term of 1 year imprisonment and a mandatory fine of at least $5,000. Cultivation of 5 pounds or more but less than 25 pounds, or 50 plants or more but less than 100 plants, of marijuana receives a mandatory minimum fixed term of 3 years imprisonment and a mandatory fine of at least $10,000. Cultivation of 25 pounds or more, or 100 plants or more, of marijuana receives a mandatory minimum fixed term of 5 years imprisonment and a mandatory fine of at least $15,000. The maximum number of years of imprisonment for trafficking shall be 15 years and the maximum fine shall be $50,000. Suspension and deferral are not available for trafficking in marijuana offenses, and parole may not be granted until the minimum sentences are completed. A second offense of trafficking in marijuana will receive a mandatory minimum term of imprisonment that is double that authorized for the offense.

See
- Idaho Code Ann. § 37-2732(a)(B)
- Idaho Code Ann. §§ 37-2732B(a)(1), (7)-(8)

A conviction for cultivation is punishable by a mandatory minimum of 3 years to life imprisonment if it is within 10 years of a conviction in any U.S. territory for an offense related to dealing, selling, or trafficking controlled substances that was punishable by imprisonment of more than 1 year.

See
- Idaho Code Ann. § 37-2739A

Cultivation on premises where a person under the age of 18 is present is a felony punishable by up to 5 years imprisonment and/or a fine up to $5,000.

See
- Idaho Code Ann. § 37-2737A

Hash & Concentrates

Hashish is classified as a Schedule I drug in Idaho. The Definitions section of the statute includes Hashish and Marijuana Concentrates when it defines Marijuana as the plant and every derivative preparation of it. The Penalties section reinforces this interpretation by explicitly including, as Marijuana, any extract or preparation of cannabis which contains tetrahydrocannabinol. The statute never explicitly refers to Hashish or Marijuana Concentrates as being separate from Marijuana. Therefore, the penalties for hashish and THC concentrates should be the same as for marijuana. Please see the above marijuana section for further information.

See
- Idaho Code Ann. §37-2705(d)(27)
- Idaho Code Ann. §37-2701(t)
- Idaho Code Ann. §37-2732(e)

Paraphernalia

Use or possession of paraphernalia is a misdemeanor punishable by up to 1 year imprisonment and/or a fine up to $1,000.

See
- Idaho Code Ann. § 37-2734A

Manufacture or sale of drug paraphernalia is a felony punishable by up to 9 years imprisonment and/or a fine up to $30,000.

See
- Idaho Code Ann. § 37-2734B

Sentencing

For violations of possession, cultivation, and sale of marijuana, all offenders are required to undergo a substance abuse evaluation. This requirement may be waived if the violation is the offenders first, the charge is for simple possession, and the court finds no reason to believe that the offender is in need of treatment. This evaluation will be used in determining the sentence of the offender, which may include mandatory treatment.

See
- Idaho Code Ann. § 37-2738(2)

Judgment may be withheld if the offender has no prior felony convictions, convictions for driving under the influence, or convictions for possession, sale, or cultivation of a controlled substance, the offender has been cooperative with law enforcement efforts for drug-related crime, and the court believes that they will complete the terms of probation. When a person pleads guilty or is found guilty of possession, sale, or cultivation, if they are granted a probationary period, it will include a minimum of 100 hours of community service.

See
- Idaho Code Ann. §§ 37-2738(4)-(5)

Second Offense

A second or subsequent offense is subject to twice the term of imprisonment and twice the fine authorized for the offense. An offense for this provision is any conviction under the Idaho Uniform Controlled Substances Act or under a federal statute or statute of another state relating to controlled substances.

See
- Idaho Code Ann. § 37-2739

Forfeiture

Criminal

Anyone who pleads guilty to or is convicted of an offense under the Idaho Uniform Controlled Substances Act which is punishable by more than 1 year imprisonment must forfeit certain property to the state of Idaho. This includes any property constituting or derived from profits of the violation and any property used in or used to facilitate the violation.

See
- Idaho Code Ann. § 37-2801

Civil

Vehicles and other property may be seized for violations of the Idaho Uniform Controlled Substances Act. Proceedings must commence within 30 days after the seizure. For certain properties, a notice of forfeiture must be provided to all those with an interest in it. Interested partied have 20 days to file an answer from the time that the notice is mailed or published.

See
- Idaho Code Ann. § 37-2744
- Idaho Code Ann. § 37-2744A

Miscellaneous

Use or intoxication in public

Using or being under the influence of marijuana on public property or on private property open to the public is a misdemeanor punishable by up to 6 months imprisonment and/or a fine up to $1,000. The court may assess an additional cost of up to $200 for reimbursement to the arresting or prosecuting authority. A public use or intoxication offense that occurs within 5 years of 2 or more separate public use or intoxication convictions is punishable by a mandatory minimum of 120 days imprisonment to a maximum of 1 year if the offender refuses to complete treatment.

See
- Idaho Code Ann. § 37-2732C

Presence at location where marijuana is cultivated or stored

Presence at or on the premises where marijuana is cultivated or held for distribution, transportation, delivery, or use is a misdemeanor punishable by up to 90 days imprisonment and/or a fine up to $300.

See
- Idaho Code Ann. § 37-2732(d)

Knowingly maintaining a structure used for drug offenses

It is a misdemeanor punishable by up to 1 year imprisonment and/or a fine up to $25,000 to maintain a structure (including vehicles and houses) that the owner knows is used for selling, storing, or using marijuana.

See
- Idaho Code Ann. §§ 37-2733(a)(5), (b)

Fees for investigation

Upon a felony or misdemeanor conviction of the Idaho Uniform Controlled Substances Act, the offender may be ordered to pay for the costs of investigating their offense incurred by law enforcement.

See
- Idaho Code Ann. § 37-2732(k)

Drug hotline fee

Any violation of the Idaho Uniform Controlled Substances Act results in a fee of $10, which is deposited in the drug and driving under the influence enforcement donation fund.

See
- Idaho Code Ann. § 37-2735A

Driver's license revocation

Any person who pleads guilty or is found guilty of possessing of marijuana and is under 18 shall have their license revoked for a period of not more than 1 year.

See
- Idaho Code Ann. § 18-1502C(3)(a)

ILLINOIS
LAWS & PENALTIES

Offense	Penalty	Incarceration	Max. Fine
POSSESSION			
2.5 g or less	Misdemeanor	30 days	$ 1,500
2.5 - 10 g	Misdemeanor	6 months	$ 1,500
More than 10 - 30 g (first offense)	Misdemeanor	1 year	$ 2,500
More than 10 - 30 g (subsequent offense)	Felony	1* - 6 years	$ 25,000
More than 30 - 500 g (first offense)	Felony	1* - 6 years	$ 25,000
More than 30 - 500 g (subsequent offense)	Felony	2* - 10 years	$ 25,000
More than 500 - 2000 g	Felony	2* - 10 years	$ 25,000
More than 2000 - 5000 g	Felony	3* - 14 years	$ 25,000
More than 5000 g	Felony	4* - 30 years	$ 25,000

* Mandatory minimum sentence

Offense	Penalty	Incarceration	Max. Fine
SALE OR TRAFFICKING			
2.5 g or less	Misdemeanor	6 months	$ 1,500
More than 2.5 - 10 g	Misdemeanor	1 year	$ 2,500
More than 10 - 30 g	Felony	1* - 6 years	$ 25,000
More than 30 - 500 g	Felony	2* - 10 years	$ 50,000
More than 500 - 2000 g	Felony	3* - 14 years	$ 100,000
More than 2000 - 5000 g	Felony	4* - 30 years	$ 150,000
More than 5000 g	Felony	6* - 60 years	$ 200,000

* Mandatory minimum sentence

Delivery on school grounds carries increased incarceration and fines

Bringing 2500 grams or more of marijuana into the State of Illinois is Trafficking and brings a mandatory minimum sentence of twice the minimum sentence as sale of marijuana.

Offense	Penalty	Incarceration	Max. Fine
CULTIVATION			
5 plants or less	Misdemeanor	1 year	$ 2,500
More than 5 - 20 plants	Felony	1* - 6 years	$ 25,000
More than 20 - 50 plants	Felony	2* - 10 years	$ 25,000
More than 50 - 200 plants	Felony	3* - 14 years	$ 100,000
More than 200 plants	Felony	4* - 30 years	$ 100,000

* Mandatory minimum sentence

HASH & CONCENTRATES

Penalties for hashish are the same as for marijuana. Please see the marijuana penalties section for further details.

Offense	Penalty	Incarceration	Max. Fine
PARAPHERNALIA			
Possession of paraphernalia	Misdemeanor	1 year	$ 2,500
Sale of paraphernalia	Felony	1* - 6 years	$ 25,000
Sale to a minor	Felony	2* - 10 years	$ 25,000
Sale to a pregnant woman	Felony	3* - 14 years	$ 25,000

* Mandatory minimum sentence

MISCELLANEOUS

Civil Asset Forfeiture - Property is subject to forfeiture.

Penalty Details

Possession for Personal Use

Possession of less than 2.5 grams of marijuana is a Class C misdemeanor, punishable by a jail term of up to 30 days and a maximum fine of up to $1,500.

Possession of more than 2.5 - 10 grams of marijuana is a Class B misdemeanor, punishable by up to 6 months imprisonment and a maximum fine of up to $1,500.

Possession of more than 10 - 30 grams of marijuana is a Class A misdemeanor for a first offense, which is punishable by a jail term of up to 1 year and a max fine of up to 2,500. For a second or subsequent offense, possession of more than 10 - 30 grams of marijuana is a Class A felony, punishable by a minimum sentence of 1 year and a maximum sentence of 6 years, as well as a fine of $25,000.

Possession of more than 30 - 500 grams of marijuana is a Class 4 felony for a first offense, which is punishable by a minimum sentence of 1 year and a maximum sentence of 6 years, as well as a fine of $25,000. For a second or subsequent offense, possession of between more than 30 - 500 grams of marijuana is a Class 3 felony, punishable by a minimum sentence of 2 years and a maximum sentence of 5 years, as well as a fine of $25,000.

Possession of more than 500 - 2,000 grams of marijuana is a Class 3 felony, punishable by a minimum sentence of 2 years and a maximum sentence of 10 years, as well as a fine of $25,000.

Possession of more than 2,000 - 5,000 grams of marijuana is a Class 2 felony, punishable by a minimum jail term of 3 years and a maximum sentence of 14 years, as well as a fine of $25,000.

Possession of over 5,000 grams of marijuana is a Class 1 felony, punishable by imprisonment of a minimum of 4 years and a maximum of 30 years, as well as a fine of $25,000.

See
• 720 Illinois Comp. Stat. 550/1 - /19   • 730 Illinois Comp. Stat. 5/5-4.5-25 - 70

Sale

Selling or possessing with the intent to sell, 2.5 grams or less of marijuana is a Class B misdemeanor, punishable by up to 6 months imprisonment and a maximum fine of $1,500.

Selling or possessing with the intent to sell, more than 2.5 - 10 grams of marijuana is a Class A misdemeanor, punishable by a maximum sentence of 1 year in prison and a maximum fine of $2,500.

Selling or possessing with the intent to sell, more than 10 - 30 grams of marijuana is a Class 4 felony, punishable by a minimum sentence of 1 year and a maximum sentence of 6 years, as well as a maximum fine of $25,000.

Selling or possessing with the intent to sell, more than 30 - 500 grams of marijuana is a Class 3 felony, punishable by a minimum sentence of 2 years and a maximum sentence of 10 years, and a maximum fine of $50,000.

Selling or possessing with the intent to sell, more than 500 - 2,000 grams of marijuana is a Class 2 felony, punishable by a minimum jail term of 3 years and a maximum sentence of 14 years, and a maximum fine of $100,000.

Selling or possessing with the intent to sell, more than 2,000 - 5,000 grams of marijuana is a Class 1 felony, punishable by imprisonment of a minimum of 4 years and a maximum of 30 years, and a maximum fine of $150,000.

Selling, manufacturing, or possessing with the intent to sell, more than 5,000 grams of marijuana is a Class X felony, punishable by a minimum sentence of 6 years and a maximum sentence of 60 years, and a maximum fine of $200,000.

See
• 720 Illinois Comp. Stat. 550/1 - /19   • 730 Illinois Comp. Stat. 5/5-4.5-25 - 70

Delivery on School grounds

Any person who delivers less than 2.5 grams of cannabis on school grounds is guilty of a Class A misdemeanor punishable by a fine not to exceed $2,500, for each offense, and a term of imprisonment of less than 1 year.

Any person who delivers more than 2.5 – 10 grams of cannabis on school grounds is guilty of a Class 4 felony, the fine for which shall not exceed $25,000 and a term of imprisonment of 1 – 6 years.

Any person who delivers more than 10 – 30 grams of cannabis on school grounds is guilty of a Class 3 felony, the fine for which shall not exceed $50,000 and a term of imprisonment of 2 – 10 years.

Any person who delivers more than 30 – 500 grams of cannabis on school grounds is guilty of a Class 2 felony, the fine for which shall not exceed $100,000 and a term of imprisonment of 3 – 14 years.

Any person who delivers more than 500 – 2000 g on any school grounds is guilty of a Class 1 felony, the fine for which shall not exceed $200,000 and a term of imprisonment of 4 – 30 years.

See
• 720 Illinois Comp. Stat. 550/5.2   • 730 Illinois Comp. Stat. 5/5-4.5-25 - 70

Delivery to a minor

Any person who is at least 18 years of age who delivers cannabis to a person under 18 years of age who is at least 3 years his junior may be sentenced to imprisonment for a term up to twice the maximum term otherwise authorized.

See
• 720 Illinois Comp. Stat. 550/7

Trafficking

Bringing 2,500 grams or more of marijuana into the State of Illinois brings a mandatory minimum sentence of twice the minimum sentence for the sale or manufacture of the same weight of marijuana, a maximum sentence of twice the maximum sentence for the sale of the same weight of marijuana, and a fine equal to the fine for distributing the same weight of marijuana, as listed above under "Sale".

See
• 720 Illinois Comp. Stat. 550/5.1

Cultivation

Possessing 5 or less marijuana plants is a Class A misdemeanor, punishable by a maximum sentence of 1 year in prison.

Possessing more than 5 - 20 plants is a Class 4 felony, punishable by a minimum sentence of 1 year and a maximum sentence of 6 years, as well as a fine of $25,000.

Possessing more than 20 - 50 plants is a Class 3 felony, punishable by a minimum sentence of 2 years and a maximum sentence of 10 years, as well as a fine of $25,000.

Possessing more than 50 - 200 plants is a Class 2 felony, which is punishable by a minimum jail term of 3 years and a maximum sentence of 14 years, along with a maximum fine of $100,000

Possessing more than 200 marijuana plants is a Class 1 felony, punishable by imprisonment of a minimum of 4 years and a maximum of 30 years, as well as a maximum fine of $100,000.

See
• 720 Illinois Comp. Stat. 550/8   • 730 Illinois Comp. Stat. 5/5-4.5-25 - 70

Hash & Concentrates

Offenses involving Hashish and Marijuana Concentrates are punished to the same extent as those offenses involving plant Cannabis. The Illinois Cannabis Control Act explicitly includes Hashish under the definition of Cannabis in the statute. The statute also includes all derivatives, compounds, and preparations of the plant under the definition of Cannabis, effectively including any other Marijuana Concentrates. There is no reference to any difference in penalties between Hashish or Marijuana Concentrates and plant Cannabis in the statute. Illinois state case law also refers to Hashish as a form of Marijuana.

See
• 720 Illinois Comp. Stat. 550/3(a)   • People v. Hopkins, 276 N.E.2d 413 (Ill. Ct. App. 1971).

Paraphernalia

Possession of paraphernalia is a Class A misdemeanor, punishable by up to one year in prison, as well as a minimum fine of $750 and a maximum fine of $2,500.

Sale of paraphernalia is a Class 4 felony, punishable by a minimum sentence of 1 year and a maximum sentence of 6 years, as well as a minimum fine of $1,000 and a maximum fine of $25,000.

Sale of paraphernalia to a minor is a Class 3 felony, punishable by a minimum sentence of 2 years and a maximum sentence of 10 years, as well as a minimum fine of $1,000 and a maximum fine of $25,000.

Sale of paraphernalia to an obviously pregnant woman is a Class 2 felony, punishable by a minimum jail term of 3 years and a maximum sentence of 14 years, as well as a minimum fine of $1,000.

All paraphernalia is subject to forfeiture.

See
• 720 Illinois Comp. Stat. 600/1 - /6   • 730 Illinois Comp. Stat. 5/5-4.5-25 - 70

Miscellaneous

Property forfeiture in IL is governed by:

See
• 725 Illinois Comp. Stat. 150/1 - 150/14
• 720 Illinois Comp. Stat. 5/37
• 720 Illinois Comp. Stat. 5/36.5-5
• 720 Illinois Comp. Stat. 5/36-1

INDIANA
LAWS & PENALTIES

Offense	Penalty	Incarceration	Max. Fine
POSSESSION			
Any amount	Misdemeanor	180 days	$ 1,000
Less than 30 g and prior drug offense	Misdemeanor	1 year	$ 5,000
30 g or more and prior drug offense	Felony	6 months - 2 1/2 years	$ 10,000
Conditional discharge may be available for first-time offenders.			
SALE OR CULTIVATION			
Less than 30 g	Misdemeanor	1 year	$ 5,000
30 g - less than 10 lbs	Felony	6 months - 2 1/2 years	$ 10,000
10 lbs or more	Felony	1 - 6 years	$ 10,000
To a minor	Felony	1 - 6 years	$ 10,000
Prior drug offense carries a greater penalty. See details section for more information.			
HASH & CONCENTRATES			
Possession			
5 g or more	Felony	6 months - 2 1/2 years	$ 10,000
Manufacture			
Less than 5 g	Misdemeanor	1 year	$ 5,000
5 g – less than 300 g	Felony	6 months - 2 1/2 years	$ 10,000
300 g or more	Felony	1 - 6 years	$ 10,000
Prior drug offense carries a greater penalty. See details section for more information.			
PARAPHERNALIA			
Possession, Dealing or Manufacture	Infraction	N/A	$ 10,000
Possession, Dealing or Manufacture (subsequent conviction)	Felony	6 months - 2 1/2 years	$ 10,000
MISCELLANEOUS			
Presence where knowledge of drug activity occurs	Misdemeanor	6 months	$ 1,000
Possession, sale, or distribution conviction will result in a driver's license suspension.			

Penalty Details

Marijuana, which includes hash and hash oil under the Indiana Criminal Code, is listed as a Schedule I drug.

See
- 35-48-2-1, et seq. of the Indiana Criminal Code
- 35-48-2-4(d)(22) of the Indiana Criminal Code
- 35-48-4-10,11 of the Indiana Criminal Code

Possession for Personal Use

Possession of marijuana is a Class B misdemeanor punishable by not more than 180 days and a possible fine of not more than $1,000. Possession of less than 30 grams and a prior drug offense is a Class A misdemeanor punishable by up to 1 year imprisonment and a fine of not more than $5,000. Possession of at least 30 grams of marijuana with a prior conviction for a drug offense is a Level 6 felony punishable by 6 months - 2 ½ years imprisonment, with the advisory sentence being 1 year and may be fined not more than $10,000. Possession with intent to manufacture, finance the manufacture of, deliver, or, finance the delivery of shall follow the violations listed under "Sale or Cultivation." Conditional discharge may be available for first-time offenders.

See
- 35-48-4-11 of the Indiana Code
- 35-48-4-12 of the Indiana Code
- 35-50-2-7(b) of the Indiana Code
- 35-50-3-3 of the Indiana Code

Sale/Cultivation

The sale of less than 30 grams is a Class A misdemeanor punishable by a maximum sentence of 1 year imprisonment and a maximum fine of $5,000. A subsequent offense is a level 6 felony punishable by 6 months - 2 ½ years imprisonment and a maximum fine of $10,000.

The sale of 30 grams - less than 10 pounds is a Level 6 felony punishable by 6 months - 2 ½ years imprisonment and a maximum fine of $10,000.

The sale of 10 pounds or more is a level 5 felony punishable by 1 - 6 years imprisonment and a maximum fine of $10,000.

The sale of any amount to a minor is a level 5 felony punishable by 1 - 6 years imprisonment and a maximum fine of $10,000.

See
- 35-48-4-10 of the Indiana Code

Hash & Concentrates

A person who knowingly or intentionally possesses (pure or adulterated) marijuana, hash oil, or hashish commits a Class A misdemeanor, punishable by a maximum sentence of one year imprisonment and a maximum fine of $5,000. Conditional discharge may be available for first-time offenders.

Possession of more than 2 grams of hashish or concentrate, or if the person has a prior conviction of an offense involving marijuana, hash oil, or hashish and is in possession less than 2 grams, then the crime is a level 6 felony, punishable by 6 months to 2 ½ years imprisonment and a maximum fine of $10,000.

See
- § 35-48-4-10 of the Indiana Code
- § 35-48-4-11 of the Indiana Code
- § 35-48-4-12 of the Indiana Code
- § 35-50-3-2 of the Indiana Code
- § 35-5-2-7 of the Indiana Code

Manufacture or sale of less than 5 grams of hash oil, or hashish is a class A misdemeanor punishable by a maximum sentence of one year imprisonment and a maximum fine of $5,000. A subsequent offense is a level 6 felony punishable by 6 months - 2 ½ years imprisonment and a maximum fine of $10,000.

If the amount is at least 5 - but less than 300 grams the offense is a level 6 felony punishable by 6 months - 2 ½ years imprisonment and a maximum fine of $10,000. A subsequent offense if a person has a prior drug dealing offense is a level 5 felony punishable by 1 - 6 years imprisonment and a maximum fine of $10,000.

If the amount involved is at least 300 grams the offense is a level 5 felony punishable by a fixed term of imprisonment of 1 - 6 years with the advisory sentence being 3 years and a fine of not more than $10,000.

If the offense involved a sale to a minor the offense is a level 5 felony punishable by a fixed term of imprisonment of 1 - 6 years with the advisory sentence being 3 years and a fine of not more than $10,000.

See
- § 35-48-4-10 of the Indiana Code

Paraphernalia

Manufacture

Manufacture of paraphernalia is a Class A infraction punishable by up to a $10,000 fine. A Subsequent conviction is a Level 6 felony punishable by 6 months – 2 ½ years imprisonment and a maximum fine of $10,000.

See
- 34-28-5-4 of the Indiana Code
- 35-48-4-8.1 of the Indiana Code

Possession

Possession of paraphernalia is a Class A infraction punishable by up to a $10,000 fine. A subsequent conviction is a Level 6 felony punishable by 6 months – 2 ½ years imprisonment and a maximum fine of $10,000.

See
- 34-28-5-4 of the Indiana Code
- 35-48-4-8.3 of the Indiana Code

Sale

Dealing in paraphernalia is a Class A infraction punishable by up to a $10,000 fine. A person is dealing in paraphernalia and has a prior unrelated judgment or conviction may be convicted of a Level 6 felony punishable by 6 months – 2 ½ years imprisonment and a maximum fine of $10,000.

See
- 34-28-5-4 of the Indiana Code
- 35-48-4-8.5 of the Indiana Code

Miscellaneous

Presence "where knowledge of drug activity occurs" is a misdemeanor punishable by a maximum sentence of six months imprisonment and a maximum fine of $1,000

A possession, sale, or distribution conviction will result in a driver's license suspension for 6 months- 2 years.

See
- 9-30-4-6(b)(6) of the Indiana Code

IOWA
LAWS & PENALTIES

Offense	Penalty	Incarceration	Max. Fine
POSSESSION			
Any amount (first offense)	Misdemeanor	6 months	$ 1,000
Any amount (second offense)	Misdemeanor	1 year	$ 1,875
Any amount (third offense)	Misdemeanor	2 years	$ 6,250
Offenders who are chronic abusers of marijuana may be sent to rehab.			
CULTIVATION OR DISTRIBUTION			
50 kg or less	Felony	5 years	$ 7,500
More than 50 - 100 kg	Felony	10 years	$ 50,000
More than 100 - 1000 kg	Felony	25 years	$ 100,000
More than 1000 kg	Felony	50 years	$ 1,000,000
Involving a minor	Felony	5* - 25 years	$ 100,000
To a minor within 1000 feet of a park, elementary or middle school, or school bus	Felony	10 years*	$ 100,000
* Mandatory minimum sentence			
Distribution includes possession With Intent to Distribute			
HASH & CONCENTRATES			
Penalties for hashish are the same as for marijuana except in one circumstance. Please see the marijuana penalties section for further details.			
PARAPHERNALIA			
Possession, distribution, or manufacture of paraphernalia	Misdemeanor	6 months	$ 1,000
MISCELLANEOUS			
Sponsoring, promoting, or assisting in a gathering where marijuana will be used, distributed, or possessed	Misdemeanor	1 year	$ 1,875
Possession with intent to sell large amounts can lead to an automatic driver's license suspension.			

Penalty Details

Marijuana is a schedule I hallucinogenic substance under the Iowa Controlled Substances Act.

See
• Iowa Code § 124.204(4)(m)

Possession for Personal Use

For first offenders, possession of any amount of marijuana is a misdemeanor and is punishable by a fine of up to $1,000 and/or up to 6 months of imprisonment. Second offenders are subject to a fine of $315-$1875 and/or up to 1 year of imprisonment. Third offenses are considered aggravated misdemeanors and are punishable by a fine of $625-$6250 and/or up to 2 years of imprisonment.

See
• Iowa Code § 124.401(c)(5)   • Iowa Code § 124.409
• Iowa Code § 903.1

Offenders who are chronic abusers of marijuana may be sent to rehab. If this program is successfully completed the court may place the defendant on probation.

See
• Iowa Code § 124.409

Possession of marijuana within 1,000 feet of an elementary school, secondary school, public park, or school bus is punishable by the penalty for possession and 100 hours of community service.

See
• Iowa Code § 124.401B

Cultivation or Distribution

Distribution of marijuana includes possessing marijuana with the intent to distribute it.

Delivery or possession with intent to deliver one half ounce or less of plant-form marijuana without remuneration is equivalent to simple possession in Iowa, with penalties for a first offense being a misdemeanor with incarceration of no more than 6 months, and a fine of no more than $1000 dollars. Subsequent convictions for delivery without remuneration will be punished more severely, just as subsequent simple possession convictions would be.

See
• Iowa Code § 124.410

Distribution or cultivation of 50 kilograms of marijuana or less is a class D felony punishable by a fine of $750-$7,500 and up to 5 years of imprisonment. Distribution or cultivation of more than 50-100 kilograms of marijuana is a class C felony and is punishable by a fine of $1,000-$50,000 and up to 10 years of imprisonment. Distribution or cultivation of more than 100-1,000 kilograms of marijuana is a class B felony and is punishable by a fine of $5,000-$100,000 and up to 25 years of imprisonment. Distribution or cultivation of more than 1,000 kilograms of marijuana is a class B felony and is punishable by a fine of not more than $1,000,000 and up to 50 years of imprisonment.

See
• Iowa Code § 124.401

If a person over the age of 18 solicits a person under the age of 18 to assist in the distribution or cultivation of marijuana this act is punishable as a class C felony by a fine of $1,000-$50,000 and up to 10 years of imprisonment.

If a person over the age of 18 distributes marijuana to someone under the age of 18 this constitutes a Class B felony punishable by a fine of $5,000-$100,000 and up to 25 years of imprisonment, in addition a mandatory minimum term of 5 years will apply. If the sale to a minor occurs within 1,000 feet of a park, elementary school, middle school, or marked school bus a mandatory minimum term of 10 years will apply.

See
• Iowa Code § 124.406

Hash & Concentrates

Iowa classifies Marijuana and Tetrahydrocannabinols separately as hallucinogenic substances in Schedule 1 of the Iowa Controlled Substances Schedule. For the purposes of criminal justice, plant Marijuana and all Tetrahydrocannabinol derivatives thereof, including hashish and marijuana concentrates, are defined as Marijuana and punished equally in all but one circumstance. The only circumstance where plant-form Marijuana is treated differently is for a charge of delivery or possession with intent to deliver one half ounce or less without remuneration. In that circumstance, plant-form marijuana is punished equivalent to the penalties for simple possession, whereas delivery, or possession with intent to deliver an equivalent amount of hashish, hash oil, or other derivatives are punished in accordance with the regular penalties for distribution.

See
• Iowa Code § 124.101   • Iowa Code § 124.401
• Iowa Code § 124.204   • Iowa Code § 124.410

Paraphernalia

Possession, distribution, or manufacture of marijuana paraphernalia is simple misdemeanor and is punishable by a fine of up to $1,000 and/or up to 6 months imprisonment. Paraphernalia includes any item that is knowingly used to ingest, inhale, manufacture, enhance, or test marijuana quality.

See
• Iowa Code § 124.414

Miscellaneous

Sponsoring, promoting, or assisting in the sponsorship or promotion of a gathering with the knowledge that marijuana will be used, distributed, or possessed at that event is a serious misdemeanor punishable by a fine of $315-$1875 and/or up to 1 year of imprisonment.

See
• Iowa Code § 124.407

Possession with intent to sell large amounts of pot (100-1000kg) can lead to an automatic driver's license suspension.

See
• Iowa Code § 124.401(1)(6)

KANSAS
LAWS & PENALTIES

Offense	Penalty	Incarceration	Max. Fine
POSSESSION			
Less than 450 g	Misdemeanor	1 year	$ 2,500
Any amount (subsequent offense)	Felony	10 months* - 3.5 years	$ 100,000
With Intent to Distribute			
450 g or more	Felony	10 months probation – 42 months*	$ 100,000

* Sentence determined by category and severity drug severity level

Offense	Penalty	Incarceration	Max. Fine
SALE OR DISTRIBUTION			
Less than 25 g	Felony	14 months probation – 51 years*	$ 300,000
25 – less than 450 g	Felony	46 – 83 months	$ 300,000
450 g – less than 30 kg	Felony	92 – 144 months	$ 500,000
30 kg or more	Felony	138 – 204 months	$ 500,000
Within 1000 feet of a school zone	Felony	4** - 7 years	$ 300,000

* Sentence determined by category and severity drug severity level

** Mandatory minimum sentence

Offense	Penalty	Incarceration	Max. Fine
CULTIVATION			
More than 4 – less than 50 plants	Felony	46 – 83 months	$ 300,000
50 – less than 100 plants	Felony	92 – 144 months	$ 500,000
100 plants or more	Felony	138 – 204 months	$ 500,000
HASH & CONCENTRATES			

Penalties for hashish are the same as for marijuana. Please see the marijuana penalties section for further details.

Offense	Penalty	Incarceration	Max. Fine
PARAPHERNALIA			
Store, Ingest	Misdemeanor	1 year	$ 2,500
Paraphernalia to cultivate less than 5 plants	Misdemeanor	1 year	$ 2,500
Paraphernalia to cultivate 5 plants or more	Felony	5 months probation – 17 months	$ 100,000
Sale	Misdemeanor	1 year	$ 2,500
Sale to a minor or within 1,000 ft of a school	Felony	5 months probation – 17 months	$ 100,000
MISCELLANEOUS			

Kansas has a marijuana tax stamp law enacted.

Penalty Details

Possession

Possession of less than 450 grams is a Class A misdemeanor punishable by a maximum of 1 year imprisonment and a maximum fine of $2,500. There is a rebuttable presumption of intent to distribute if possession is 450 grams or more, which is a drug severity level 5 felony punishable by a fine not to exceed $100,000 and a term of imprisonment ranging from 10 months probation - 42 months imprisonment.

A subsequent conviction is a drug severity level 5 felony punishable by imprisonment for 10 months probation - 42 months imprisonment and a maximum fine of $100,000.

See
- 65-4101 of the Kansas Code
- 65-4105 of the Kansas Code
- 21-5705 of the Kansas Code
- 21-5706 of the Kansas Code
- 21-6602 of the Kansas Code
- 21-6611 of the Kansas Code

Sale or Distribution

Sale of less than 25 grams is a drug severity level 4 felony punishable by 14 months probation - 51 years imprisonment and a fine not to exceed $300,000.

Distribution of 25 - less than 450 grams is a drug severity level 3 felony punishable by 46 - 83 months imprisonment and a fine not to exceed $300,000.

Sale of 450 - less than 30 kilograms is a drug severity level 2 felony punishable by 92 - 144 months imprisonment and a fine not to exceed $500,000.

Sale of 30 kilograms or more is a drug severity level 1 felony punishable by 138 - 204 months imprisonment and a fine not to exceed $500,000.

Sale within 1,000 feet of a school zone will increase a drug severity level.

See
- 65-4101 of the Kansas Code
- 65-4105 of the Kansas Code
- 21-5705 of the Kansas Code
- 21-6611 of the Kansas Code

Cultivation

Cultivation of more than 4 - less than 50 plants is a drug severity level 3 felony punishable by 46 - 83 months imprisonment and a fine not to exceed $300,000.

Cultivation of 50 - less than 100 plants is drug severity level 2 felony punishable by 92 - 144 months imprisonment and a fine not to exceed $500,000.

Cultivation of 100 or more plants is a drug severity level 1 felony punishable by 138 - 204 months imprisonment and a fine not to exceed $500,000

See
- 21-5705 of the Kansas Code
- 21-6611 of the Kansas Code
- 65-4101 of the Kansas Code

Hash & Concentrates

Hashish and marijuana concentrates are classified as cannabinoids and are Schedule I controlled substances. The penalties for hashish and marijuana concentrates are the same as those for marijuana.

See
- 21-5701(j) of the Kansas Code
- 21-6602 of the Kansas Code
- 21-6611 of the Kansas Code
- 65-4105 of the Kansas Code

Paraphernalia

Use of or possession with intent to use paraphernalia to cultivate is a drug severity drug severity level 5 felony punishable by a fine not to exceed $100,000 and a sentence ranging from 10 months probation - 42 months imprisonment.

Paraphernalia used to cultivate less than 5 marijuana plants is a class A nonperson misdemeanor punishable by a maximum of 1 year imprisonment and a fine not to exceed $2,500.

Use of or possession with intent to use paraphernalia to store, ingest is a class A nonperson misdemeanor punishable by a maximum of 1 year imprisonment and a fine not to exceed $2,500.

Sale of paraphernalia is a Class A nonperson misdemeanor punishable by a maximum of 1 year imprisonment and a fine not to exceed $2,500.

Sale to a minor or on or within 1,000 feet of any school property has a nondrug severity level 9, nonperson felony punishable by 5 months probation - 17 months imprisonment and a fine not to exceed $500,000

See
- Section 9.50.040 of the Kansas Code
- 21-5709 of the Kansas Code
- 21-5710 of the Kansas Code
- 21-6602 of the Kansas Code
- 21-6611 of the Kansas Code

Miscellaneous

Kansas has a marijuana tax stamp law enacted. Those who possess marijuana are legally required to affix state-issued stamps to the contraband. Failure to do so may result in a fine and/or a criminal sanction.

See
- 79-5204 of the Kansas Code

KENTUCKY
LAWS & PENALTIES

Offense	Penalty	Incarceration	Max. Fine
POSSESSION			
Less than 8 oz	Misdemeanor	45 days	$ 250
SALE OR TRAFFICKING			
Less than 8 oz (first offense)	Misdemeanor	1 year	$ 500
Less than 8 oz (subsequent offense)	Felony	1 - 5 years	$ 10,000
8 oz - 5 lbs (first offense)	Felony	1 - 5 years	$ 10,000
8 oz - 5 lbs (subsequent offense)	Felony	5 - 10 years	$ 10,000
5 lbs or more (first offense)	Felony	5 - 10 years	$ 10,000
5 lbs or more (subsequent offense)	Felony	10 - 20 years	$ 10,000
To a minor (first offense)	Felony	5 - 10 years	$ 10,000
To a minor (subsequent offense)	Felony	10 - 20 years	$ 10,000
Within 1000 yards of a school or park	Felony	1 - 5 years	$ 10,000
CULTIVATION			
Less than 5 plants (first offense)	Misdemeanor	1 year	$ 500
Less than 5 plants (subsequent offense)	Felony	1 - 5 years	$ 10,000
5 plants or more (first offense)	Felony	1 - 5 years	$ 10,000
5 plants or more (subsequent offense)	Felony	5 - 10 years	$ 10,000
HASH & CONCENTRATES			
Penalties for hashish are the same as for marijuana. Please see the marijuana penalties section for further details.			
PARAPHERNALIA			
Possession of paraphernalia	Misdemeanor	1 year	$ 500

Penalty Details

Possession

Possession of up to 8 ounces of marijuana is a Class B misdemeanor, which is punishable by a maximum sentence of 45 days imprisonment and a maximum fine of $250.

Possession of 8 ounces or more of marijuana shall be prima facie evidence that the person possessed the marijuana with the intent to sell or transfer it. - See Sale or Trafficking for penalties

See
- KRS § 218A.050(3)
- KRS § 218A.276
- KRS § 218A.1421 & .1422

Sale or Trafficking

The sale or trafficking of less than 8 ounces is a Class A misdemeanor for a first offense which is punishable by a maximum sentence of 1 year imprisonment and a maximum fine of $500.

A second or subsequent offense for trafficking or selling less than 8 ounces of marijuana is a Class D felony, punishable by a sentence of 1-5 years imprisonment and a fine of not more than $10,000.

The sale or trafficking of 8 ounces- less than 5 pounds is a Class D felony which is punishable for a first offense by 1-5 years imprisonment and a fine of $1,000-$10,000. A second of subsequent violation of this section is a Class C felony, punishable by a sentence of 5-10 years imprisonment and a fine of not over $10,000.

The sale or trafficking of 5 pounds or more is a Class C felony which is punishable for a first offense by a sentence of 5-10 years imprisonment and a fine of $1,000-$10,000. For a second or subsequent violation of this section, the offender will be guilty of a Class B felony, which is punishable by a sentence of 10-20 years imprisonment.

The sale to a minor is a Class C felony which is punishable by a sentence of 5-10 years imprisonment and a fine of $1,000-$10,000.

A subsequent conviction for the sale to a minor is a Class B felony which is punishable by a sentence of 10-20 years imprisonment and a fine of $1,000-$10,000.

The sale within 1,000 yards of a school or park is a felony which is punishable by 1-5 years imprisonment and a fine of $1,000-$10,000.

See
- KRS § 218A.1401 & 1421
- KRS §§ 532.020, .060, .090
- KRS §§ 534.030 & .040

Cultivation

Cultivation of fewer than 5 plants is a Class A misdemeanor for a first offense, which is punishable by a maximum sentence of 12 months imprisonment and a maximum fine of $500. For a second or subsequent offense, the offender will be charged with a Class D felony, which is punishable by 1-5 years imprisonment and a fine of $1,000-$10,000.

Cultivation of 5 plants or more is a Class D felony for a first offense, which is punishable by 1-5 years imprisonment and a fine of $1,000-$10,000. A second or subsequent offense is a Class C felony which is punishable by 5-10 years imprisonment and a fine of $1,000-$10,000.

See
- KRS § 218A.1423
- KRS § 532.060 & .090

Hash & Concentrates

Hashish is listed as Schedule I hallucinogenic substance, but is punished exactly the same as marijuana infractions. See the penalties for marijuana above for further details on specific penalties.

See
- KRS § 218A.010(21)
- KRS § 218A.050(3)

Com. v. McGinnis, 641 S.W.2d 45 (Ky. Ct. App. 1982).

Paraphernalia

Possession of paraphernalia is a Class A misdemeanor which is punishable by a maximum sentence of one year imprisonment and a maximum fine of $500.

See
- KRS § 218A.500

Miscellaneous

Prohibited activities

Unless another specific penalty is provided, any person who violates one of the following:

- Trafficking in any controlled substance except as authorized by law.
- Dispensing, prescribing, distributing, or administering any controlled substance except as authorized by law, for a first offense, shall be guilty of a Class D felony and a Class C felony for subsequent offenses.
- Any person who possesses any controlled substance except as authorized by law shall be guilty of a Class A misdemeanor.

See
- KRS § 218A.1404

Firearm

Any person who is convicted of any violation above who, at the time of the commission of the offense and in furtherance of the offense, was in possession of a firearm, shall:

- Be penalized one (1) class more severely than provided in the penalty provision pertaining to that offense if it is a felony; or
- Be penalized as a Class D felony if the offense would otherwise be a misdemeanor.

See
- KRS § 218A.992

LOUISIANA
LAWS & PENALTIES

Offense	Penalty	Incarceration	Max. Fine
POSSESSION			
14 g or less (first offense)	Not Classified	15 days	$ 300
More than 14 g – less than 2.5 lbs (first offense)	Not Classified	6 months	$ 500
2.5 - less than 60 lbs	Not Classified	2* - 10 years	$ 30,000
60 - less than 2000 lbs	Felony	5* - 30 years	$ 100,000
2000 - less than 10,000 lbs	Felony	10* - 40 years	$ 400,000
10,000 lbs or more	Felony	25* - 40 years	$ 1,000,000

First and second offenders may be eligible for probation.

* Mandatory minimum sentence

DISTRIBUTION OR CULTIVATION OF MARIJUANA			
Any amount (first offense)	Not Classified	5* - 30 years	$ 50,000
Any amount (subsequent offense)	Not Classified	10* - 60 years	$ 100,000
To a minor (first offense)	Not Classified	5* - 45 years	$ 100,000
To a minor (subsequent offense)	Not Classified	10* - 90 years	$ 200,000

Includes possession With Intent to Distribute

* Mandatory minimum sentence

HASH & CONCENTRATES

Penalties for hashish are the same as for marijuana. Please see the marijuana penalties section for further details.

MISCELLANEOUS

Possession, distribution, or Cultivation of marijuana within 2000 feet of a drug free zone is punishable by 1.5 times the maximum sentence.

Conviction of any crime involving controlled substances results in denial of driving privileges for not less than 30 days but not more than 1 year.

Penalty Details

Marijuana is a schedule I(C) hallucinogenic substance under Louisiana law.

Possession for Personal Use

For first offenders, possession of 14 grams or less of marijuana is punishable by a fine of up to $300 and/or up to 15 days of imprisonment.

For first offenders, possession of more than 14 grams but less than 2 ½ pounds of marijuana is punishable by a fine of up to $500 and/or up to 6 months of imprisonment.

There is a one-time two-year cleansing period for first time convictions.

All second convictions regarding less than 2 ½ pounds are punishable by a fine of $1,000 and/or up to 6 months of imprisonment.

All third convictions regarding less than 2 ½ pounds are punishable by a fine of up to $2,500 and/or up to 2 years of imprisonment.

All fourth convictions regarding less than 2 ½ pounds are punishable by a fine of up to $5,000 and/or up to 8 years of imprisonment.

See
- Louisiana Rev. Stat. § 40:966(E)

Possession of 2 ½ - less than 60 pounds of marijuana is punishable by 2 -10 years of imprisonment and a fine of $30,000.

Possession of 60 - less than 2,000 pounds of marijuana is a felony and is punishable by 5-30 years of imprisonment and a fine of $50,000-$100,000. Possession of 2,000 - less than 10,000 pounds is a felony and is punishable by 10-40 years of imprisonment and a fine of $100,000-$400,000. Possession of 10,000 pounds or more of marijuana is a felony and is punishable by 25-40 years of imprisonment.

See
- Louisiana Rev. Stat. § 40:966(F)

Distribution or Cultivation of Marijuana

Distribution of marijuana includes possessing marijuana with the intent to distribute it.

See
- Louisiana Rev. Stat. § 40:966(A)

Distribution or cultivation of marijuana is punishable by a fine of up to $50,000 and 5-30 years of imprisonment. Subsequent offenses are punishable by 10-60 years of imprisonment and a fine of up to $100,000. Prior offenses include any drug crime convictions, no matter where they occurred. If the defendant is 18 or older and is selling to a minor under the age of 18 who is at least 3 years younger than the defendant a maximum term of 45 years may be imposed for first offenders or 90 years for subsequent offenders. Distributing marijuana to an elementary, middle, or high school student is punishable by a maximum term of 45 years imprisonment for first offenders and up to 90 years imprisonment for subsequent offenses. For first offenders a fine of up to $100,000 may also be imposed. For subsequent offenders a fine of $200,000 may be imposed. Soliciting a minor to distribute marijuana is punishable for first offenders by 45 years of imprisonment and a fine of up to $100,000. For subsequent offenders imprisonment for up to 90 years and a fine of up to $200,000 may be imposed

See
- Louisiana Rev. Stat. § 40:966(B)(3)
- Louisiana Rev. Stat. § 40:982
- Louisiana Rev. Stat. § 40:981(C)
- Louisiana Rev. Stat. § 40:981.1
- Louisiana Rev. Stat. § 40:981.2

Hash & Concentrates

Louisiana classifies both plant-form Marijuana and Tetrahydro-cannabinols, including Hashish and Marijuana Concentrates, in schedule I of the Louisiana Controlled Substances Schedule. For the purposes of criminal justice, the statute defines Marijuana as including tetrahydrocannabinols and derivatives thereof. The penalties for offenses involving tetrahydrocannabinols and derivatives thereof have the same penalties as for plant-form Marijuana.

See
- Louisiana Rev. Stat. §40:964(C) (19), (27)
- Louisiana Rev. Stat. §40-961(25)
- Louisiana Rev. Stat. §40-966(E)

Miscellaneous

Violation in a Drug Free Zone

Possession, distribution, or cultivation of marijuana within 2,000 feet of a drug free zone is punishable by 1.5 times the maximum sentence allowed for the underlying offense. A drug free zone includes: Elementary schools, high schools, colleges or universities, playgrounds, drug treatment facilities, religious buildings, public housing, and child care centers.

See
- Louisiana Rev. Stat. § 40:981.3

Driver's license privileges

Whenever any person who has attained the age of 19 is convicted of any crime, offense, violation, or infraction involving the possession, use, or abuse of one or more controlled dangerous substances, the court... shall issue an order of denial of driving privileges for not less than 30 days but not more than 1 year.

See
- Louisiana Rev. Stat. § 32:430(2)

MAINE
LAWS & PENALTIES

Offense	Penalty	Incarceration	Max. Fine
POSSESSION			
1.25 oz or less	Civil Violation	N/A	$ 600
More than 1.25 - 2.5 oz	Civil Violation	N/A	$ 1,000
More than 2.5 - 8 oz	Crime	6 months	$ 1,000
More than 8 oz - 1 lb	Crime	1 year	$ 2,000
More than 1 - 20 lbs	Crime	5 years	$ 5,000
More than 20 lbs	Crime	10 years	$ 20,000
Possession of a "usable amount" with proof of a physician's recommendation is not punishable.			
SALE OR DISTRIBUTION			
1 lb or less	Crime	1 year	$ 2,000
More than 1 – less than 20 lbs	Crime	5 years	$ 5,000
20 lbs or more	Crime	10 years	$ 20,000
To a minor or within 1000 feet of a school or school bus	Crime	5 years	$ 5,000
CULTIVATION			
5 plants or less	Crime	6 months	$ 1,000
More than 5 - less than 100 plants	Crime	1 year	$ 2,000
100 - less than 500 plants	Crime	5 years	$ 5,000
500 plants or more	Crime	10 years	$ 20,000
HASH & CONCENTRATES			
Possession	Crime	1 year	$ 2,000
Trafficking	Crime	5 years	$ 5,000
Trafficking (prior conviction, use of minor, other)	Crime	10 years	$ 20,000
PARAPHERNALIA			
Possession of paraphernalia	Civil Violation	N/A	$ 300
Sale of paraphernalia	Crime	6 months	$ 1,000
Sale to a minor younger than 16 years of age	Crime	1 year	$ 2,000
MISCELLANEOUS			
Driver's license restriction will be imposed for aggravated furnishing any amount of pot or hash.			

Penalty Details

Marijuana is a schedule Z drug.

Possession for Personal Use

Possession of a "usable amount" with proof of a physician's recommendation is not punishable.

Possession of up to 1 ¼ ounces of marijuana is a civil violation punishable by a fine of $350 - $600.

Possession of 1 ¼ to 2.5 oz. is a civil violation punishable by a $700-$1000 fine. Subsequent offenses within 6 months are punishable by a $550 fine.

Possession of between 2.5-8 oz. is a Class E crime punishable by a maximum sentence of 6 months imprisonment and a maximum fine of $1,000.

Possession of between 8-16 oz. is a Class D crime punishable by a maximum sentence of 1 year imprisonment and a maximum fine of $2,000.

Possession of between 1-20 lbs. is a Class C crime punishable by a maximum sentence of 5 years imprisonment and a maximum fine of $5,000.

Possession of over 20 lbs. is a Class B crime punishable by a maximum sentence of 10 years imprisonment and a maximum fine of $20,000.

See
- 22 Section 2382 of the Maine Revised Statutes
- 22 Section 2383 of the Maine Revised Statutes
- Tit. 17A Section 1102 of the Maine Revised Statutes
- Tit. 17-A Section 4-A of the Maine Revised Statutes
- Tit. 17-A Section 1107-A of the Maine Revised Statutes
- Tit. 17-A Section 1252 of the Maine Revised Statutes
- Tit. 17-A Section 1301 of the Maine Revised Statutes

Sale or Distribution

The sale of 1 lb. or less is a Class D crime punishable by a maximum sentence of 1 year imprisonment and a maximum fine of $2,000.

The sale of more than 1 - less than 20 lbs. is a Class C crime punishable by a maximum sentence of 5 years imprisonment and a maximum fine of $5,000.

The sale of 20 lbs. or more is a Class B crime punishable by a maximum of 10 years imprisonment and a maximum fine of $20,000.

Sale to a minor or within 1,000 feet of a school or school bus is a felony punishable by a maximum sentence of 5 years imprisonment and a $5,000 fine.

See
- Tit. 17A Section 1101 of the Maine Revised Statutes
- Tit. 17A Section 1102 of the Maine Revised Statutes
- Tit. 17A Section 1103 of the Maine Revised Statutes
- Tit. 17-A Section 1252 of the Maine Revised Statutes
- Tit. 17-A Section 1301 of the Maine Revised Statutes
- Tit. 17-A Section 4-A of the Maine Revised Statutes

Cultivation

The cultivation of 5 plants or less is a Class E crime punishable by a maximum sentence of 6 months imprisonment and a maximum fine of $1,000.

The cultivation of 5-99 plants is a Class D crime punishable by a maximum sentence of 1 year imprisonment and a maximum fine of $2,000.

The cultivation of 100-499 plants is a Class C crime punishable by a maximum sentence of 5 years imprisonment and a maximum fine of $5,000.

The cultivation of 500 or more plants is a Class B crime punishable by a maximum of 10 years imprisonment and a maximum fine of $20,000.

See
- Title 17A Section 1117 of the Maine Revised Statutes
- Tit. 17-A Section 4-A of the Maine Revised Statutes
- Tit. 17A Section 1103 of the Maine Revised Statutes
- Tit. 17-A Section 1252 of the Maine Revised Statutes
- Tit. 17-A Section 1301 of the Maine Revised Statutes

Hash & Concentrates

The definition of Marijuana in the Maine statute is written explicitly not to cover Hashish or Marijuana Concentrates. The statute defines Hashish separately as the resin extracted from the Cannabis plant including any derivative, mixture, or compound of the resin, effectively including all Concentrates. Hashish is classified in Schedule X of the Maine Controlled Substances Schedule.

See
- Tit. 17A Section 1101(1), (5) of the Maine Revised Statutes
- Tit. 17A Section 1102 of the Maine Revised Statutes

Trafficking any amount of Hashish is a Class C Crime, subject to 5 years incarceration and a fine of no more than $5000.

See
- Tit. 17A Section 1103 of the Maine Revised Statutes
- Tit. 17-A Section 1252 of the Maine Revised Statutes
- Tit. 17-A Section 1301 of the Maine Revised Statutes

Using a minor child to traffic any amount of Hashish is a Class C Crime, subject to 10 years incarceration and a fine of no more than $20,000.

Trafficking any amount of Hashish when you have at least one prior conviction for a similar drug crime is a Class B Crime, subject to 10 years incarceration and a fine of no more than $20,000.

Use or possession of a firearm when trafficking any amount of Hashish is a Class B crime, subject to 10 years incarceration and a fine of no more than $20,000.

Trafficking any amount of Hashish while within 1000 feet from a school or other designated safe zone is a Class B crime, subject to 10 years incarceration and a fine of no more than $20,000.

Soliciting with, conspiring with, or enlisting the assistance of a minor child in trafficking any amount of hashish is a Class B crime, subject to 10 years incarceration and a fine of no more than $20,000.

Using a motor vehicle to traffic in scheduled drugs in Maine may result in a driver's license being revoked for up to 5 years.

See
- Tit. 17A Section 1105-A of the Maine Revised Statutes
- Tit. 17-A Section 1252 of the Maine Revised Statutes
- Tit. 17-A Section 1301 of the Maine Revised Statutes

Furnishing any amount of Hashish to a minor child is a Class C crime, subject to 5 years incarceration and a fine of no more than $5000.

Furnishing any amount of Hashish when you have at least one prior conviction for a similar drug crime is a Class C crime, subject to 5 years imprisonment and a fine of no more than $5000.

Use or possession of a firearm while furnishing any amount of Hashish is a Class C crime, subject to 5 years imprisonment and a fine of no more than $5000.

Furnishing any amount of Hashish on a school bus or within 1000 feet of a school or other designated safe zone is a Class C crime, subject to 5 years incarceration and a fine of no more than $5000.

Soliciting with, conspiring with, or enlisting the assistance of a minor child in furnishing any amount of Hashish is a Class C crime subject to 5 years imprisonment, and a fine of no more than $5000.

Using a motor vehicle to furnish any amount of Hashish may result in your driver's license being revoked for up to 5 years.

See
- Tit. 17A Section 1105-C of the Maine Revised Statutes
- Tit. 17-A Section 1252 of the Maine Revised Statutes
- Tit. 17-A Section 1301 of the Maine Revised Statutes

Furnishing any amount of Hashish is a Class D crime subject to 1 year's imprisonment and a fine not to exceed $2000.

See
- Tit. 17A Section 1106 of the Maine Revised Statutes
- Tit. 17-A Section 1252 of the Maine Revised Statutes
- Tit. 17-A Section 1301 of the Maine Revised Statutes

Possessing any amount of Hashish is a Class D crime subject to 1 year's imprisonment and a fine not to exceed $2000.

See
- Tit. 17A Section 1107-A of the Maine Revised Statutes
- Tit. 17-A Section 1252 of the Maine Revised Statutes
- Tit. 17-A Section 1301 of the Maine Revised Statutes

Importing any amount of Hashish into Maine from another state or country is a Class D crime subject to 1 year's imprisonment and a fine not exceeding $2000.

See
- Tit. 17A Section 1118 of the Maine Revised Statutes
- Tit. 17A Section 1252 of the Maine Revised Statutes
- Tit. 17-A Section 1301 of the Maine Revised Statutes
- Tit. 17-A Section 1252 of the Maine Revised Statutes
- Tit. 17-A Section 1301 of the Maine Revised Statutes

Paraphernalia

Possession of paraphernalia is a civil violation punishable by a maximum $300 fine.

The sale of paraphernalia is a person at least 16 years old is a Class E crime misdemeanor punishable by a maximum sentence of 6 months imprisonment and a maximum fine of $1,000.

The sale of paraphernalia to a person less than 16 years old is a Class D crime misdemeanor punishable by a maximum sentence of 1 year imprisonment and a maximum fine of $2,000.

See
- Title 17A Section 1111 of the Maine Revised Statutes
- Tit. 17-A Section 1252 of the Maine Revised Statutes
- Tit. 17-A Section 1301 of the Maine Revised Statutes

Miscellaneous

Will impose a license restriction for the aggravated trafficking of over 1 pound of marijuana if a vehicle is used in doing so. Aggravated is met by using a minor in the trafficking, or having a prior drug record in Maine or another state (but the amount of pot must be over 1 pound) or possession of a firearm at the time of the offense. They will also deprive of a license for aggravated furnishing any amount of pot or hash, aggravation based on the same as above.

See
- Title 17-A, Sec. 1105-A(2)
- Title 17-A, Sec. 1105-C(2)

MARYLAND
LAWS & PENALTIES

Offense	Penalty	Incarceration	Max. Fine
POSSESSION			
Personal Use			
Less than 10 g	Civil Offense	None	$ 100
10g - less than 50 lbs	Misdemeanor	1 year	$ 1,000
50 lbs or more	Felony	5 years*	$ 100,000
Increased fines for subsequent offenders			
With Intent to Distribute			
Less than 50 lbs	Felony	5 years	$ 15,000
50 lbs or more**	Felony	5 years*	$ 15,000
More than 50 lbs (drug kingpin)	Felony	20* - 40 years	$ 1,000,000
In a school vehicle, or in, on, or within 1000 feet of an elementary or secondary school	Felony	20 years	$ 20,000
Subsequent violation	Felony	5* - 40 years	$ 40,000
Involving a minor	Felony	20 years	$ 20,000

* Mandatory minimum sentence

** Subsequent offense carries a mandatory minimum sentence of 2 years

Offense	Penalty	Incarceration	Max. Fine
TRAFFICKING			
More than 5 - less than 45 kg	Felony	10 years	$ 10,000
45 kg or more	Felony	25 years	$ 50,000
In possession of a firearm while Trafficking	Felony	5* - 20 years	$ 0

* Mandatory minimum sentence

CULTIVATION
See Possession section for details.

HASH & CONCENTRATES
Penalties for hashish are the same as for marijuana. Please see the marijuana penalties section for further details.

Offense	Penalty	Incarceration	Max. Fine
PARAPHERNALIA			
Possession/Sale/Advertising distribution of drug paraphernalia	Misdemeanor	None	$ 500
Subsequent violation	Misdemeanor	2 years	$ 2,000
Selling to a minor who is at least 3 years younger	Misdemeanor	8 years	$ 15,000
Possession/Sale controlled paraphernalia	Misdemeanor	1 year	$ 1,000

Paraphernalia includes all equipment and materials used in the use, manufacture, or distribution of marijuana.

Penalty Details

Possession for Personal Use

In Maryland marijuana is listed as a Schedule I controlled hallucinogenic substances. Simple possession (possession without the intent to distribute) of less than 10 grams in Maryland is a civil offense (fine not exceeding $100 for first-time offenders, $250 for second-time offenders, and $500 for third or subsequent offenders).

Possession of between 10 grams and less than 50 pounds of marijuana is a misdemeanor with a punishment of up to one year imprisonment and a fine not exceeding $1,000.

Possession of 50 pounds or more of marijuana carriers a punishment of a minimum of 5 years imprisonment and a fine not exceeding $100,000.

See
- MD CODE ANN. §5-402(d)(vii)
- MD CODE ANN. §5-601
- MD CODE ANN. §5-612

Possession With Intent to Distribute

Possession with intent to distribute less than 50 pounds of marijuana in Maryland is a felony with a punishment of up to 5 years imprisonment and a fine not exceeding $15,000.

See
- MD. CODE ANN. §5-607(a)

If a person is found to be in possession of 50 pounds or more of marijuana (acts in proceeding 90 days can be aggregated), then the punishment for this felony is imprisonment of not less than 5 years and a fine not exceeding $100,000.

See
- MD. CODE ANN. §§5-612 (a)-(c).

Possessing marijuana with the intent to distribute in a school vehicle, or in, on, or within 1,000 feet of real property owned by or leased to an elementary school or secondary school, is a felony and is punishable by, for a first violation, imprisonment not exceeding 20 years and a fine not exceeding $20,000, and for each subsequent violation, imprisonment not less than 5 years and not exceeding 40 years and a fine not exceeding $40,000. These penalties are in addition to any other conviction.

See
- MD. CODE ANN. § 5-627

If an offender has previously been convicted of possession with intent to distribute, then there is a mandatory minimum sentence of 2 years.

See
- MD. CODE ANN. §5 607(b)(1)

If an individual is found to be a "drug kingpin" (an organizer, supervisor, financier, or manager who acts as a co-conspirator in a conspiracy to manufacture, distribute, dispense, transport in, or bring into the State a controlled dangerous substance), and dealt with 50 pounds or more of marijuana, then are guilty of a felony and subject to imprisonment for not less than 20 years and not exceeding 40 years without the possibility of parole and a fine not exceeding $1,000,000.

See
- MD. CODE ANN. §5-613. (Does not merge. §5-613(d).)

If an adult uses or solicits a minor in a conspiracy to distribute, deliver or manufacture marijuana, then the adult is guilty of a felony and is subject to imprisonment not exceeding 20 years or a fine not exceeding $20,000.

See
- MD. CODE ANN. §5-628

Cultivation

Cultivation in Maryland is punished as either simple possession or as possession with intent to deliver, depending on the amount of marijuana being produced and other factors that may lead to the conclusion that the marijuana was being grown for reasons other than strict personal use. See the Possession for Personal Use" and "Possession with Intent to Distribute" sections for further penalty details.

Trafficking

If a person brings 45 kilograms or more of marijuana into the state of Maryland, then they are guilty of a felony and are subject to imprisonment not exceeding 25 years and a fine not exceeding $50,000.

See
- MD. CODE ANN. §5-614(a)

If a person brings less than 45 kilograms of marijuana into the state, but more than 5 kilograms, then said person is guilty of a felony and subject to imprisonment not exceeding 10 years and a fine not exceeding $10,000.

See
- MD. CODE ANN. §5-614(b)

If a person is in possession of a firearm at the time they are arrested for trafficking marijuana into MD, then said person is guilty of a felony and may be punished with, for a first violation, imprisonment for not less than 5 years and not exceeding 20 years, and for each subsequent violation, imprisonment for not less than 10 years and not exceeding 20 years.

See
- MD. CODE ANN. §5-621(c)(1)

Hash & Concentrates

In Maryland, hashish and marijuana concentrates are punished at the same level as plant-form marijuana, and are Schedule I controlled hallucinogenic substances. See the Maryland marijuana penalty section for further details.

See
- MD. CODE ANN. §5-101(q)
- MD. CODE ANN. §5-402(d)(vii)
- MD. CODE ANN. §5-402(d)(xii)
- Hignut v. State, 17 Md.App. 399 (Md. Spec. App. 1973)
- Ertwine v. State, 18 Md.App. 619, 308 A.2d 414 (Md. Spec. App. 1973)

Paraphernalia

Under MD law, paraphernalia includes all equipment and materials used in the use, manufacture, or distribution of marijuana. This includes all agricultural materials used in the growing process, including electronic equipment and typical gardening supplies, such as lights, fertilizer, and top soil. §5-101 also includes under its definition items such as scales, plastic bags, and others used in the distribution process. Hash bubble sacks are paraphernalia. These items are joined by the typical forms of paraphernalia involved in the ingestion of marijuana, including pipes, bongs, and roach clips. Rolling papers and blunt wraps are not included under the statutory definition.

See
- MD. CODE ANN. §5-101

If a person is convicted of possessing or selling drug paraphernalia, then they are guilty of a misdemeanor and can be sentenced, for a first violation, a fine not exceeding $500, and for each subsequent violation, imprisonment not exceeding 2 years and a fine not exceeding $2,000.

See
- §5-619 (d)(2)

If a person is caught in possession of controlled paraphernalia and marijuana, then they are guilty of a misdemeanor and subject to imprisonment not exceeding 1 year and a fine not exceeding $1,000.

See
- MD. CODE ANN. § 5-620(d)(2)

If an adult delivers drug paraphernalia to a minor who is at least 3 years younger than the person, the person is guilty of a separate misdemeanor and on conviction is subject to imprisonment not exceeding 8 years and a fine not exceeding $15,000.

See
- MD. CODE ANN. § 5-619(d)(4).

Advertising the distribution of paraphernalia is a misdemeanor and can be punished for a first violation, with a fine not exceeding $500, and for each subsequent violation, with imprisonment for not exceeding 2 years and a fine not exceeding $2,000.

See
- MD. CODE ANN. §5-619(e)(1)

Mandatory Minimum

Maryland has a mandatory minimum sentences for:

1. Repeat offenders who have been convicted of possession to distribute on 2 or more occasions (2 years).
2. Repeat offenders who have previously been convicted of possession with intent to distribute within 1,000 ft. of a school on 2 or more occasions (5 years).
3. Any offender convicted of possessing 50 pounds or more of marijuana, including any acts of possession within the last 90 days (5 years).
4. Any offender convicted of being a "drug kingpin" who dealt in more than 50 pounds of marijuana (20 years).
5. Any offender who is in possession of a firearm at the time they are arrested for trafficking marijuana into MD (10 years)

See
- MD. CODE ANN. §5-607(b)(1)
- MD. CODE ANN. §§5-612 (a)-(c)
- MD. CODE ANN. § 5-621(c)(1)
- MD. CODE ANN. §5-613
- MD. CODE ANN. § 5-621(c)(1)

Miscellaneous

Medical Necessity Defense

"In a prosecution for the use or possession of marijuana, the defendant may introduce and the court shall consider as a mitigating factor any evidence of medical necessity.

(ii) Notwithstanding paragraph (2) of this subsection, if the court finds that the person used or possessed marijuana because of medical necessity, on conviction of a violation of this section, the maximum penalty that the court may impose on the person is a fine not exceeding $100."

Even with the defense, the crime is still a misdemeanor. Additional fines/penalties are applicable if use is in public or more than one ounce is in possession at one time.

See
- MD. CODE ANN. §§5-601(c)(3) (i)-(ii)

For more information concerning Maryland's marijuana laws, please visit NORML's Maryland Medical Marijuana page.

MASSACHUSETTS
LAWS & PENALTIES

Offense	Penalty	Incarceration	Max. Fine
POSSESSION			
Personal Use			
1 oz or less	Civil Offense	N/A	$ 100
More than 1 oz (first offense)	Misdemeanor	6 months	$ 500
More than 1 oz (subsequent offense)	Misdemeanor	2 years	$ 2,000
With Intent to Distribute			
Less than 50 lbs (first offense)	Not Classified	0 - 2 years	$ 5,000
Less than 50 lbs (subsequent offense)	Not Classified	1 - 2.5 years	$ 10,000
50 - less than 100 lbs	Felony	1* - 15 years	$ 10,000
100 - less than 2000 lbs	Felony	2* - 15 years	$ 25,000
2000 - less than 10,000 lbs	Felony	3.5* - 15 years	$ 50,000
10,000 lbs or more	Felony	8* - 15 years	$ 200,000
Within 300 feet of a school, or within 100 feet of a public park	Felony	2* - 15 years	$ 10,000
Causing or inducing someone under 18 years to commit offenses	Felony	5* - 15 years	$ 100,000
* Mandatory minimum sentence			
DISTRIBUTION OR CULTIVATION			
Less than 50 lbs (first offense)	Not Classified	0 - 2 years	$ 5,000
Less than 50 lbs (subsequent offense)	Not Classified	1 - 2.5 years	$ 10,000
50 - less than 100 lbs	Felony	1* - 15 years	$ 10,000
100 - less than 2000 lbs	Felony	2* - 15 years	$ 25,000
2000 - less than 10,000 lbs	Felony	3.5* - 15 years	$ 50,000
10,000 lbs or more	Felony	8* - 15 years	$ 200,000
Within 300 feet of a school, or within 100 feet of a public park	Felony	2* - 15 years	$ 10,000
Causing or inducing someone under 18 years to commit offenses	Felony	5* - 15 years	$ 100,000
* Mandatory minimum sentence			
HASH & CONCENTRATES			
Possession of 1 oz or less	Civil Offense	N/A	$ 100
Possession of more than 1 oz	N/A	1 year	$ 1,000
Manufacture or distribution	N/A	2.5 - 5 years	$ 5,000
Manufacture or distribution to a minor	N/A	2 - 15 years	$ 25,000
Using a minor to manufacture or distribute	N/A	5* - 15 years	$ 100,000
* Mandatory minimum sentence			
PARAPHERNALIA			
Selling, possessing, or purchasing paraphernalia	Not Classified	1 - 2 years	$ 5,000
Selling to someone under 18 years of age	Felony	3 - 5 years	$ 5,000
FORFEITURE			
Marijuana, vehicles, and money are subject to forfeiture.			
MISCELLANEOUS			
Conspiracy to commit any marijuana related offense is punishable by up to the maximum punishment.			
Possession of 1 oz or less cannot result in the suspension of driving privileges.			

Penalty Details

Marijuana is a class D controlled substance under the Massachusett's Controlled Substances Act.

See
- Mass. Gen. Laws. ch. 94C, § 31

Possession for Personal Use

Possession of 1 ounce or less of marijuana is decriminalized and is punishable as a civil offense. If the offender is over the age of 18 they must pay a fine of $100. Offenders under the age of 18 must pay a $100 fine and must attend a drug awareness program. Possession of less than an ounce of marijuana cannot result in denial of public financial assistance or the right to a driver's license.

See
- Mass. Gen. Laws. ch. 94C, § 32L

Possession of more than one ounce of marijuana is punishable by a fine of $500 and/or imprisonment of up to 6 months. However, first offenders of the controlled substances act will be placed on probation and all official records relating to the conviction will be sealed upon successful completion of probation. Subsequent offenses may result in a fine of $2000 and/or imprisonment of up to 2 years. Individuals previously convicted of felonies under the controlled substances act who are arrested with over an ounce of marijuana may be subject to a fine of $2000 and/or up to 2 years of imprisonment.

See
- Mass. Gen. Laws. ch. 94C, § 34

Possession with Intent to Distribute

For first offenders, possessing less than 50 pounds of marijuana with the intent to manufacture, distribute, dispense or cultivate is punishable by a fine of $500-$5,000 and/or imprisonment of up to 2 years. Subsequent offenses are punishable by a fine of $1,000-$10,000 and/or imprisonment of 1-2.5 years.

See
- Mass. Gen. Laws, ch. 94C, § 32C

Possessing 50 - less than 100 pounds of marijuana with intent to distribute is a felony punishable by a fine of $500-$10000 and imprisonment of 2.5-15 years. There is a mandatory minimum sentence of 1 year for this offense.

Possessing 100 - less than 2000 pounds if marijuana with intent to distribute is a felony punishable by a fine of $2,500-$25,000 and imprisonment for 2-15 years. There is a mandatory term of 2 years imprisonment.

Possessing 2,000 - less than 10,000 pounds of marijuana with intent to distribute is a felony punishable by a fine of $5,000-$50,000 and imprisonment for 3 ½ - 15 years. There is a mandatory minimum term of 3 ½ years imprisonment.

Possessing 10,000 pounds or more of marijuana with intent to distribute is a felony punishable by a fine of $20,000-$200,000 and imprisonment of 8-15 years. There is a mandatory minimum term of 8 years of imprisonment for this offense.

See
- Mass. Gen. Laws. ch. 94C, § 32E

If any of the above offenses are committed within 300 feet of a school and if the violation occurs between 5:00 a.m. and midnight, whether or not in session, or within 100 feet of a public park that offense is punishable by a fine of $1,000-$10,000 and imprisonment for 2 - 15 years. This offense has a mandatory minimum term of 2 years of imprisonment.

See
- Mass. Gen. Laws. ch. 94C, § 32J

Causing or inducing someone under 18 to commit any of the above offenses is punishable by a fine of $1,000-$100,000 and imprisonment for 5 - 15 years. This offense has a mandatory minimum term of 5 years of imprisonment.

See
- Mass. Gen. Laws. ch. 94C, § 32K

Distribution or Cultivation

For first offenders, selling or cultivating less than 50 pounds of marijuana is punishable by a fine of $500-$5,000 and/or imprisonment of up to 2 years. Subsequent offenses are punishable by a fine of $1,000-$10,000 and/or imprisonment for 1 - 2.5 years.

See
- Mass. Gen. Laws. ch. 94C, § 32C

Selling or cultivating 50 - less than 100 pounds of marijuana is a felony punishable by a fine of $500-$10,000 and imprisonment for 1 - 15 years. There is a mandatory minimum term of 1 year for this offense.

Selling or cultivating 100 - less than 2000 pounds of marijuana is a felony punishable by a fine of $2,500-$25,000 and imprisonment for 2 - 15 years. There is a mandatory minimum term of 2 years imprisonment.

Selling or cultivating 2,000 - less than 10,000 pounds of marijuana with is a felony punishable by a fine of $5,000-$50,000 and is punishable by imprisonment for 3 ½ - 15 years. There is a mandatory term of 3 ½ years imprisonment.

Selling or cultivating 10,000 pounds or more of marijuana with intent to distribute is a felony punishable by a fine of $20,000-$200,000 and imprisonment for 8 - 15 years. There is a mandatory minimum term of 8 years imprisonment.

See
- Mass. Gen. Laws. ch. 94C, § 32E

If any of these offenses are committed within 300 feet of a school and if the violation occurs between 5:00 a.m. and midnight, whether or not in session, or within 100 feet of a public park, that offense is punishable by a fine of $1,000-$10,000 and imprisonment for 2 - 15 years. This offense has a mandatory minimum term of 2 years imprisonment.

See
- Mass. Gen. Laws. ch. 94C, § 32J

Causing or inducing someone under 18 to commit any of the above offenses is punishable by a fine of $1,000-$100,000 and imprisonment for 5-15 years. This offense has a mandatory minimum term of 5 years of imprisonment.

See
- Mass. Gen. Laws. ch. 94C, § 32K

Hash & Concentrates

Massachusetts statute defines Marijuana as including the resin extracted from the Cannabis plant and any derivatives or compounds thereof. The statute also defines Tetrahydrocannabinol separately as any compound that contains Tetrahydrocannabinol that is not itself Marijuana. The Massachusetts Controlled Substances Schedule classifies Marijuana as a Class D drug whereas Tetrahydrocannabinol as a Class C drug. Case law indicates that Hashish and Concentrates are meant to be prosecuted as Tetrahydrocannabinol, using the penalties for Class C drugs.

See
- Mass. Gen. Laws. ch. 94C, §1
- Mass. Gen. Laws. ch. 94C, §31
- Commonwealth v. Weeks, 431 N.E.2d 586 (Mass. App. Ct. 1982).

The Massachusetts decriminalization law explicitly reduced penalties for the possession of less than one ounce of either Tetrahydrocannabinols or Marijuana, though it does not modify any other penalties relating to Hashish.

Possession of one ounce or less of hashish is decriminalized and is punishable as a civil offense. If the offender is over the age of 18 they must pay a fine of $100. Offenders under the age of 18 must pay a $100 fine and must attend a drug awareness program. Possession of less than an ounce of hashish cannot result in denial of public financial assistance or the right to a driver's license.

See
- Mass. Gen. Laws ch. 94C §32L, 32M

Possession of any amount of Hashish greater than one ounce is subject to no more than one year's imprisonment and a fine of no greater than $1000. Diversionary probation is available for first time offenders.

See
- Mass. Gen Laws. ch. 94C §34

Manufacture, distribution, dispensing, or possession with intent to manufacture, distribute, or dispense Hashish is punishable by up to five years imprisonment in a state prison or two and one half years in a jail or house of correction, as well as a fine of between $500 - $5000.

Engaging in any of the above conduct when one has at least one prior conviction for a similar drug crime is punishable by up to ten years in a state prison or two and one half years in a jail or house of correction, as well as a fine of between $1,000 - $10,000. This crime is subject to a mandatory minimum of two years imprisonment.

See
- Mass. Gen Laws ch 94C §32B

The manufacture, distribution, dispensing, or possession with intent to manufacture, distribute, or dispense Hashish to a minor under eighteen years is punishable by up to fifteen years imprisonment in a state prison or two and one half years in a jail or house of correction, as well as a fine of between $1,000 - $25,000. There is a mandatory minimum sentence of two years imprisonment.

See
- Mass Gen Laws. ch. 94C § 32F

If a police officer finds a child under seventeen years old in a place where Hashish, or what the officer reasonable believes is Hashish, is present, the police officer may lawfully take the child into protective custody for a period not to exceed four hours.

See
- Mass Gen Laws ch. 94C § 36

Using or inducing a minor to manufacture, dispense, distribute, or possess with intent to manufacture, dispense, or distribute Hashish is punishable by up to fifteen years imprisonment in the state prison and a fine of no more than $100,000. This offence carries a mandatory minimum sentence of five years.

See
- Mass Gen. Laws ch. 94C §32K

Paraphernalia

Selling, possessing, or purchacing devices used in the cultivation or smoking/ingestion of marijuana is punishably by a fine of $500-$5,000 and/or 1-2 years of imprisonment.

Sec
- Mass. Gen. Laws. ch. 94C, § 32I(a)

Selling marijuana paraphernalia to someone under 18 years of age is a felony and is punishable by a fine of $1,000-$5,000 and/or 3-5 years of imprisonment.

See
- Mass. Gen. Laws. ch. 94C, § 32I(b)

Forfeiture

All marijuana is subject to forfeiture, even in amounts under an ounce which is decriminalized in the state.

See
- Mass. Gen. Laws. ch. 94C, § 47(a)(1)

Vehicles are subject to forfeiture if they are used to distribute marijuana or possess marijuana that a person intends to distribute.

See
- Mass. Gen. Laws. ch. 94C, § 47(a)(3)

All money or proceeds that can be traced to a sale of marijuana are subject to forfeiture.

See
- Mass. Gen. Laws. ch. 94C, § 47(a)(5)

Miscellaneous

Conspiracy

Conspiring with another person to commit any marijuana related offense is punishable by up to the maximum punishment for the crime which was the object of the conspiracy.

See
- Mass. Gen. Laws. ch. 94C, § 40

Driving Under the Influence

Failure to pass a sobriety test can result in a fine and/or imprisonment. Massachusetts does not test for THC in blood, urine, or hair when deciding if an individual has been driving while intoxicated.

Driver's License Suspension

Simple possession of one ounce or less of pot cannot result in the suspension of driving privileges.

See
- Mass. Gen. Laws. ch. 94C, § 32L

MICHIGAN
LAWS & PENALTIES

Offense	Penalty	Incarceration	Max. Fine
POSSESSION			
Any amount	Misdemeanor	1 year	$ 2,000
In a park	Misdemeanor or Felony	2 years	$ 2,000
Use of marijuana	Misdemeanor	90 days	$ 100
SALE			
Sale without remuneration	Misdemeanor	1 year	$ 1,000
Less than 5 kg	Felony	4 years	$ 20,000
5 - less than 45 kg	Felony	7 years	$ 500,000
45 kg or more	Felony	15 years	$ 10,000,000
CULTIVATION			
Less than 20 plants	Felony	4 years	$ 20,000
20 - less than 200 plants	Felony	7 years	$ 500,000
200 plants or more	Felony	15 years	$ 10,000,000
HASH & CONCENTRATES			
Penalties for hashish are the same as for marijuana. Please see the marijuana penalties section for further details.			
PARAPHERNALIA			
Sale of paraphernalia	Misdemeanor	90 days	$ 5,000
MISCELLANEOUS			
In Ann Arbor	N/A	N/A	$ 100
Any conviction will result in a driver's license suspension for 6 months.			

Penalty Details

Possession

Under Michigan law marijuana is listed as a Schedule I controlled substance.

Possession of any amount is a misdemeanor which is punishable by a maximum sentence of 1 year imprisonment and a maximum fine of $2,000. A conditional discharge is possible.

Use of marijuana is a misdemeanor which is punishable by a maximum sentence of 90 days imprisonment and a maximum fine of $100.

Possession in or within 1,000 feet of a park is either a felony or a misdemeanor, based on the judge's discretion, and is punishable by a maximum of 2 years imprisonment and a maximum fine of $2,000.

See

Michigan Code Section 333.7212

Michigan Code Section 333.7403(d)

Michigan Code Section 333.7404(d)

Michigan Code Section 333.7410a

Michigan Code Section 333.7411

Sale

Sale without remuneration is a misdemeanor punishable by a maximum sentence of 1 year imprisonment and a maximum fine of $1,000.

The sale of less than 5 kilograms is a felony punishable by a maximum sentence of 4 years imprisonment and a maximum fine of $20,000.

The sale of 5 kilograms - less than 45 kilograms is a felony, which is punishable by a maximum sentence of 7 years imprisonment and a maximum fine of $500,000.

The sale of 45 kilograms or more is a felony, which is punishable by a maximum sentence of 15 years imprisonment and a maximum fine of $10,000,000.

See

Michigan Code Section 333.7401(2)(d)

Michigan Code Section 333.7410

Cultivation

The cultivation of fewer than 20 plants is a felony punishable by a maximum sentence of 4 years imprisonment and a maximum fine of $20,000.

The cultivation of 20 - less than 200 plants is a felony, which is punishable by a maximum sentence of 7 years imprisonment and a maximum fine of $500,000.

The cultivation of more than 200 plants is a felony, which is punishable by a maximum sentence of 15 years imprisonment and a maximum fine of $10,000,000.

See

Michigan Code Section 333.7401

Hash & Concentrates

In Michigan, marijuana and hashish are punished in the same manner. The statutory definition of "marijuana" includes "all parts of the plant Cannabis sativa L., growing or not; the seeds thereof; the resin extracted from any part of the plant; and every compound, manufacture, salt, derivative, mixture, or preparation of the plant or its seeds or resin." Hashish, hashish oil, and extracts clearly fall under this definition. Please see the marijuana penalties section for further details on Michigan's criminal sanction on cannabis.

See
• Michigan Code § 333.7106

People v. Campbell, 72 Mich App. 411 (1977).

Paraphernalia

The sale of paraphernalia is a misdemeanor which is punishable by a maximum sentence of 90 days imprisonment and a maximum fine of $5,000. Bongs, dugouts, and pipes are exempted from the definition of paraphernalia, however."

See
• Michigan Code § 333.7453(1)

Gauthier v. Alpena County Prosecutor, 267 Mich.App. 167, 703 N.W.2d 818 (MI Ct. App. 2005)

Miscellaneous

Any conviction will result in a driver's license suspension for 6 months.

See
• Michigan Code § 257.319e

Ann Arbor

In Ann Arbor, the penalty for being caught with marijuana is a $25 fine for the first offense, $50 for the second, and $100 for the third offense. Marijuana is not decriminalized on the University of Michigan's campus.

MINNESOTA
LAWS & PENALTIES

Offense	Penalty	Incarceration	Max. Fine
POSSESSION			
42.5 g or less*	Misdemeanor	N/A	$ 200
More than 42.5 g - less than 10 kg	Felony	5 years	$ 10,000
10 - less than 50 kg	Felony	20 years	$ 250,000
50 - less than 100 kg	Felony	25 years	$ 500,000
100 kg or more	Felony	30 years	$ 1,000,000
More than 1.4 grams inside one's vehicle (except the trunk)	Misdemeanor	90 days	$ 1,000

* A conditional discharge is possible for first time offenders.

* There is a possible drug education course requirement.

Offense	Penalty	Incarceration	Max. Fine
SALE			
42.5 g or less* without remuneration	Misdemeanor	N/A	$ 200
More than 42.5 g - less than 5 kg	Felony	5 years	$ 10,000
5 - less than 25 kg	Felony	20 years	$ 250,000
25 - less than 50 kg	Felony	25 years	$ 500,000
50 kg or more	Felony	30 years	$ 1,000,000
Importing 100 kg or more or using a minor to import	Felony	35 years	$ 1,250,000
To a minor	Felony	20 years	$ 250,000
Within a school zone or other specified areas	Felony	15 years	$ 100,000
5 – less than 25 kg in a school zone	Felony	25 years	$ 500,000
25 kg or more in a school zone	Felony	30 years	$ 1,000,000

* There is a possible drug education course requirement.

CULTIVATION

See Possession section for details.

HASH & CONCENTRATES

Penalties for hashish and marijuana are generally treated equally under the law. Please see details below.

Offense	Penalty	Incarceration	Max. Fine
PARAPHERNALIA			
Possession of paraphernalia	Misdemeanor	N/A	$ 300
Sale/Advertise	Misdemeanor	N/A	$ 1,000
Sale to a minor	Misdemeanor	1 year	$ 3,000

MISCELLANEOUS

Conviction for possession or sale while driving may result in a 30 day driver's license suspension.

Penalty Details

Possession for Personal Use

The Minnesota statute lists Marijuana as a Schedule 1 controlled substances.

Possession of 42.5 grams or less is a misdemeanor punishable by a maximum fine of $200.*

* A conditional discharge is possible for first time offenders.
* There is a possible drug education course requirement.

Possession of more than 42.5 grams - less than 10 kilograms is a felony punishable by a maximum sentence of 5 years imprisonment and a maximum fine of $5,000. Subsequent convictions shall be committed to the commissioner of corrections for 6 mos - 10 years and a possible fine of not more than $20,000.

Possession of 10 - less than 50 kilograms is a felony punishable by a maximum sentence of 20 years imprisonment and a maximum fine of $250,000. Subsequent convictions shall be committed to the commissioner of corrections for 2 - 30 years and a possible fine of not more than $250,000.

Possession of 50 - less than 100 kilograms is a felony punishable by a maximum sentence of 25 years imprisonment and a maximum fine of $500,000. Subsequent convictions shall be committed to the commissioner of corrections for 3 - 40 years and a possible fine of not more than $500,000.

Possession of 100 kilograms or more is a felony punishable by a maximum sentence of 30 years imprisonment and a maximum fine of $1,000,000. Subsequent convictions shall be committed to the commissioner of corrections for 4 - 40 years and a possible fine of not more than $1,000,000.

Possession of more than 1.4 grams inside one's vehicle (except the trunk) is a misdemeanor punishable by a maximum sentence of 90 days imprisonment and a maximum fine of $1,000.

See
* Section 152.02 of the Minnesota Statute
* Section 152.021 of the Minnesota Statutes
* Section 152.022 of the Minnesota Statute
* Section 152.023 of the Minnesota Statute
* Section 152.024 of the Minnesota Statute
* Section 152.025 of the Minnesota Statute
* Section 152.027 of the Minnesota Statute

Sale

The distribution of 42.5 grams or less without remuneration is a misdemeanor punishable by a maximum fine of $200.*

* There is a possible drug education course requirement.

The sale of more than 42.5 grams - less than 5 kilograms is a felony punishable by a maximum sentence of 5 years imprisonment and a maximum fine of $10,000. Subsequent convictions shall be committed to the commissioner of corrections for 6 mos - 10 years and a possible fine of not more than $20,000.

The sale of 5 - less than 25 kilograms is a felony punishable by a maximum sentence of 20 years imprisonment and a maximum fine of $250,000. Subsequent convictions shall be committed to the commissioner of corrections for 2 - 30 years and a possible fine of not more than $250,000.

The sale of 25 - less than 50 kilograms is a felony punishable by a maximum sentence of 25 years imprisonment and a maximum fine of $500,000. Subsequent convictions shall be committed to the commissioner of corrections for 3 - 40 years and a possible fine of not more than $500,000.

The sale of 50 kilograms or more is a felony punishable by a maximum sentence of 30 years imprisonment and a maximum fine of $1,000,000. Subsequent convictions shall be committed to the commissioner of corrections for 4 - 40 years and a possible fine of not more than $1,000,000.

Importing 100 kilograms or more or using a minor to import into the state is a felony punishable by a maximum sentence of 35 years imprisonment and a maximum fine of $1,250,000.

Sale to a minor is a felony punishable by a maximum sentence of 20 years imprisonment and a maximum fine of $250,000.

Distribution within a school zone or other specified areas is a felony punishable by a maximum sentence of 15 years imprisonment and a maximum fine of $100,000. Subsequent convictions shall be committed to the commissioner of corrections for 1 - 30 years and a possible fine of not more than $100,000.

Distribution of 5 kg - less than 25kg within a school zone or other specified areas is a felony punishable by a maximum sentence of 25 years imprisonment and a maximum fine of $500,000.

Distribution of 25 kg or more within a school zone or other specified areas is a felony punishable by a maximum sentence of 30 years imprisonment and a maximum fine of $1,000,000. Subsequent convictions shall be committed to the commissioner of corrections for 4 - 40 years and a possible fine of not more than $1,000,000.

See
* Section 152.021 of the Minnesota Statutes
* Section 152.022 of the Minnesota Statute
* Section 152.023 of the Minnesota Statute
* Section 152.024 of the Minnesota Statute
* Section 152.025 of the Minnesota Statute
* Section 152.027 of the Minnesota Statute
* Section 152.0261 of the Minnesota Statute

Cultivation

Cultivation in Minnesota will be punished based upon the aggregate weight of the plants found. See the "Possession for Personal Use" section for further penalty details.

Hash & Concentrates

The Minnesota statute lists Marijuana and Tetrahydrocannabinol separately in Schedule 1 of the Minnesota controlled substances schedule. Tetrahydrocannabinols are defined as any mixture, compound, or preparation that contains the active THC component of the Cannabis plant or its resinous extractives. Case law refers to Hashish as the resinous form of Marijuana and generally holds that Marijuana and Hashish should be treated equally under the law.

The punishments enumerated in the statutes are equal for Marijuana and Tetrahydrocannabinols in all but one instance. The only difference is the decreased penalties for the possession of, or distribution without remuneration of, a small amount of plant-form Marijuana. This provision does not include Tetrahydrocannabinols. The statute specifically excludes the "resinous form" of Marijuana from inclusion in the definition.

Possession, distribution without remuneration, or sale of less than 5kg of Tetrahydrocannabinols is therefore subject to a term of incarceration not to exceed 5 years, and a fine not to exceed $10,000. For any of the above crimes, if a person has previously been convicted of a drug crime, the maximum period of incarceration and the maximum fine both double, and a mandatory minimum of 6 months imprisonment is imposed.

See
* § 152.02 of the Minnesota Statutes
* § 152.01 of the Minnesota Statutes
* § 152.027 of the Minnesota Statutes
* § 152.025 of the Minnesota Statutes
* Soutor v. State, 342 N.W.2d 175 (Ct. App. Min. 1984)

Paraphernalia

Possession of paraphernalia is a petty misdemeanor punishable by a maximum fine of $300.

Sale or advertising of paraphernalia is a misdemeanor punishable by a fine not to exceed $1,000.

Sale to a minor is a gross misdemeanor punishable by a fine not to exceed $3,000 and a maximum sentence of imprisonment of up to 1 year.

See
* Section 152.092 of the Minnesota Statutes

Miscellaneous

When a person is convicted of possession or sale of marijuana, the sentencing court shall determine whether the person unlawfully sold or possessed the controlled substance while driving a motor vehicle. If so, the court shall notify the commissioner of public safety of its determination and order the commissioner to revoke the person's driver's license for 30 days.

See
* Section 152.0271 of the Minnesota Statutes

MISSISSIPPI
LAWS & PENALTIES

Offense	Penalty	Incarceration	Max. Fine
POSSESSION			
30 g or less (first offense)	N/A	N/A	$ 250
30 g or less (second offense)	N/A	5* - 60 days	$ 250
30 g or less (third offense)	N/A	5 days* - 6 months	$ 500
30 - 250 g	Felony	3 years	$ 3,000
250 - 500 g	Felony	2* - 8 years	$ 50,000
500 g - 1 kg	Felony	4* - 16 years	$ 250,000
1 - 5 kg	Felony	6* - 24 years	$ 500,000
5 kg or more	Felony	10* - 30 years	$ 1,000,000
In any part of a vehicle besides the trunk	Misdemeanor	90 days	$ 1,000

* Mandatory minimum sentence

Offense	Penalty	Incarceration	Max. Fine
SALE			
Up to 30 g	Felony	3 years	$ 3,000
30 g - 1 kg	Felony	5 years	$ 30,000
1 kg - 10 lbs	Felony	30 years	$ 1,000,000
More than 10 lbs	Felony	life	$ 1,000,000

To a minor or within 1500 feet of a school, church, or other designated area is a felony that carries double incarceration period and fines.

CULTIVATION			
See Possession and Sale sections for details.			

Offense	Penalty	Incarceration	Max. Fine
HASH & CONCENTRATES			
Possession of .1 g or less	Misdemeanor or Felony	1 - 4 years	$ 10,000
Possession of .1 g - 2 g	Felony	2* - 8 years	$ 50,000
Possession of 2 g - 10 g	Felony	4* - 16 years	$ 250,000
Possession of 10 g - 30 g	Felony	6* - 24 years	$ 500,000
Possession of more than 30 g	Felony	10* - 30 years	$ 1,000,000
Sale, barter, manufacture, transfer, or distribution	N/A	30 years	$ 1,000,000
Trafficking	N/A	30 years*	$ 1,000,000

*Mandatory Minimum Sentence

Offense	Penalty	Incarceration	Max. Fine
PARAPHERNALIA			
Possession of paraphernalia	Misdemeanor	6 months	$ 500

MISCELLANEOUS			
Any conviction will result in a 6 months driver's license suspension.			
Subsequent convictions will result in double penalties.			

Penalty Details

Possession

A first offense for possession of 30 grams or less is punishable by a fine of $100-$250.

A subsequent conviction will result in 5-60 days imprisonment and a fine of up to $250.

A third conviction will result in 5 days-6 months imprisonment as well as a maximum fine of $500.

See
- Miss. Ann. Code § 41-29-139

Possession of between 30 and 250 grams is a felony punishable by a maximum of 3 years imprisonment and a maximum fine of $3,000.

See
- Miss. Ann. Code § 41-29-139(c)(2)
  (C)

Possession of between 250 and 500 grams is a felony punishable by 2-8 years imprisonment and/or a maximum fine of $50,000.

See

Miss. Ann. Code § 41-29-139(c)(2)(D)

Possession of between 500 grams and 1 kilogram is a felony punishable by 4-16 years imprisonment and/or a maximum fine of $250,000.

See
- Miss. Ann. Code § 41-29-139 (c)
  (2)(E)

Possession of between 1 and 5 kilograms is a felony punishable by between 6 and 24 years in prison and/or a maximum fine of up to $500,000.

See
- Miss. Ann. Code § 41-29-139 (c)
  (2)(F)

Possession of 5 kilograms or more is a felony punishable by 10-30 years imprisonment as well as a maximum fine of $1,000,000.

See
- Miss. Ann. Code § 41-29-139(c)(2)
  (G)

Sale

Selling up to 30 grams of marijuana is a felony punishable by up to 3 years imprisonment and/ or a maximum fine of $3,000.

See
- Miss. Ann. Code § 41-29-139 (b)
  (3)

Selling between 30 grams and one kilogram is a felony punishable by a maximum sentence of 5 years imprisonment and/or a maximum fine of $30,000.

See
- Miss. Ann. Code § 41- 29- 139 (b)
  (2)

Selling 10lbs or marijuana within a 12-month period is a felony, punishable with a life term of imprisonment without parole. Providing the prosecution information on others who violate the law can reduce this penalty

See
- Miss. Ann. Code § 41-29-139 (f)

The sale to a minor or within 1,500 feet of a school, church, or other designated area is a felony that carries with it a doubling of the incarceration period and the fine.

See
- Miss. Ann. Code § 41-29-139

Cultivation

Cultivation in Mississippi will be punished based upon the aggregate weight of the plants found. See the "Possession" and "Sale, Trafficking, or Distribution" sections for further penalty details.

Hash & Concentrates

Under the Mississippi Code, hashish is defined as the resin extracted from the cannabis plant and any preparation, derivative, or mixture of that resin.

See
- Miss. Ann. Code §
  41-29-113

The sale, barter, manufacture, transfer, or distribution of hashish, or possession of hashish with intent to take any of the above actions is subject to up to 30 years imprisonment and a fine of no more than $1,000,000 and no less than $5000.

See
- Miss. Ann. Code §
  41-29-139(a)-(b)

Trafficking hashish is subject to a mandatory minimum penalty of 30 years imprisonment without the possibility of parole or a reduction in the sentence. It is also subject to a fine no less than $5000 and no more than $1,000,000.

See
- Miss. Ann. Code § 41-29-139(g)

Possession of .1g or less of hashish may be prosecuted either as a felony or misdemeanor. If prosecuted as a misdemeanor, it is subject to imprisonment for no more than 1 year and a fine of no more than $1000. If prosecuted as a felony, it is subject to no more than 4 years imprisonment, with a 1-year mandatory minimum, and a fine of no more than $10,000.

See
- Miss. Ann. Code § 41-29-139(c)

Possession of between .1g and 2g of hashish is a felony punishable by a maximum of 8 years imprisonment, with a 2-year mandatory minimum, and a fine no greater than $50,000.

See
- Miss. Ann. Code § 41-29-139(c)

Possession of between 2g and 10g of hashish is a felony, punishable by a maximum of 16 years imprisonment, with a 4-year mandatory minimum, and a fine no greater than $250,000.

See
- Miss. Ann. Code § 41-29-139(c)

Possession of between 10g and 30g of hashish is a felony subject to no more than 24 years imprisonment, with a 6-year mandatory minimum, and a fine of no more than $500,000.

See
- Miss. Ann. Code § 41-29-139(c)

Possession of more than 30g of hashish is a felony subject to no more than 30 years imprisonment, with a 10-year mandatory minimum, and a fine of no more than $1,000,000.

See
- Miss. Ann. Code § 41-29-139(c)

Sale or distribution of hashish by a person over 21 years old to a person under 21 years old doubles the maximum allowable period of incarceration for that offense. The fine for the offense does not change.

See
- Miss. Ann. Code § 41-29-145

Sale, barter, distribution, transfer, or manufacture of hashish or possession with intent to commit any of the above offenses within 1500 feet of a school building or other designated place or within 1000 feet of the property a school building or other designated place resides on doubles the maximum allowable period of incarceration for that offense. The fine for the offense can also be doubled in this situation. A subsequent conviction under this statute will lead to the imposition of the maximum allowable fine and incarceration period.

See
- Miss. Code Ann. § 411-29-142

The maximum period of incarceration and maximum fine for any crime under this section may be doubled for any person who, at the time of their conviction, has a prior conviction for any similar drug crime.

See
- Miss. Ann. Code § 41-29-147

The use of a gun in the commission of any drug crime or possession of a gun at the time of arrest for a drug crime doubles both the maximum allowable period of incarceration and the maximum fine for any given offense.

See
- Miss. Ann. Code § 41-29-152

Paraphernalia

Using, or possessing paraphernalia is a misdemeanor, punishable by up to 6 months in jail and a maximum fine of $500. This does not apply to individuals convicted of one ounce or less; in that case the possession punishment would be the only penalty.

See
- Miss. Ann. Code § 41-29-139(d)
  (1)

Selling paraphernalia is a misdemeanor, punishable by up to a $500 fine or up to 6 months in jail. Additionally, selling paraphernalia to a minor is punishable of up to $1,000 and/or up to one year in jail.

See
- Miss. Ann. Code § 41-29-139 (d)
  (2)-(3)

It is illegal to advertise the sale of paraphernalia in any print or electronic publication. The penalty for such activity is a fine of up to $500 and/or 6 months in jail.

See
- Miss. Ann. Code § 41-29-139(d)
  (4)

Miscellaneous

Any conviction will result in a 6-month driver's license suspension.

See
- Miss. Ann. Code § 63-1-71(1)

Possession of between one and 30 grams kept in a vehicle is punishable of a fine up to $1,000 and up to 90 days in jail. This only applies to areas in the vehicle occupied by passengers and does not apply to a locked glove compartment or trunk.

See
- Miss. Ann. Code § 41-29-139(c)(2)
  (B)

Offense	Penalty	Incarceration	Max. Fine
POSSESSION			
Less than 35 g	Misdemeanor	1 year	$ 1,000
35 g - 30 kg	Felony	1 year	$ 5,000
More than 30 - less than 100 kg	Felony	5 - 15 years	$ 20,000
100 kg or more	Felony	10 years - life	$ 20,000
Possession of more than 100 kilograms is considered Trafficking.			
SALE, TRAFFICKING, OR DISTRIBUTION			
Less than 5 g	Felony	7 years	$ 5,000
5 g - 30 kg	Felony	5 - 15 years	$ 20,000
More than 30 - less than 100 kg	Felony	5 - 15 years	$ 20,000
100 kg or more	Felony	10 years - life*	$ 20,000
500 plants or more	Felony	10 years - life*	$ 20,000
Within 2000 feet of a school or 1000 feet of public housing	Felony	10 years - life	$ 20,000
To a minor	Felony	5 - 15 years	$ 20,000
* No probation or parole			

CULTIVATION

See Possession and Sale sections for details.

HASH & CONCENTRATES

Penalties for hashish are the same as for marijuana. Please see the marijuana penalties section for further details.

PARAPHERNALIA			
Possession of paraphernalia	Misdemeanor	1 year	$ 1,000
Sale of paraphernalia	Felony	4 years	$ 5,000

MISCELLANEOUS

Possession or use of marijuana results in a driver's license suspension if under the age of 21.

Penalty Details

Legislation was approved in 2014 to rewrite Missouri's criminal code that includes provisions reducing marijuana possession penalties. Under the future law, the possession of ten grams or less of cannabis will be punishable by a fine only though the offense will remain classified as a criminal misdemeanor. The possession of greater quantities of cannabis will remain punishable by jail time. The changes to the Missouri criminal code will not go into effect until Jan. 1, 2017.

Possession

Possession of less than 35 grams is a Class A misdemeanor which is punishable by a maximum sentence of 1 year imprisonment and a maximum fine of $1,000.

Possession of 35 grams- 30 kilograms is a Class C felony which is punishable by a maximum sentence of 1 year imprisonment and a maximum fine of $5,000.

Possession of more than 30 - less than 100 kilograms is considered trafficking and is a Class B felony punishable by a sentence of 5-15 years and a fine of $5,000-$20,000.

Possession of 100 kilograms or more is considered trafficking and is a Class A felony punishable by 10 years-life imprisonment and fine of $5,000-$20,000.

See
- Section 195.202.1 of the Missouri Criminal Code
- Section 195.222 of the Missouri Criminal Code
- Section 195.223 of the Missouri Criminal Code
- Section 558.011 of the Missouri Criminal Code
- Section 560.011 of the Missouri Criminal Code
- Section 560.016 of the Missouri Criminal Code

Sale, Trafficking, or Distribution

The sale or manufacture of 5 grams or less is a Class C felony which is punishable by up to 7 years imprisonment and a maximum fine of $5,000.

The sale or manufacture of 5 grams-30 kilograms is a Class B felony which is punishable by a sentence of 5 - 15 years imprisonment and a fine of $5,000-$20,000.

The sale of more than 30 less than 100 kilograms is a Class A felony which is punishable by a sentence of 5 - 15 years imprisonment and a fine of $5,000-$20,000.

The sale of 100 kilograms or more is a Class A felony which is punishable by a sentence of 10 years-life imprisonment with no probation or parole and a fine of $5,000 $20,000.

Sale within 2,000 feet of a school or 1,000 feet of public housing is punishable by a sentence of 10 years-life imprisonment and a fine of $5,000-$20,000.

See
- Section 195.211 of the Missouri Criminal Code
- Section 195.212 of the Missouri Criminal Code
- Section 195.222 of the Missouri Criminal Code
- Section 195.223 of the Missouri Criminal Code
- Section 558.011 of the Missouri Criminal Code
- Section 560.011 of the Missouri Criminal Code

Cultivation

Cultivation of 500 plants or more is a Class A felony, which is punishable by a sentence of 10 years-life imprisonment with no probation or parole and a fine of $5,000-$20,000.

All other cultivation in Missouri will be punished based upon the aggregate weight of the plants found. See the "Possession" and "Sale, Trafficking, or Distribution" sections for further penalty details.

See
- Section 195.223 of the Missouri Criminal Code
- Section 558.011 of the Missouri Criminal Code
- Section 560.011 of the Missouri Criminal Code

Hash & Concentrates

The penalties for hashish and concentrates are exactly the same as for marijuana in Missouri.

See
- Section 195.010(24) of the Missouri Criminal Code
- State v. Randall, 540 S.W.2d 156, 159
- State v. Evans, 637 S.W.2d 62 (Mo App. 1982)

(Mo.App.1976) ("Although 'hashish' is not specifically listed in the schedules, it is clearly included within the statutory definition of marijuana.")

Paraphernalia

The possession of paraphernalia is a misdemeanor which is punishable by a maximum sentence of 1 year imprisonment and a maximum fine of $1,000.

The sale of paraphernalia is a felony which is punishable by a maximum sentence of 5 years imprisonment and a maximum fine of $5,000.

See
- Section 195.233 of the Missouri Criminal Code
- Section 195.235 of the Missouri Criminal Code
- Section 558.011 of the Missouri Criminal Code
- Section 560.011 of the Missouri Criminal Code
- Section 560.016 of the Missouri Criminal Code

Miscellaneous

Possession or use of marijuana results in a driver's license suspension if the offender is under the age of 21 at the time the offense was committed.

MONTANA
LAWS & PENALTIES

Offense	Penalty	Incarceration	Max. Fine
POSSESSION			
Personal Use			
60g or less (first offense)	Misdemeanor	6 months	$ 500
60g or less (second offense)	Misdemeanor	3 years	$ 1,000
More than 60g	Felony	5 years	$ 50,000
With Intent to Distribute			
Any amount	Felony	20 years	$ 50,000
SALE OR DELIVERY			
Any amount with or without compensation	Felony	1 year* - life	$ 50,000
From an adult to a minor	Felony	2 years*	$ 50,000
Within 1000 feet of school grounds	Felony	3 years* - life	$ 50,000
* Mandatory minimum sentence			
CULTIVATION			
1 lb or less or 30 plants or less	Felony	10 years	$ 50,000
More than 1 lb or more than 30 plants	Felony	2 years - life	$ 50,000
Second or subsequent offense is punishable by twice the term of imprisonment and twice the authorized fine.			
HASH & CONCENTRATES			
Possession of 1 gram or less (first offense)	Misdemeanor	6 months	$ 500
Possession of 1 gram or less (subsequent offense)	Misdemeanor	3 years	$ 1,000
Possession of more than 1 g	Felony	5 years	$ 1,000
Manufacture	Felony	10 years	$ 50,000
Penalties for the sale or possession with the intent to sell hashish are the same as for marijuana. Please see the marijuana penalties section for further details.			
PARAPHERNALIA			
Possession, manufacture, or delivery of paraphernalia	Misdemeanor	6 months	$ 500
To a person under 18 who is at least 3 years younger	Misdemeanor	1 year	$ 1,000
CIVIL ASSET FORFEITURE			
Vehicles and other property may be seized.			
MISCELLANEOUS			
Use or possession of property subject to criminal forfeiture	Felony	10 years	$ 0
Continuing criminal enterprise results is a felony punishable by double or triple fine and imprisonment.			
Possession of marijuana on a train results in additional penalties.			
Storing marijuana results in additional fines.			
Anyone convicted of a misdemeanor must attend a mandatory drug education course.			
Imprisonment for felonies may be eligible for suspended or deferred imposition, which may include commitment to a drug treatment facility, community service, or driver's license revocations.			

Penalty Details

Marijuana is a Schedule I hallucinogenic substance under the Controlled Substances Chapter of the Montana Code Annotated. It is also considered a dangerous drug.

See
- Montana Code Ann. § 50-32-101
- Montana Code Ann. § 50-32-222(4)(t)

Possession for Personal Use

Possession of 60 grams or less of marijuana is a misdemeanor punishable by up to 6 months imprisonment and a fine of $100 - $500. A second offense is punishable by up to 3 years imprisonment and/or a fine up to $1,000. Possession of more than 60 grams is a felony punishable by up to 5 years imprisonment and/or a fine up to $50,000.

See
- Montana Code Ann. § 45-9-102

Possession with Intent to Distribute

Possession of any amount of marijuana with intent to distribute is a felony punishable by up to 20 years imprisonment and/or a fine up to $50,000.

See
- Montana Code Ann. § 45-9-103(3)

Sale/Delivery

Distribution of any amount of marijuana, with or without compensation, is punishable by a mandatory minimum of 1 year and a maximum sentence of life imprisonment and/or a fine up to $50,000.

See
- Montana Code Ann. § 45-9-101(4)

Distribution of any amount, with or without compensation, from an adult to a minor is punishable by a mandatory minimum of 2 years imprisonment and/or a fine up to $50,000. Penalties significantly increase for repeat offenses.

See
- Montana Code Ann. § 45-9-101(5)

Distribution of any amount, with or without compensation, within 1,000 feet of school grounds is a felony punishable by a minimum of 3 years and maximum of life imprisonment and a fine up to $50,000. It is an affirmative defense to this charge if the distribution occurred within the confines of a private residence and no one under the age of 18 was present in the residence.

See
- Montana Code Ann. § 45-9-109

Cultivation

Cultivation of up to 1 pound or 30 plants of marijuana is a felony punishable by up to 10 years imprisonment and/or a fine up to $50,000. Cultivation of more than 1 pound or 30 plants is a felony punishable by a minimum of 2 years to a maximum of life imprisonment and a fine up to $50,000. A second or subsequent offense for cultivation of marijuana is punishable by twice the term of imprisonment and twice the authorized fine for the first offense.

See
- Montana Code Ann. § 45-9-110

Hash & Concentrates

Montana lists both Marijuana and Tetrahydrocannabinols in Schedule I of the Montana Controlled Substances Schedule. The statute defines Marijuana as all plant material of the genus Cannabis containing THC. Tetrahydrocannabinols are defined as substances contained in the resinous extractives of Cannabis, not requiring any plant matter be present.

See
- Montana Code Ann. §50-32-101
- Montana Code Ann. §50-32-222

The penalties for the sale of any amount of Marijuana and Tetrahydrocannabinols are equal.

See
- Montana code Ann. §45-9-101(4)

The penalties for possession of Tetrahydrocannabinols are differentiated by weight:

For the first offense, possession of 1 gram or less of Tetrahydrocannabinol is a misdemeanor punishable by a fine of no less than $100 and no greater than $500, as well as a term of incarceration not to exceed 6 months in a county jail.

For all subsequent offenses, possession of one gram or less of Tetrahydrocannabinol is a misdemeanor, punishable by up to 1 year in a county jail, or a felony punishable by up to 3 years in a state prison, as well as a fine not to exceed $1000.

Possession of any amount of Tetrahydrocannabinol greater than 1 gram is a felony punishable by up to 5 years in a state prison as well as a fine not to exceed $50,000.

See
- Montana Code Ann. §45-9-102(2), (5)

The penalties for possession with intent to distribute any amount of Tetrahydrocannabinol are equal to those for the possession with intent to distribute any amount of Marijuana.

See
- Montana Code Ann. §45-9-103

Distribution of Tetrahydrocannabinol within 1000 feet of the real property of a school, whether public or private, elementary or secondary, is a felony punishable by up to life imprisonment, with a 3 year mandatory minimum and a fine not to exceed $50000.

See
- Montana Code Ann. §45-9-109

For the first offense, manufacture of any amount Tetrahydrocannabinol is a felony punishable by up to 10 years imprisonment and a fine not to exceed $50,000. For any offense occurring after a prior conviction for manufacture of a dangerous drug, manufacture of Tetrahydrocannabinol is a felony punishable by up to 20 years in prison and a fine of no less than $100,000.

See
- Montana Code Ann. §45-9-110

Paraphernalia

Possession, manufacture, or delivery of paraphernalia is a misdemeanor punishable by up to 6 month imprisonment and/or a fine up to $500. However, if the delivery was from a person aged 18 or older to a person under the age of 18 who is at least 3 years younger, then the offense is a misdemeanor punishable by up to 1 year imprisonment and/or a fine up to $1,000.

See
- Montana Code Ann. § 45-10-103 to 105

Sentencing

Imprisonment for felonies involving dangerous drugs may be eligible for suspended or deferred imposition. Conditions of this suspension or deferral may include commitment to a drug education or treatment facility, 2,000 hours community service in a drug education or treatment facility, driver's license revocations (6 months for first offense, 1 year for a second offense, and 3 years for a third or subsequent offense), among others.

See
- Montana Code Ann. § 45-9-202

Those convicted of a first-time possession of 60 grams or less offense are presumed to be eligible for deferred imposition of a sentence of imprisonment. For suspended or deferred sentencing of a first time possession offense of under 60 grams, the minimum fine of $100 must be imposed as a condition.

See
- Montana Code Ann. § 45-9-102

Forfeiture

Vehicles and other property may be seized for controlled substance violations. However, a vehicle may not be seized if it was used or intended for use for transported 60 grams of marijuana or less. Within 45 days of seizure of the property, the seizing agency must file a forfeiture proceeding. The court will then issue a summons and notice to all those with interest in the property. Those with an interest must file an answer within 20 days after the service of the summons, or the property is forfeited to the state.

See
- Montana Code Ann. §§ 44-12-102 to 103
- Montana Code Ann. §§ 44-12-201 to 203
- Montana Code Ann. § 45-9-206

Miscellaneous

Use or possession of property subject to criminal forfeiture

Use or possession of property that one knows is subject to criminal forfeiture for involvement with drug offenses is a felony punishable by up to 10 years imprisonment.

See
- Montana Code Ann. § 45-9-206

Continuing criminal enterprise

Any person who commits a felony under the Controlled Substances Chapter which was part of a series of 2 or more violations on separate occasions, included 5 people or more, and from which substantial income was made is guilty of a felony punishable by twice the term of imprisonment and fine authorized for the underlying offense. A second or subsequent violation of this offense results in triple the penalties authorized for the underlying offense.

See
- Montana Code Ann. § 45-9-125

Carrying dangerous drugs on a train

Possession of marijuana on a train is an offense that is punishable by the same penalties of and in addition to the possession itself.

See
- Montana Code Ann. § 45-9-127

Mandatory fine for possession and storage of dangerous drugs

Every person found to have possessed or stored marijuana shall be fined, in addition to other fines, an amount which is 35% of the market value of the marijuana.

See
- Montana Code Ann. § 45-9-130

Mandatory drug education course

Anyone who is convicted of drug offense characterized as a misdemeanor must attend a dangerous drug information course.

See
- Montana Code Ann. § 45-9-208

Suspended or deferred imposition

Imprisonment for felonies involving dangerous drugs may be eligible for suspended or deferred imposition. Conditions of this suspension or deferral may include commitment to a drug treatment facility for up to 1 year, up to 2,000 hours community service in a drug education or treatment facility, driver's license revocations (6 months for first offense, 1 year for a second offense, and 3 years for a third or subsequent offense), among others.

See
- Montana Code Ann. § 45-9-202

NEBRASKA
LAWS & PENALTIES

Offense	Penalty	Incarceration	Max. Fine
POSSESSION			
1 oz or less (first offense)	Infraction	N/A	$ 300
1 oz or less (second offense)	Misdemeanor	N/A	$ 500
1 oz or less (third offense)	Misdemeanor	7 days	$ 500
More than 1 oz - I lb	Misdemeanor	3 months	$ 500
More than I lb	Felony	5 years	$ 10,000
SALE			
Any amount	Felony	1* - 20 years	$ 25,000
To a minor within 1000 feet of a school or between 100-1000 feet of other designated areas (first offense)	Felony	1* - 50 years	$ 0
Subsequent offense	Felony	3 years* - life	$ 0
* Mandatory minimum sentence			
CULTIVATION			
See Possession section for penalty details.			
HASH & CONCENTRATES			
Possession	Felony	5 years	$ 10,000
Selling, manufacturing, or possessing with the intent to distribute	Felony	1 - 20 years	$ 25,000
PARAPHERNALIA			
Possession of paraphernalia (first offense)	Infraction	N/A	$ 100
Sale	Misdemeanor	6 months	$ 1,000
Sale to a minor	Misdemeanor	1 year	$ 1,000
Advertise	Misdemeanor	3 months	$ 500

Penalty Details

Nebraska law lists Marijuana as a Schedule I controlled substance.

Possession

Possession of 1 ounce or less is an infraction, which is punishable by a maximum fine of $300. The judge may order the offender to complete a drug education course.

A second conviction for possession of 1 ounce or less is a Class IV misdemeanor punishable by a maximum fine of $500.

Third and subsequent convictions for possession of 1 ounce or less are a Class IIIA misdemeanor and are punishable by a maximum sentence of 7 days imprisonment and a maximum fine of $500.

Possession of more than 1 ounce - 1 pound is a class III misdemeanor punishable by a maximum sentence of 3 months imprisonment and a maximum fine of $500.

Possession of more than 1 pound is a class IV felony which is punishable by a maximum sentence of 5 years imprisonment and a maximum fine of $10,000.

See
- § 28-416 of the Nebraska Revised Statutes
- § 28-105 of the Nebraska Revised Statutes

Sale

The sale of any amount is a class III felony, which is punishable by a 1 year mandatory minimum sentence and up to 20 years imprisonment as well as a maximum fine of $25,000.

The sale to a minor within 1,000 feet of a school or between 100-1,000 ft. of other designated areas is a class II felony, which is punishable by a 1 year mandatory minimum sentence and up to 50 years imprisonment.

A second or subsequent violation is a class ID felony punishable by a mandatory minimum sentence of 3 years and up to 50 years imprisonment.

See
- § 28-416 of the Nebraska Revised Statutes
- § 28-105 of the Nebraska Revised Statutes

Cultivation

Cultivation in Nebraska will be punished based upon the aggregate weight of the plants found. See the "Possession" section for further penalty details.

Hash & Concentrates

Hashish and THC Concentrates are individually named Schedule I controlled substances in Nebraska. Possession of hash is a Class IV felony, punishable by a maximum sentence of 5 years imprisonment and a maximum fine of $10,000. Selling, manufacturing, or possessing with the intent to distribute hashish is a Class III felony, punishable by a minimum sentence of 1 year, a maximum of 20 years imprisonment, and a maximum fine of $25,000.

See
- § 28-405(c)(23) of the Nebraska Revised Statutes
- § 28-416 of the Nebraska Revised Statutes
- § 28-416 of the Nebraska Revised Statutes
- § 28-105 of the Nebraska Revised Statutes

Paraphernalia

Possession of paraphernalia is an infraction which is punishable by a maximum fine of $100.

Each additional conviction is punishable by a fine of $200-$500.

Sale of paraphernalia is a Class II misdemeanor, which is punishable by a maximum fine not exceeding $1,000 and a term of imprisonment not exceeding 6 months.

Sale of paraphernalia to a person under 18 at least 3 years younger is a Class I misdemeanor, which is punishable by a maximum fine not exceeding $1,000 and a term of imprisonment not exceeding 1 year.

Advertisement of is a Class III misdemeanor, which is punishable by a maximum fine not exceeding $500 and a term of imprisonment not exceeding 3 months.

See
- 28-106 of the Nebraska Revised Statutes
- 28-441 of the Nebraska Revised Statutes
- 28-439 of the Nebraska Revised Statutes
- 28-440 of the Nebraska Revised Statutes
- 28-442 of the Nebraska Revised Statutes
- 28-443 of the Nebraska Revised Statutes
- 28-444 of the Nebraska Revised Statutes

NEVADA
LAWS & PENALTIES

Offense	Penalty	Incarceration	Max. Fine
POSSESSION			
Personal Use			
1 oz or less (first offense)	Misdemeanor	N/A	$ 600
1 oz or less (second offense)	Misdemeanor	N/A	$ 1,000
1 oz or less (third offense)	Misdemeanor	365 days	$ 2,000
1 oz or less (fourth offense)	Felony	1* - 4 years	$ 5,000

Or mandatory assessment or treatment for first and second offense
* Mandatory minimum sentence

Offense	Penalty	Incarceration	Max. Fine
SALE OR DELIVERY			
Less than 100 lbs (first offense)	Felony	1* - 4 years	$ 5,000
Less than 100 lbs (second offense)	Felony	1* - 5 years	$ 10,000
Less than 100 lbs (subsequent offense)	Felony	3* - 15 years	$ 20,000
100 - less than 2000 lbs	Felony	1* - 5 years	$ 25,000
2000 - less than 10,000 lbs	Felony	2* - 10 years	$ 50,000
10,000 lbs or more	Felony	5* - life	$ 200,000
To a minor	Felony	5* - life	$ 20,000

* Mandatory minimum sentence

Offense	Penalty	Incarceration	Max. Fine
CULTIVATION			
12 plants or more	Felony	1* - 4 years	$ 5,000
100 - less than 2000 lbs	Felony	1* - 5 years	$ 25,000
2000 - less than 10,000 lbs	Felony	2* - 10 years	$ 50,000
10,000 lbs or more	Felony	5* - life	$ 200,000

* Mandatory minimum sentence

HASH & CONCENTRATES

Penalties for hashish are the same as for marijuana. Please see the marijuana penalties section for further details.

Offense	Penalty	Incarceration	Max. Fine
PARAPHERNALIA			
Possession or use of paraphernalia or advertising	Misdemeanor	6 months	$ 1,000
Sale, delivery, manufacture, or possession with intent	Felony	1* - 4 years	$ 5,000
Sale to a minor who is at least 3 years younger	Felony	1* - 5 years	$ 10,000

* Mandatory minimum sentence

CIVIL ASSET FORFEITURE

Vehicles and other property may be seized.

Offense	Penalty	Incarceration	Max. Fine
MISCELLANEOUS			
Knowingly maintaining a structure used for drug offenses	Felony	1* - 6 years	$ 10,000
100 - 2000 lbs	Civil Penalty	N/A	$ 350,000
2000 - 10,000 lbs	Civil Penalty	N/A	$ 700,000
10,000 lbs or more	Civil Penalty	N/A	$ 1,000,000

* Mandatory minimum sentence

Penalty Details

Marijuana is a Schedule I hallucinogenic substance under rule by the Nevada State Board of Pharmacy as authorized by the Nevada Uniform Controlled Substances Act.

See
- Nevada Rev. Stat. § 453.146

Possession for Personal Use

Possession of 1 ounce or less of marijuana is a misdemeanor punishable by a fine up to $600 or mandatory assessment for addiction for the first offense. A second offense is a misdemeanor punishable by up to $1,000 or mandatory treatment. A third offense is a gross misdemeanor punishable by up to 365 days imprisonment and/or a fine up to $2,000. A fourth or subsequent offense is a category E felony punishable by a minimum of 1 year and maximum of 4 years imprisonment and a fine up to $5,000. The court shall, in most situations, defer imposition of this sentence and have the defendant enter into conditional probation.

See
- Nevada Rev. Stat. § 193.130
- Nevada Rev. Stat. § 193.140
- Nevada Rev. Stat. § 193.150
- Nevada Rev. Stat. § 453.336

Use of marijuana without authorization is a category E felony punishable by a minimum of 1 year and maximum of 4 years imprisonment and a fine up to $5,000.

See
- Nevada Rev. Stat. § 453.411

Sale/Delivery

Sale or delivery of less than 100 pounds of marijuana is a category D felony punishable by a minimum of 1 and maximum of 4 years imprisonment and fine up to $5,000 for the first offense. A second offense is a category C felony punishable by a minimum of 1 and maximum of 5 years imprisonment and fine up to $10,000. A third or subsequent offense is a category B felony punishable by a minimum of 3 and maximum of 15 years imprisonment and a fine up to $20,000. Sale or delivery of 100 pounds or more but less than 2,000 pounds of marijuana is a category C felony punishable by a minimum of 1 year and maximum of 5 years imprisonment and a fine up to $25,000. Sale or delivery of 2,000 pounds or more but less than 10,000 pounds is a category B felony punishable by a minimum of 2 years and maximum of 10 years imprisonment and fine up to $50,000. Sale or delivery of 10,000 pounds or more is a category A felony punishable by life with the possibility of parole after a minimum of 5 years has been served, or for a definite term of 15 years with possibility for parole after a minimum of 5 years has been served, and a fine up to $200,000.

See
- Nevada Rev. Stat. § 193.130
- Nevada Rev. Stat. § 453.321
- Nevada Rev. Stat. § 453.337
- Nevada Rev. Stat. § 453.339

Selling marijuana to a minor is a category A felony punishable by life with the possibility of parole after a minimum of 5 years has been served, or for a definite term of 15 years with possibility for parole after a minimum of 5 years has been served, and a fine up to $20,000. The person may additionally be responsible for paying for the costs of the minor's drug treatment costs.

See
- Nevada Rev. Stat. § 453.334

Cultivation

Cultivation of 12 plants or more is a category E felony punishable by a minimum of 1 year and maximum of 4 years imprisonment and a fine up to $5,000.

Cultivation of 100 pounds or more but less than 2,000 pounds of marijuana is a category C felony punishable by a minimum of 1 year and maximum of 5 years imprisonment and a fine up to $25,000. Cultivation of 2,000 pounds or more but less than 10,000 pounds is a category B felony punishable by a minimum of 2 years and maximum of 10 years imprisonment and a fine up to $50,000. Cultivation of 10,000 pounds or more is a category A felony punishable by up to life imprisonment and a fine up to $200,000.

See
- Nevada Rev. Stat. § 193.130
- Nevada Rev. Stat. § 453.339
- Nevada Rev. Stat. § 453.3393

Hash & Concentrates

In Nevada, hashish and marijuana concentrates are punished under the State's marijuana penalties, with penalty levels based on the weight of the hashish present. See Nevada's marijuana penalties section above for further details.

See
- Nevada Rev. Stat. § 453.096

Paraphernalia

Possession or use of paraphernalia or advertising to promote the sale of paraphernalia is a misdemeanor punishable by up to 6 months imprisonment and/or a fine up to $1,000. Sale, delivery, manufacture, or possession with intent to sell or deliver paraphernalia is a category E felony punishable by a minimum of 1 year and maximum of 4 years imprisonment and a fine up to $5,000.

Sale or delivery of paraphernalia to a minor by an individual aged 18 years or older who is at least 3 years older than the minor is a category C felony punishable by minimum of 1 year and maximum of 5 years imprisonment and a fine up to $10,000. The offender may also be ordered to pay restitution to the minor for treatment costs.

See
- Nevada Rev. Stat. § 193.130
- Nevada Rev. Stat. § 193.150
- Nevada Rev. Stat. § 453.560
- Nevada Rev. Stat. § 453.562
- Nevada Rev. Stat. § 453.566

Sentencing

The court may suspend proceedings against persons who are charged with first time possession or use offenses after a finding of guilty and instead impose conditional probation which will include either a drug education or treatment program. Upon successful completion of the terms of the probation, the proceedings against the defendant will be dismissed.

See
- Nevada Rev. Stat. § 453.3363

First time offenders may be eligible for probation, but probation is generally not allowed for second or subsequent offenses.

See
- Nevada Rev. Stat. § 453.321(3)

Misdemeanor sentences may be replaced in part or whole by community service.

See
- Nevada Rev. Stat. § 193.150

Forfeiture

Vehicles and other property may be seized for controlled substance violations. The state has 60 days after seizure to file a forfeiture proceeding. They must notify all those who have an interest in the property. A person with an interest in the property must file a response within 20 days of service.

See
- Nevada Rev. Stat. §§ 179.1164 - 179.1171
- Nevada Rev. Stat. § 453.301

Miscellaneous

Knowingly maintaining a structure used for drug offenses

Opening or maintaining a place for the purpose of selling, giving away, or using marijuana is a category B felony punishable by a minimum of 1 year and maximum of 6 years imprisonment and a fine up to $10,000. A second offense of this type or a first offense of this type if the offender had a previous drug-related felony is a category B felony punishable by a minimum of 2 years and maximum of 10 years imprisonment and a fine up to $20,000.

See
- Nevada Rev. Stat. § 453.316

Controlled substances homicide

If marijuana proximately causes the death of a person, the person who delivered the marijuana to him may be guilty of murder.

See
- Nevada Rev. Stat. § 453.333

Civil penalties

The state of Nevada is entitled to civil penalties recoverable from certain marijuana offenders. If the amount involved was 100 pounds or more but less than 2,000 pounds, the state is entitled up to $350,000. If the amount was 2,000 pounds or more but less than 10,000 pounds, the state is entitled up to $700,000. If the amount was 10,000 pounds or more, the state is entitled to $1,000,000.

See
- Nevada Rev. Stat. § 453.5531(1)

Driver's license suspension

If a child is adjudicated delinquent for the unlawful act of using, possessing, selling or distributing a controlled substance... the juvenile court shall: (a) if the child possesses a driver's license, issue an order suspending the driver's license of the child for at least 90 days but not more than 2 years.

See
- Nevada Rev. Stat. § 62E.630

NEW HAMPSHIRE
LAWS & PENALTIES

Offense	Penalty	Incarceration	Max. Fine
POSSESSION			
Any amount	Misdemeanor	1 year	$ 2,000
SALE OR POSSESSION WITH INTENT TO SELL			
Less than 1 oz (first offense)	Felony	3 years	$ 25,000
1 oz - less than 5 lbs (first offense)	Felony	7 years	$ 100,000
5 lbs or more (first offense)	Felony	20 years	$ 300,000
Subsequent offense carries a greater sentence and fine. See Penalty Details section for information.			
Within 1000 feet of a school zone carries a double sentence and fine.			
CULTIVATION			
See Possession and Sale sections for details.			
HASH & CONCENTRATES			
Possession of 5 g or less	Misdemeanor	1 year	$ 2,000
Possession of more than 5 g	Misdemeanor	1 year	$ 5,000
Manufacturing, selling, or possessing with intent to sell of less than 5 g	Felony	3 years	$ 25,000
Manufacturing, selling, or possessing with intent to sell of 5 g - less than 1 lb	Felony	7 years	$ 100,000
Manufacturing, selling, or possessing with intent to sell of 1 lb or more	Felony	20 years	$ 30,000
Subsequent offense carries a greater sentence and fine. See Penalty Details section for information.			
PARAPHERNALIA			
Sale or possession of paraphernalia	Misdemeanor	1 year	$ 2,000
MISCELLANEOUS			
Persons under 21 years will face a driver's license suspension for 90 days - 1 year.			
Persons under 18 years will face a driver's license suspension for 1 - 5 years.			

Penalty Details

Possession

Possession of any amount is a Class A misdemeanor punishable by a maximum sentence of 1 year imprisonment and a maximum fine of $2,000.

See
- 318 B:2 of the New Hampshire Criminal Code
- 318 B:1 et seq. of the New Hampshire Criminal Code
- 318-B:26 of the New Hampshire Criminal Code
- 651:2 of the New Hampshire Criminal Code

Sale

Includes possession with intent to sell.

The sale of less than 1 ounce for a first offense is a felony punishable by a maximum sentence of 3 years imprisonment and a maximum fine of $25,000. A Subsequent offense is a felony punishable by a maximum sentence of 6 years imprisonment and a maximum fine of $50,000.

The sale of 1 ounce - less than 5 pounds for a first offense is a felony punishable by a maximum sentence of 7 years imprisonment and a maximum fine of $100,000. A Subsequent offense is a felony punishable by a maximum sentence of 15 years imprisonment and a maximum fine of $200,000.

The sale of 5 pounds or more for a first offense is a felony punishable by a maximum sentence of 20 years imprisonment and a maximum fine of $300,000. A Subsequent offense is a felony punishable by a maximum sentence of 30 years imprisonment and a maximum fine of $500,000.

Sale within 1,000 feet of a school zone is a felony punishable by a doubling of the sentence and the fine.

See
- 318 B:2 of the New Hampshire Criminal Code
- 318 B:1 et seq. of the New Hampshire Criminal Code
- 318-B:26 of the New Hampshire Criminal Code

Cultivation

Cultivation in New Hampshire will be punished based upon the aggregate weight of the plants found. See the "Possession" and "Sale" sections for further penalty details.

Hash & Concentrates

Possessing 5 grams or less of hashish or concentrates is a class A misdemeanor punishable by a fine no greater than $2,000 and a term of imprisonment no greater than 1 year. Possessing 5 grams or more of hashish is a misdemeanor punishable by a fine no greater than $5,000 and a term of imprisonment no greater than 1 year.

See
- 318-B:26(II) of the New Hampshire Criminal Code
- 651:2 of the New Hampshire Criminal Code

The sale of less than 5 grams for a first offense is a felony punishable by a maximum sentence of 3 years imprisonment and a maximum fine of $25,000. A Subsequent offense is a felony punishable by a maximum sentence of 6 years imprisonment and a maximum fine of $50,000.

The sale of 5 grams - less than 1 pound for a first offense is a felony punishable by a maximum sentence of 7 years imprisonment and a maximum fine of $100,000. A Subsequent offense is a felony punishable by a maximum sentence of 15 years imprisonment and a maximum fine of $200,000.

The sale of 1 pound or more for a first offense is a felony punishable by a maximum sentence of 20 years imprisonment and a maximum fine of $300,000. A Subsequent offense is a felony punishable by a maximum sentence of 30 years imprisonment and a maximum fine of $500,000.

If any of the offenses occurred with 1,000 feet of a school the fines and terms of imprisonment double.

See
- 318-B:26 of the New Hampshire Criminal Code

Any device or equipment used to manufacture hashish or concentrates is considered drug paraphernalia. Manufacturing, or delivering any such device or equipment is a misdemeanor punishable by a fine no greater than $2,000 and/or a term of imprisonment no greater than 1 year.

See
- 318-B1(X-a) of the New Hampshire Criminal Code
- 318-B:26(III) of the New Hampshire Criminal Code

Paraphernalia

The sale or possession of paraphernalia is a misdemeanor punishable by a maximum sentence of 1 year imprisonment and a maximum fine of $2,000.

See
- 318 B:1 et seq. of the New Hampshire Criminal Code
- 318 B:2 318 B:1 et seq. of the New Hampshire Criminal Code
- 318-B:26 of the New Hampshire Criminal Code

Miscellaneous

Persons under 21 years of age will face a driver's license suspension for 90 days- 1 year.

See
- 318 B:2 of the New Hampshire Criminal Code

Any person under 18 years of age who is convicted sale or possession with intent to sell controlled drugs shall be subject to revocation or denial of a driver's license or privilege to drive for a mandatory period of at least one year and a maximum period of up to 5 years. In the case of denial of an application for a license under this section, the period imposed shall begin on the date the person is eligible by age for the issuance of a license.

See
- 263:50-b of the New Hampshire Criminal Code

NEW JERSEY
LAWS & PENALTIES

Offense	Penalty	Incarceration	Max. Fine
POSSESSION			
50 g or less	Disorderly Person	6 months	$ 1,000
More than 50 g	Crime	1.5 years	$ 25,000
Within 1000 feet of a school adds 100 hours of community service, as well as an additional fine.			
DISTRIBUTION			
Less than 1 oz	Crime	1.5 years	$ 25,000
1 oz - less than 5 lbs	Crime	3* - 5 years	$ 25,000
5 - less than 25 lbs	Crime	5* - 10 years	$ 150,000
25 lbs or more	Crime	10* - 20 years	$ 300,000
Within 1000 feet of a school or school bus	Crime	3* - 5 years	$ 150,000
Includes possession with the intent to distribute			
To minors or pregnant women carries a double term of imprisonment and fine.			
* Mandatory minimum sentence			
CULTIVATION			
1 oz - less than 5 lbs (less than 10 plants)	Crime	3* - 5 years	$ 25,000
5 - less than 25 lbs (10 - less than 50 plants)	Crime	5* - 10 years	$ 150,000
More than 25 lbs (50 plants or more)	Crime	10* - 20 years	$ 300,000
* Mandatory minimum sentence			
HASH & CONCENTRATES			
Possession of 5 g or less	Disorderly Person	6 months	$ 1,000
Possession of more than 5 g	Crime	6 months	$ 25,000
Manufacturing, distributing, dispensing, or possessing with intent of less than 5 g	Crime	18 months	$ 10,000
Manufacturing, distributing, dispensing, or possessing with intent of 5 g - less than 1 lb	Crime	3* - 5 years	$ 25,000
Manufacturing, distributing, dispensing, or possessing with intent of 1 lb - less than 5 lbs	Crime	5* - 10 years	$ 150,000
Manufacturing, distributing, dispensing, or possessing with intent of 5 lbs or more	Crime	10* - 20 years	$ 300,000
Within 1000 feet of a school or school bus	Crime	3* - 5 years	$ 150,000
* Mandatory minimum sentence			
PARAPHERNALIA			
Possession or use of paraphernalia	Disorderly Person	6 months	$ 1,000
Sale of paraphernalia	Crime	18 months	$ 10,000
MISCELLANEOUS			
Failure to turn over marijuana to a police officer is a misdemeanor. Being under the influence of marijuana is a misdemeanor. Potential punishment is listed in Penalty Details.			
If under 17 years, driving privileges shall be suspended for 6 months, 2 years			

Penalty Details

See

24:21-1, et seq. of the New Jersey Criminal Code

Possession

Possession of 50 grams or less is a "Disorderly Person" offense punishable by a maximum sentence of 6 months imprisonment and a maximum fine of $1,000.

Possession of more than 50 grams is a crime in the 4th degree punishable by a maximum sentence of 18 months imprisonment and a maximum fine of $25,000.

Possession within 1,000 feet of a school adds a sentence of 100 hours of community service to the sentence, as well a variable (depending on quantity) additional fine.

See
- Section 2C:21-7.4 of the New Jersey Statutes Annotated
- Section 2C:35-10 of the New Jersey Statutes Annotated

Distribution or Possession with the Intent to Distribute

Sale or distribution of less than 1 ounce is a crime in the 4th degree punishable by a maximum sentence of 18 months imprisonment and a maximum fine of $25,000.

Sale or distribution of 1 ounce- less than 5 pounds is a crime in the 3rd degree punishable by a sentence of 3-5 years imprisonment and a maximum fine of $25,000.

Sale or distribution of 5 pounds - less than 25 pounds is a crime in the 2nd degree punishable by a sentence of 5-10 years imprisonment and a maximum fine of $150,000.

Sale or distribution of 25 pounds or more is a crime in the 1st degree punishable by a sentence of 10-20 years imprisonment and a maximum fine of $300,000.*

* A mandatory minimum sentence (with limited exceptions) shall be imposed.

Sale within 1,000 feet of school property or a school bus is a crime in the 3rd degree punishable by a sentence of 3-5 years imprisonment and a maximum fine of $150,000.

If the violation involves less than 1 ounce, a mandatory minimum sentence of either 1/2 or 1/3 of the sentence shall be imposed.

Sale or distribution of less than 1 ounce within 500 feet of certain public property is a crime in the 3rd degree punishable by 3-5 years imprisonment and a maximum fine of $25,000.

Sale or distribution of more than 1 ounce within 500 feet of certain public property is a felony punishable by 5-10 years imprisonment and a maximum fine of $150,000.

Sale to minors or pregnant women is a felony which carries with a doubling of the term of imprisonment and the fine.

See
- Section 2C:35-5 of the New Jersey Statutes Annotated
- Section 2C:35-7 of the New Jersey Statutes Annotated
- Section 2C:43-3 of the New Jersey Statutes Annotated
- Section 2C:43-6 of the New Jersey Statutes Annotated

Cultivation

Cultivation of 1 ounce - less than 5 pounds (less than 10 plants) is a crime in the 3rd degree punishable by a sentence of 3-5 years imprisonment and a maximum fine of $25,000.

Cultivation of 5 pounds - less than 25 pounds (10 - less than 50 plants) is a crime in the 2nd degree punishable by a sentence of 5-10 years imprisonment and a maximum fine of $150,000.

Cultivation of 25 pounds or more (50 or more plants) is a crime in the 1st degree punishable by a sentence of 10-20 years imprisonment and a maximum fine of $300,000.*

* A mandatory minimum sentence shall be imposed.

See
- Section 2C:35-5 of the New Jersey Statutes Annotated
- Section 2C:43-6 of the New Jersey Statutes Annotated

Hash & Concentrates

New Jersey defines hashish as "the resin extracted from any part of the plant Genus Cannabis L. and any compound, manufacture, salt, derivative, mixture, or preparation of such resin." Hashish is a Schedule I controlled substance.

See
- Section 24:21-2 of the New Jersey Statutes Annotated
- Section 24:21-5(e) of the New Jersey Statutes Annotated

Possessing less than 5 grams of hashish is a disorderly person offense punishable by a fine no greater than $1,000 and/or a term of imprisonment no greater than 6 months. Possessing 5 grams or more of hashish is a crime in the 4th degree punishable by a fine no greater than $25,000 and/or a term of imprisonment no greater than 18 months.

See
- Section 2C:35-10 of the New Jersey Statutes Annotated
- Section 2C:43-3 of the New Jersey Statutes Annotated
- Section 2C:43-6 of the New Jersey Statutes Annotated
- Section 2C:43-8 of the New Jersey Statutes Annotated

Manufacturing, distributing, dispensing, or possessing with intent to manufacture, distribute, or dispense less than 5 grams of hashish is a crime in the 4th degree punishable by a fine no greater than $25,000 and/or a term of imprisonment no greater than 18 months. If the amount of hashish is 5 grams or more but less than 1 pound, the offense is a crime in the 3rd degree punishable by a fine no greater than $25,000 and/or a term of imprisonment no less than 3 years and no greater than 5 years. If the amount of hashish involved was 1 pound or greater but less than 5 pounds, the offense is a crime in the second degree punishable by a fine no greater than $150,000 and/or a term of imprisonment no less than 5 years and no greater than 10 years. If the amount of hashish involved was 5 pounds or greater, the offense is a crime in the first degree punishable by a fine no greater than $200,000 and/or a term of imprisonment no less than 10 years and no greater than 20 years.

See
- Section 2C:35-5 of the New Jersey Statutes Annotated
- Section 2C:43-3 of the New Jersey Statutes Annotated
- Section 2C:43-6 of the New Jersey Statutes Annotated

Manufacturing, distributing, dispensing, or possessing with intent to manufacture, distribute, or dispense hashish within 1,000 feet of a school or school bus stop is a crime in the 3rd degree punishable by a fine no greater than $150,000 and/or a term of imprisonment no less than a mandatory 3 years and no greater than 5 years.

See
- Section 2C:35-7 of the New Jersey Statutes Annotated
- Section 2C:43-3 of the New Jersey Statutes Annotated
- Section 2C:43-6 of the New Jersey Statutes Annotated

Paraphernalia

Possession or use of paraphernalia is a "Disorderly Persons Offense" punishable by a maximum sentence of 6 months imprisonment and a maximum fine of $1,000.

Sale of paraphernalia is a crime in the 4th degree punishable by a maximum sentence 18 months imprisonment and a maximum fine of $10,000.

Sale of paraphernalia to minors is a crime in the 3rd degree punishable by a sentence of 3-5 years imprisonment and a maximum sentence of $25,000.

Advertising the sale of any such device or equipment is a crime in the 4th degree punishable by a fine no greater than $10,000 and/or a term of imprisonment no greater than 18 months.

See
- Section 2C:36-2 of the New Jersey Statutes Annotated
- Section 2C:36-4 of the New Jersey Statutes Annotated
- Section 2C:36-5 of the New Jersey Statutes Annotated
- Section 2C:43-3 of the New Jersey Statutes Annotated
- Section 2C:43-6 of the New Jersey Statutes Annotated
- Section 2C:43-8 of the New Jersey Statutes Annotated

Miscellaneous

In NJ, failure to turn over marijuana or hashish to a nearby police officer is a misdemeanor. In addition, being under the influence of marijuana or hashish (whether you are driving a car or not), is also a misdemeanor. These offenses can be punished by:

- Up to six months imprisonment (N.J.S.A. 2C:43-8)
- A fine of up to $1000 (N.J.S.A. 2C:43-3(c))
- Loss of Public Housing (N.J.S.A. 2A:18-61.1)
- Potential Eviction from leased residential premises (N.J.S.A. 2A:18-61.1)
- Loss of driving privileges for not less than six months and up to two years. (2C:35-16)
- Mandatory loss of driving privileges for two years if the marijuana is in a motor vehicle. (N.J.S.A. 39:4-49.1)
- A term of community service (N.J.S.A. 2C:43-2b(5))
- A mandatory $75 Safe Neighborhoods Services assessment (N.J.S.A. 2C:43-3.2)
- A mandatory $50 lab fee (2C:35-20)
- A mandatory $50 Victims of Crime Compensation Board penalty (2C:43-3.1a(2)(a))
- A mandatory $500 Drug Enforcement Demand Reduction penalty (N.J.S.A. 2C:35-15(e))
- A period of probation of up to five years (N.J.S.A. 2C:43-2b(2); State v. Dove, 202 N.J.Super. 540, (Law Div. Jan 29, 1985))

See
- Section 2C:35-10(c) of the New Jersey Statutes Annotated
- Section 2C:35-10(b) of the New Jersey Statutes Annotated

Driver's license suspension

Shall suspend, revoke or postpone the driving privileges for a period not less than six months or more than two years of every person convicted of or adjudicated delinquent for not less than 6 months and no more than two years. If less than 17 years old, the suspension shall not run less than six months or more than two years after they turn 17.

See
- 17. 39:5-30.13 of the New Jersey Statutes Annotated

NEW MEXICO
LAWS & PENALTIES

Offense	Penalty	Incarceration	Max. Fine
POSSESSION			
1 oz or less (first offense)	Misdemeanor	15 days	$ 100
1 oz or less (second offense)	Misdemeanor	1 year	$ 1,000
More than 1 - less than 8 oz	Misdemeanor	1 year	$ 1,000
8 oz or more	Felony	1.5 years	$ 5,000
DISTRIBUTION			
100 lbs or less (first offense)	Felony	1.5 years	$ 5,000
Less than 100 lbs or less (second offense)	Felony	3 years	$ 5,000
100 lbs or more (first offense)	Felony	3 years	$ 5,000
100 lbs or more (second offense)	Felony	9 years	$ 10,000
To a minor (first offense)	Felony	3 years	$ 5,000
To a minor (second offense)	Felony	9 years	$ 10,000
Within a drug-free school zone	Felony	18 years	$ 15,000
Includes possession with the intent to distribute			
If no payment, exchange of small amount of marijuana is treated as possession only.			
CULTIVATION			
Any amount (first offense)	Felony	9 years	$ 10,000
Any amount (second offense)	Felony	18 years	$ 15,000
Within a drug-free school zone	Felony	18 years	$ 15,000
HASH & CONCENTRATES			
Possession	Misdemeanor	1 year	$ 1,000
Distributing or possessing With Intent to Distribute	Felony	3 years	$ 5,000
Subsequent convictions or within 1,000 feet of non-secondary school carries increased incarceration and fines.			
PARAPHERNALIA			
Possession or distribution of paraphernalia	Misdemeanor	1 year	$ 100
Distribution of paraphernalia to a minor	Felony	1.5 years	$ 5,000
MISCELLANEOUS			
If a person who is 15 years or older is found delinquent of violating the Controlled Substances Act, their license may revoked.			

Penalty Details

Marijuana is a schedule I(c) hallucinogenic substance under New Mexico's Controlled Substances Act.

See
• New Mexico Stat. Ann. § 30-31-6

Possession for Personal Use

For first offenders, possession of 1 ounce or less of marijuana is a petty misdemeanor and is punishable by a fine of $50-$100 and/or up to 15 days of imprisonment. For subsequent offenses possession of 1 ounce or less of marijuana is a misdemeanor and is punishable by a fine of $100-$1000 and/or up to 1 year of imprisonment.

Possession of more than 1 - less than 8 ounces of marijuana is a misdemeanor punishable by a fine of $100-$1000 and imprisonment for up to 1 year. Possession of 8 ounces or more of marijuana is a fourth degree felony and is punishable by 1.5 years of imprisonment and a fine of up to $5,000.

See
• New Mexico Stat. Ann. § 30-31-23
• New Mexico Stat. Ann. § 31-18-15

Distribution

Distribution of marijuana is treated the same as possessing marijuana with the intent to distribute it.

For first offenders, distribution of 100 pounds or less of marijuana is a fourth degree felony and is punishable by 1.5 years of imprisonment and a fine of up to $5,000. Subsequent offenses are punished as a third degree felony and offenders may be imprisoned for 3 years, a fine of $5,000 may also be imposed.

For first offenders, distribution of more than 100 pounds of marijuana is third degree felony and is punishable by 3 years of imprisonment and a fine of $5,000. Subsequent offenses are punished as a second degree felony and offenders may be imprisoned for 9 years, a fine of $10,000 may also be imposed.

If no payment is given, exchange of a small amount of marijuana is treated as possession only.

Distribution of marijuana to a minor occurs when a person over the age of 18 distributes marijuana to a person under the age of 18. For first offenders, distribution of marijuana to a minor is a third degree felony and is punishable by 3 years of imprisonment and a fine of $5,000. Subsequent offenses are punishable as a second degree felony and offenders may be imprisoned for 9 years, a fine of $10,000 may also be imposed

Distributing marijuana within a drug-free school zone is a first degree felony and is punishable by 18 years of imprisonment and a fine of $15,000. There is an exception if the sale occurs in a private residence that is located in a drug-free school zone.

See
• New Mexico Stat. Ann. §30-31-20(C)
• New Mexico Stat. Ann. §30-31-21
• New Mexico Stat. Ann. §30-31-22
• New Mexico Stat. Ann. § 31-18-15

Cultivation

For first offenders cultivation of marijuana is a second degree felony and is punishable by 9 years of imprisonment and a fine of $10,000. Subsequent offenses are considered a first degree felony and are punishable by 18 years of imprisonment and a fine of $15,000.

Cultivating marijuana within a drug-free school zone is a first degree felony and is punishable by 18 years of imprisonment and a fine of $15,000.

See
• New Mexico Stat. Ann. §30-31-20

Hash & Concentrates

New Mexico defines hashish as: "the resin extracted from any part of marijuana, whether growing or not, and every compound, manufacture, salt, derivative, mixture or preparation of such resins". Hashish is a Schedule I controlled substance.

Possessing hashish is a misdemeanor punishable by a fine no less than $500 and no greater than $1,000 and/or a term of imprisonment no greater than 1 year. Possessing hashish within 1,000 feet of non-secondary school is a fourth degree felony punishable by a fine no greater than $5,000 and/or a term of imprisonment no greater than 18 months. Drug-free zones do not include private residences, nor vehicles in transit.

Distributing or possessing with intent to distribute hashish is a third degree felony punishable by a fine no greater than $5,000 and a term of imprisonment no greater than 3 years. Subsequent convictions are second degree felonies punishable by a fine no greater than $10,000 and a term of imprisonment no greater than 9 years. Distributing or possessing with intent to distribute hashish within 1,000 feet of a non-secondary school is a second degree felony punishable by a fine no greater than $10,000 and/or a term of imprisonment no greater than 9 years. Subsequent convictions are first degree felonies punishable by a fine no greater than $15,000 and/or a term of imprisonment no greater than 18 years.

See
• New Mexico Stat. Ann. § 30-31-2(L)
• New Mexico Stat. Ann. § 30-31-6(C)(18)
• New Mexico Stat. Ann. § 30-31-22
• New Mexico Stat. Ann. § 30-31-23(D),(F)
• New Mexico Stat. Ann. § 31-18-15

Paraphernalia

Possession or distribution of marijuana paraphernalia used for the cultivation, distribution, or inhalation/ingestion of marijuana is a misdemeanor and is punishable by a fine of $50-$100 and/ or up to 1 year imprisonment.

Distribution of marijuana paraphernalia to a minor occurs when a person over the age of 18 distributes marijuana paraphernalia to a person under the age of 18. This offense is a fourth degree felony and is punishable by a fine of $5,000 and 1.5 years of imprisonment.

See
• New Mexico Stat. Ann. §30-31-25.1

Miscellaneous

In addition to any other penalty, a child 15 years or older is found delinquent of violating the Controlled Substances Act, their license may revoked.

See
• New Mexico Stat. Ann. § 32A-2-19(H)

NEW YORK
LAWS & PENALTIES

Offense	Penalty	Incarceration	Max. Fine
POSSESSION			
25 g or less (first offense)	Not Classified	N/A	$ 100
25 g or less (second offense)	Not Classified	N/A	$ 200
25 g or less (third offense)	Not Classified	15 days	$ 250
More than 25 g - 2 oz	Misdemeanor	3 months	$ 500
More than 2 - 8 oz	Misdemeanor	1 year	$ 1,000
More than 8 oz - 1 lb	Felony	4 years	$ 5,000
More than 1 - 10 lbs	Felony	7 years	$ 5,000
More than 10 lbs	Felony	15 years	$ 15,000
In public view	Misdemeanor	90 days	$ 250
SALE			
2 g or less without profit or 1 marijuana cigarette	Misdemeanor	3 months	$ 500
25 g or less	Misdemeanor	1 year	$ 1,000
More than 25 g - 4 oz	Felony	4 years	$ 5,000
More than 4 oz - 1 lb	Felony	7 years	$ 5,000
More than 1 lb	Felony	15 years	$ 15,000
Using a child to assist	Felony	4 years	$ 5,000
To a minor	Felony	7 years	$ 5,000
TRAFFICKING			
Any amount	Felony	15* - 25 years	$ 100,000

* Mandatory minimum sentence

Offense	Penalty	Incarceration	Max. Fine
CULTIVATION			
Any amount	Misdemeanor	1 year	$ 1,000

Cultivating marijuana is also possessing marijuana under current case law. See Penalty Details section.

Offense	Penalty	Incarceration	Max. Fine
HASH & CONCENTRATES			
Possession of less than 1/4 oz	Misdemeanor	1 year	$ 1,000
Possession of 1/4 - less than 1 oz	Felony	7 years	$ 5,000
Possession of 1 oz or more	Felony	15 years	$ 15,000
Sale	Felony	15 years	$ 15,000
PARAPHERNALIA			
Possession or sale of scales or balances for the purpose of weighing or measuring marijuana	Misdemeanor	1 year	$ 0
Subsequent offense	Felony	7 years	$ 5,000
CIVIL ASSET FORFEITURE			

Property can be seized if convicted of a felony.

MISCELLANEOUS

Mandatory driver's license suspension of 6 months for youthful offenders.

Penalty Details

Marijuana and its synthetic "equivalents" are considered Schedule I hallucinogenic substances under New York Public Health Law. Synthetic equivalents include resinous extracts and derivatives with similar chemical properties.

See
- New York Pub. Health §3306(d) (13)
- New York Pub. Health §3306(d) (21)

Possession for Personal Use

For a first offender, possession of up to 25 grams of marijuana is punishable by a fine of $100. If an additional offense occurs within three years of the first offense, possession of up to 25 grams of marijuana is punishable by a fine of $200. For the third or subsequent offense(s) within a three-year period, possession of up to 25 grams of marijuana is punishable by a fine of $250 and/or imprisonment of 15 days or less. Possession of marijuana in excess of 25 grams - 2 ounces is a class B misdemeanor and is punishable by no more than 3 months imprisonment and a fine not to exceed $500. Possession of marijuana in excess of 2 ounces - 8 ounces is a class A misdemeanor and is punishable by no more than 1 year of imprisonment and a fine not to exceed $1,000. Possession of marijuana in excess of 8 ounces - 16 ounces is a class E felony and is punishable by no more than 4 years of imprisonment and a fine not to exceed $5,000. Possession of marijuana in excess of 16 ounces - 10 pounds is a class D felony and is punishable by no more than 7 years of imprisonment and a fine not to exceed $5,000. Possession of marijuana in excess of 10 pounds is a class C felony and is punishable by no more than 15 years of imprisonment and a fine not to exceed $15,000.

See
- New York Pen. Code §221
- New York Pen. Code §70
- New York Pen. Code §80

Use or Display of Marijuana

Marijuana open to public view or being burnt in public is a Class B misdemeanor punishable by a fine of $250 with a maximum sentence of 90 days.

See
- New York Pen. Code §221.10

Sale

Exchange without payment of less than 2 grams of marijuana and/or one marijuana cigarette is a class B misdemeanor and is punishable by no more than 3 months imprisonment.

Sale of marijuana in any amount to a person under 18 years of age is a class D felony and is punishable by up to 7 years of imprisonment and a fine not to exceed $5,000.

Sale of marijuana in an amount 25 grams or less is a class A misdemeanor and is punishable by no more than 1 year of imprisonment and a fine not to exceed $1,000. Sale of marijuana in an amount greater than 25 grams - 4 ounces is a class E felony and is punishable by up to 4 years of imprisonment and a fine not to exceed $5,000. Sale of marijuana in an amount greater than 4 ounces - 16 ounces is a class D felony and is punishable by up to 7 years of imprisonment and a fine not to exceed $5,000. Sale of marijuana in excess of 16 ounces is a class C felony and is punishable by up to 15 years of imprisonment and a fine not to exceed $15,000.

Using a child to assist in the sale of marijuana is a class E felony and is punishable by no more than 4 years of imprisonment and a fine not to exceed $5,000. This offense includes hiding marijuana on a child or otherwise directing a child to assist in a marijuana sale.

See
- New York Pen. Code §70
- New York Pen. Code §80
- New York Pen. Code §220.28
- New York Pen. Code §221

Trafficking

A person is considered a major trafficker of marijuana if they do one of the following: Act as the director of an organization, which sells $75000 worth of marijuana over the course of a year or less; collect $75000 or more from sales of marijuana over the course of 6 months or less; possess with intent to sell $75000 or more of marijuana over the course of 6 months or less. If one or more of the above are satisfied the person may be charged as a major trafficker, this is a class A-I felony and is punishable by 15-25 years of imprisonment and a fine not to exceed $100,000.

See
- New York Pen. Code §220.77
- New York Pen. Code §70.00(i)

Cultivation

Growing cannabis is a class A misdemeanor and is punishable by up to 1 year of imprisonment and/or a fine of up to $1000.

*While technically cultivation of any amount of marijuana is a misdemeanor, a person who cultivates marijuana is also "possessing" marijuana under current case law. Parmeter v. Feinberg affirms the state's ability to charge a person with the crime of "cultivation" and "possession" any time a person is caught growing marijuana. This means the more marijuana that a person cultivates the more severe the degree of possession that the state can charge."

Hash & Concentrates

The term 'Marijuana' as used in the New York Criminal code is defined as including both plant-form Marijuana and Concentrated Cannabis. Marijuana is listed as a Schedule 1 drug on the New York Controlled Substances Schedule. Concentrated Cannabis is defined as the separated resin of the Cannabis plant, whether purified or raw, or any mixture or preparation containing at least 2.5% THC. Unlike most other states, New York uses the term Tetrahydrocannabinols exclusively to refer to synthetic cannabinoids, not Concentrates. New York does not apply its Marijuana decriminalization law to Concentrated Cannabis. There is no explicit justification for this in the statute, but specific penalties for offenses involving Concentrated Cannabis are separated from those involving plant-form Marijuana and the distinction is noted in caselaw.

Possession of any amount of Concentrated Cannabis up to one-fourth of an ounce is a class A Misdemeanor, punishable by up to 1 year imprisonment and a fine not to exceed $1000.

Possession of between one-fourth of an ounce and one ounce of Concentrated Cannabis is a class D Felony, punishable by up to 7 years imprisonment and a fine of no more than $5000.

Possession of one ounce or more of Concentrated Cannabis is a class C Felony, punishable by up to 15 years imprisonment and a fine of no more than $15,000.

The presence of any controlled substance in an automobile creates a presumption of knowing possession for all occupants of the vehicle. This principle does not apply if the controlled substance is on the person of one of the passengers and the substance is hidden from the view of other passengers.

The presence of Marijuana (including Concentrated Cannabis) in open view in a room, other than a public place, under circumstances that evince an intent to manufacture, package, or otherwise prepare the Marijuana for sale gives rise to a presumption of knowing possession for all those in close proximity to the Marijuana at the time it is found.

See
- New York Pen. Code §220.25

Sale of any amount of Concentrated Cannabis is a class C Felony subject to no more than 15 years imprisonment and a fine not to exceed $15,000.

See
- New York Pen. Code §220.34

Sale of any amount of Concentrated Cannabis on a school bus, on the grounds of a child day care or educational facility, or in a publically accessible area within 1000 feet of the real property line of such a facility is a class B Felony subject to no more than 25 years imprisonment and a fine not to exceed $30,000.

See
- New York Pen. Code §220.44

Sale of any amount of Concentrated Cannabis by a person 21 years old or more to a person 17 years old or younger is a class B Felony subject to no more than 25 years imprisonment and a fine not to exceed $30,000.

See
- New York Pen. Code §220.48

Paraphernalia

Possession or sale of scales or balances for the purpose of weighing or measuring marijuana is a class A misdemeanor and is punishable by up to 1 year of imprisonment. Any subsequent conviction of possession or sale of paraphernalia is a class D felony and is punishable by up to 7 years imprisonment and a fine of up to $5000.

See
- New York Pen. Code §220.50
- New York Pen. Code §220.55
- New York Pen. Code §70
- New York Pen. Code §80

Forfeiture

If convicted of a felony offense the following may be forfeited, unless the forfeiture would be disproportionate from what the defendant gained from the offense: the proceeds from the offense, instruments used in the offense (including a car).

See
- New York Pen. Code §480.05

Miscellaneous

Mandatory suspension for a period of six months where the holder is convicted of, or receives a youthful offender or other juvenile adjudication in connection with any crime in violation of the Federal Controlled Substances Act.

See
- New York Pen. Code § 510(2)(b) (v)

NORTH CAROLINA
LAWS & PENALTIES

Offense	Penalty	Incarceration	Max. Fine
POSSESSION			
Personal Use			
0.5 oz or less	Misdemeanor	N/A	$ 200
0.5 - 1.5 oz	Misdemeanor	1 - 45 days	$ 1,000
More than 1.5 oz - 10 lbs	Felony	3 - 8 months	$ 1,000
With Intent to Distribute			
More than 10 - less than 50 lbs	Felony	25* - 39 months	$ 5,000
50 - less than 2000 lbs	Felony	35* - 51 months	$ 25,000
2000 - less than 10,000 lbs	Felony	70* - 93 months	$ 50,000
10,000 lbs or more	Felony	175* - 222 months	$ 200,000
* Mandatory minimum sentence			
SALE OR DELIVERY			
10 lbs or less	Felony	4 - 8 months	$ 1,000
More than 10 - less than 50 lbs	Felony	25* - 39 months	$ 5,000
50 - less than 2000 lbs	Felony	35* - 51 months	$ 25,000
2000 - less than 10,000 lbs	Felony	70* - 93 months	$ 50,000
10,000 lbs or more	Felony	175* - 222 months	$ 200,000
To a minor or pregnant women	Felony	3 - 8 years	$ 0
Within 1000 feet of school, child care center, or park grounds	Felony	1 - 3 years	$ 0
* Mandatory minimum sentence			
CULTIVATION			
Less than 10 lbs	Felony	3 - 8 months	$ 1,000
10 - 50 lbs	Felony	2* - 2.5 years	$ 5,000
50 - 2000 lbs	Felony	3* - 3.5 years	$ 25,000
2000 - 10,000 lbs	Felony	6* - 7 years	$ 50,000
10,000 lbs or more	Felony	14.5* - 18 years	$ 200,000
* Mandatory minimum sentence			
HASH & CONCENTRATES			
Possession of less than .05 oz	Misdemeanor	1 - 10 days	$ 200
Possession of .05 - .15 oz	Misdemeanor	1 - 45 days	$ 200
Possession of more than .15 oz	Felony	4 - 6 months	$ 200
PARAPHERNALIA			
Use, possession, sale, delivery, or manufacture of paraphernalia	Misdemeanor	1 - 45 days	$ 1,000
To a minor who is at least 3 years younger	Felony	3 - 8 months	$ 0
CIVIL ASSET FORFEITURE			
Vehicles and other property may be seized.			
MISCELLANEOUS			
Involving a minor	Felony	8 months - 7 years	$ 0
Possession in a penal institution	Felony	4 - 8 months	$ 0

A fine of $0 is discretionary and is decided on a case-by-case basis by the sitting judge.

If convicted of a felony offense and given probation results in driver's license forfeiture.

Penalty Details

Marijuana is a Schedule VI substance under the North Carolina Controlled Substances Act.

See
- North Carolina Gen Stat. § 90-94

Possession for Personal Use

Possession of 0.5 ounces or less of marijuana is a Class 3 misdemeanor and a maximum fine of $200. Any sentence of imprisonment imposed for this offense must be suspended. Possession of more than 0.5 to 1.5 ounces is a Class 1 misdemeanor punishable by 1 to 45 days imprisonment and a discretionary fine for a first offense, and maximum fine of $1000. Possession of over 1 and a half ounces but less than or equal to 10 pounds is a Class I felony punishable by 3 to 8 months imprisonment and a discretionary fine for a first offense.

See
- North Carolina Gen Stat. § 15A-1340.17
- North Carolina Gen Stat. § 15A-1340.23
- North Carolina Gen Stat. § 90-95(d)(4)

Possession with Intent to Distribute

Possession with intent to distribute less than 10 pounds of marijuana is a class I felony punishable by 3 to 8 months imprisonment and a discretionary fine for a first offense.

See
- North Carolina Gen Stat. § 15A-1340.17
- North Carolina Gen Stat. § 90-95(b)(2)

Possession of more than 10 pounds but less than 50 pounds is a Class H felony punishable by a minimum of 25 months and maximum of 39 months imprisonment and a fine of at least $5,000. Possession of 50 pounds or more but less than 2,000 pounds is a Class G felony punishable by a minimum of 35 months and maximum of 51 months imprisonment and a fine of at least $25,000. Possession of 2,000 pounds or more but less than 10,000 pounds is a Class F felony punishable by a minimum of 70 months and maximum of 93 months imprisonment and a fine of at least $50,000. Possession of 10,000 pounds or more of marijuana is a Class D felony punishable by a minimum of 175 months and maximum of 222 months imprisonment and a fine of at least $200,000.

See
- North Carolina Gen Stat. § 90-95(h)

Sale/Delivery

Delivery of less than 5 grams of marijuana for no compensation is not considered sale or delivery, but may still be prosecuted as possession. Sale of less than 10 pounds of marijuana is a Class H felony punishable by 4 to 8 months imprisonment and a discretionary fine for the first offense. Delivery without compensation of less than 10 pounds is a Class I felony punishable by 3 to 8 months imprisonment and a discretionary fine for a first offense.

See
- North Carolina Gen Stat. § 15A-1340.17
- North Carolina Gen Stat. § 90-95(a)(2)

Sale or delivery of 10 pounds or more but less than 50 pounds is a Class H felony punishable by a minimum of 25 months and maximum of 30 months imprisonment and a fine of at least $5,000. Sale or delivery of 50 pounds or more but less than 2,000 pounds is a Class G felony punishable by a minimum of 35 months and maximum of 42 months imprisonment and a fine of at least $25,000. Sale or delivery of 2,000 pounds or more but less than 10,000 pounds is a Class F felony punishable by a minimum of 70 months and maximum of 80 months imprisonment and a fine of at least $50,000. Sale or delivery of 10,000 pounds or more of marijuana is a Class D felony punishable by a minimum of 175 months and maximum of 219 months imprisonment and a fine of at least $200,000.

See
- North Carolina Gen Stat. § 90-95(h)

Cultivation

Cultivation of less than 10 pounds of marijuana is a class I felony punishable by 3 to 8 months imprisonment and a discretionary fine for a first offense.

See
- North Carolina Gen Stat. § 90-95(a)(2)

Cultivation of 10 pounds or more but less than 50 pounds is a Class H felony punishable by a minimum of 25 months and maximum of 30 months imprisonment and a fine of at least $5,000. Cultivation of 50 pounds or more but less than 2,000 pounds is a Class G felony punishable by a minimum of 35 months and maximum of 42 months imprisonment and a fine of at least $25,000. Cultivation of 2,000 pounds or more but less than 10,000 pounds is a Class F felony punishable by a minimum of 70 months and maximum of 80 months imprisonment and a fine of at least $50,000. Cultivation of 10,000 pounds or more of marijuana is a Class D felony punishable by a minimum of 175 months and maximum of 219 months imprisonment and a fine of at least $200,000.

See
- North Carolina Gen Stat. § 90-95(h)

Hash & Concentrates

Possession of an extract of marijuana resin, commonly referred to as hashish, is a crime in North Carolina. Possession of .05 ounces or less (~1.4 grams) is a Class 3 misdemeanor, which is punishable by a $200 fine and a 1-10 day sentence that must be suspended. Possession of more than .05 ounces (~1.4 grams) but less than .15 ounces (~4.25 grams) is a Class 1 misdemeanor, which is punishable by a fine determined at the discretion of the court and a 1-45 day sentence. Possession of an amount greater than .15 ounce (~4.25 grams) is a Class I felony which has a presumptive sentence of 4-6 months and a discretionary fine may also be assessed by the court.

See
- North Carolina Gen Stat. §90-95(d)(4)
- North Carolina Gen Stat. §15A-1340.17(b)

Paraphernalia

Use, possession, sale, delivery, or manufacture of paraphernalia is a Class 1 misdemeanor punishable by 1 to 45 days imprisonment and a discretionary fine for a first offense. Delivery of paraphernalia by a person aged 18 years or older to a person under the age of 18 who is at least 3 years younger is a Class I felony punishable by 3 to 8 months imprisonment and a discretionary fine for a first offense.

See
- North Carolina Gen Stat. § 15A-1340.17
- North Carolina Gen Stat. § 15A-1340.23
- North Carolina Gen Stat. §§ 90-113.22 to 113.23

Sentencing

If a person has a previous controlled substance violation and commits a Class 1 misdemeanor, he will be punished as a Class I felon. If a person has a previous controlled substance violation and commits a Class 2 misdemeanor, he will be guilty of a Class 1 misdemeanor. If a person has a previous controlled substance violation and commits an offense that requires any sentence of imprisonment be suspended, he is guilty of Class 2 misdemeanor.

See
- North Carolina Gen Stat. §§ 90-95(e)(3)-(4), (7)

First time misdemeanor marijuana proceedings may be suspended and the offender placed on probation. The probation must include drug education, unless certain circumstances apply. Upon successful completion of the terms of probation, the charges will be dismissed and the individual discharged.

See
- North Carolina Gen Stat. § 90-96

A person convicted of a marijuana possession, cultivation, or sale/delivery offense may be eligible for probation if they are not sentenced to the maximum term of imprisonment allowed for that offense. This may include a requirement to attend treatment. This probation cannot last longer than 5 years.

See
- North Carolina Gen Stat. § 90-95(f)

Forfeiture

Vehicles and other property may be seized for controlled substance violations. Seized property is not subject to be returned to the owner unless he can prove in a forfeiture proceeding that he is the owner and was unaware that it was being used in the violation.

See
- North Carolina Gen Stat. §§ 90-122 to 112.1

Miscellaneous

Sale or delivery to a minor or pregnant women

Sale or delivery by a person aged 18 years or older to a person between 14-15 years of age or to a pregnant woman of any age is a Class D felony punishable by 38 to 80 months imprisonment and a fine to be set by the discretion of the court for the first offense. Sale or delivery by a person aged 18 years or older to a person 13 years of age or younger is a Class C felony punishable by 44 to 92 months imprisonment and a fine to be set by the discretion of the court for the first offense.

See
- North Carolina Gen Stat. § 15A-1340.17
- North Carolina Gen Stat. § 90-95(e)(5)

Employing a minor in a drug offense

A person aged 10-20 years who uses a minor in the sale, delivery, or cultivation of marijuana is guilty of a Class I felony if the minor is 14-17 years old, punishable by 8 to 16 months imprisonment and a discretionary fine for the first offense, and a Class F felony if the minor is 13 years of age or younger, punishable by 10 to 20 months imprisonment and a discretionary fine for the first offense. A person aged 21 years or older who uses a minor in the sale, delivery, or cultivation of marijuana is guilty of a Class E felony if the minor is 14-17 years old, punishable by 15 to 31 months imprisonment and a fine to be set by the discretion of the court for the first offense, and a Class D felony if the minor is 13 years of age or younger, punishable by 38 to 80 months imprisonment and a fine to be set by the discretion of the court for the first offense. A person aged 21 years or older who uses a minor in a drug offense may be liable for civil damages for drug addiction.

See
- North Carolina Gen Stat. § 15A-1340.17
- North Carolina Gen Stat. § 90-95.4
- North Carolina Gen Stat. § 90-95.5

Promoting drug sales by a minor

Any person aged 21 years or older who entices, encourages, forces, or supports a minor in selling, delivering, or cultivating marijuana is guilty of a Class D felony punishable by 38 to 80 months imprisonment and a fine to be set by the discretion of the court for the first offense.

See
- North Carolina Gen Stat. § 15A-1340.17
- North Carolina Gen Stat. § 90-95.6

Participating in a drug violation by a minor

Any person aged 21 years or older who purchases marijuana from a minor 13 years or younger is guilty of a Class G felony punishable by 8 to 16 months imprisonment and a discretionary fine for the first offense.

See
- N.C. Gen Stat. § 15A-1340.17
- North Carolina Gen Stat. § 90-95.7

Sale or delivery on school grounds

Sale or delivery in or within 1,000 feet of school, child care center, or park grounds is class E felony punishable by 15 to 31 months imprisonment and a fine to be set by the discretion of the court for the first offense. Delivery of less than 5 grams of marijuana for no compensation is not considered delivery, but still may be prosecuted for delivery.

See
- North Carolina Gen Stat. § 15A-1340.17
- North Carolina Gen Stat. §§ 90-95(e)(8), (10)

Possession in a penal institution

Possession of any amount of marijuana in a penal institution or local confinement facility is a Class H felony punishable by 4 to 8 months imprisonment and a discretionary fine for the first offense.

See
- North Carolina Gen Stat. § 15A-1340.17
- North Carolina Gen Stat. § 90-95(e)(9)

Reimbursement for undercover marijuana purchases

When a person is convicted of a marijuana offense, the court may order him to reimburse the law enforcement agency for money spent in purchasing marijuana as part of an undercover operation.

See
- North Carolina Gen Stat. § 90-95.3

Driver's license forfeiture

Any time an individual is convicted of a felony offense and is given probation, they are to have their license forfeited.

See
- North Carolina Gen Stat. § 15A-1331A

NORTH DAKOTA
LAWS & PENALTIES

Offense	Penalty	Incarceration	Max. Fine
POSSESSION			
1 oz or less	Misdemeanor	30 days	$ 1,500
More than 1 oz - 500 g	Felony	5 years	$ 10,000
More than 500 g	Felony	10 years	$ 20,000
Any amount within 1000 feet of a school	Felony	10 years	$ 20,000
SALE			
Any amount	Felony	3* - 10 years	$ 20,000
Using a minor	Felony	10 years	$ 20,000
Any amount within 1000 feet of a school	Felony	20 years	$ 20,000
* Mandatory minimum sentence for second offense			
CULTIVATION			
See Possession section for penalty details.			
HASH & CONCENTRATES			
Ingesting	Misdemeanor	1 year	$ 3,000
Possession	Felony	5 years	$ 10,000
Manufacture or delivery	Felony	10 years	$ 20,000
PARAPHERNALIA			
Possession, manufacture, delivery or advertisement of paraphernalia	Misdemeanor	1 year	$ 3,000
To a minor	Felony	5 years	$ 10,000
MISCELLANEOUS			
Any conviction requires the offender to undergo a drug addiction evaluation.			
Juveniles may have their driver's license suspended for up to 6 months.			

Penalty Details

See
- North Dakota Century Code 19-03.1-23
- North Dakota Century Code 12.1-32-01

Possession

Possession of 1 ounce [28.35 grams] or less of marijuana is a class B misdemeanor punishable by a maximum imprisonment of 30 days, a fine of one thousand five hundred dollars, or both.

The court, assuming the defendant is not subsequently convicted of another criminal offense within the following two years, will permanently seal convictions for first offenders possessing 1 ounce or less.

Possession of more than 1 ounce but less than 500 grams is a Class C felony which is punishable by a maximum sentence of 5 years imprisonment and a maximum fine of $10,000.

Possession of 500 grams or more of marijuana is a Class B Felony, which is punishable by up to 10 years imprisonment and a fine of up to $20,000.

Possession on, or within 1,000 feet of the real property comprising a public or private elementary or secondary school or a public career and technical education school is a class B felony punishable by up to 10 years imprisonment and a fine of up to $20,000.

See
- North Dakota Century Code 19-03.1-23
- North Dakota Century Code 19-03.1-23.1
- North Dakota Century Code 12.1-32-01

Sale

The sale of any amount of marijuana is a class B felony punishable by up to 10 years imprisonment and a fine of up to $20,000. For a second offense there is a minimum term of imprisonment of at least 3 years. For a third or subsequent offense there is a minimum term of imprisonment of at least 10 years.

Sale within 1,000 feet of a school is a class A felony punishable by maximum sentence of 20 years imprisonment and a maximum fine of $20,000.

See
- North Dakota Century Code 19-03.1-23
- North Dakota Century Code 12.1-32-01

Cultivation

Cultivation in North Dakota will be punished based upon the aggregate weight of the plants found. See the "Possession" section for further penalty details.

Hash & Concentrates

North Dakota defines hashish as "the resin extracted from any part of the plant cannabis with or without its adhering plant parts, whether growing or not, and every compound, manufacture, salt, derivative, mixture, or preparation of the resin." Hashish is a Schedule I controlled substance.

See
- North Dakota Century Code 19-03.1-01(14)
- North Dakota Century Code 19-03.1-05(5)(u)

Ingesting hashish is a class A misdemeanor punishable by a fine no greater than $3,000 and/or a term of imprisonment no greater than 1 year.

See
- North Dakota Century Code 19-03.1-22.3
- North Dakota Century Code 12.1-32-01(5)

Possessing any amount of hashish is a class C felony punishable by a fine no greater than $10,000 and/or a term of imprisonment no greater than 5 years. Possessing hashish within 1,000 feet of a school or career training center is a class B felony punishable by a fine no greater than $20,000 and/or a term of imprisonment no greater than 10 years.

See
- North Dakota Century Code 19-03.1-23(7)
- North Dakota Century Code 12.1-32-01(3),(4)

Manufacturing, delivering or possessing with intent to manufacture or deliver hashish is a class B felony punishable by a fine no greater than $20,000 and/or a term of imprisonment no greater than 10 years. A second conviction carries a minimum term of imprisonment of 3 years. A third or subsequent conviction carries a minimum term of imprisonment of 10 years. Manufacturing, delivering or possessing with intent to manufacture or deliver hashish within 1,000 feet of a school or career training center carries a mandatory 8 year term of imprisonment. Delivering hashish to a minor carries a mandatory 8 year term of imprisonment.

See
- North Dakota Century Code 19-03.1-23(1)(b)
- North Dakota Century Code 12.1-32-01(3)
- North Dakota Century Code 19-03.1-23(3)

Paraphernalia

Possession, manufacture, delivery, or advertisement of paraphernalia is a Class A Misdemeanor, punishable by a maximum sentence of 1 year imprisonment and a maximum fine of $3,000. Providing paraphernalia to a minor is a Class C Felony, which is punishable by a maximum sentence of 5 years imprisonment and a maximum fine of $10,000.

See
- North Dakota Century Code 19-03.4-01
- North Dakota Century Code 19-03.4-06
- North Dakota Century Code 12.1-32-01(4),(5)

Miscellaneous

Any conviction requires the offender to undergo a drug addiction evaluation.

If a juvenile is adjudicated delinquent of an offense that would be a class A misdemeanor or a felony if the offense were committed by an adult, the juvenile court may order the suspension of the juvenile's driving privileges for a period of up to six months for the first offense.

See
- North Dakota Century Code 27-20-31.1

OHIO
LAWS & PENALTIES

Offense	Penalty	Incarceration	Max. Fine
POSSESSION			
Less than 100 g	Misdemeanor	N/A	$ 150
100 - 200 g	Misdemeanor	30 days	$ 250
200 - 1,000 g	Felony	1 year	$ 2,500
1,000 - 20,000 g	Felony	1 - 5 years	$ 10,000
20,000 - 40,000 g	Felony	5* - 8 years	$ 15,000
More than 40,000 g	Felony	8 years*	$ 20,000

* Mandatory minimum sentence

SALE/DISTRIBUTION/TRAFFICKING			
A gift of 20 g or less (first offense)	Misdemeanor	N/A	$ 150
A gift of 20 g or less (second offense)	Misdemeanor	60 days	$ 500
Less than 200 g	Felony	1 year	$ 2,500
200 - 1,000 g	Felony	18 months	$ 2,500
1,000 - 20,000 g	Felony	1 - 5 years	$ 10,000
20,000 - 40,000 g	Felony	5* - 8 years	$ 15,000
More than 40,000 g	Felony	8 years*	$ 20,000

To a minor, within 1000 feet of a school, within 100 feet of a juvenile, or by one who has a previous drug conviction will increase the term of imprisonment and the fine.

* Mandatory minimum sentence

CULTIVATION			
See Possession			
HASH & CONCENTRATES			
Possession of less than 5g/1g (solid/liquid)	Misdemeanor	N/A	$ 150
Possession of 5g/1g - 10g/2g (solid/liquid)	Misdemeanor	30 days	$ 250
Possession of 10g/2g - 50g/10g (solid/liquid)	Felony	1 year	$ 2,500
Possession of 50g/10g - 1,000g/200g (solid/liquid)	Felony	3 years	$ 10,000
Possession of 1,000g/200g (solid/liquid) or more	Felony	8 years	$ 15,000
Selling less than 10g/2g (solid/liquid)	Felony	1 year	$ 2,500
Selling 10g/2g - 50g/10g (solid/liquid)	Felony	18 months	$ 5,000
Selling 50g/10g - 1,000g/200g (solid/liquid)	Felony	3 years	$ 10,000
Selling 1,000g/200g (solid/liquid) or more	Felony	8 years	$ 15,000
Manufacture	Felony	8 years	$ 15,000
PARAPHERNALIA			
Possession of paraphernalia	Misdemeanor	N/A	$ 150
Sale of paraphernalia	Misdemeanor	90 days	$ 750
MISCELLANEOUS			

Any drug conviction (including a paraphernalia conviction) may result in a driver's license suspension for a period of 6 months - 5 years.

Penalty Details

Possession

Possession of less than 100 grams is a minor misdemeanor punishable by a $150 fine.*

Possession of 100 - 200 grams is a misdemeanor punishable by a maximum sentence of 30 days imprisonment and a maximum fine of $250.

Possession of 200 - 1,000 grams is a felony, punishable by up to one year in jail and a maximum fine of $2,500.**

Possession of 1,000 - 20,000 grams is a third degree felony punishable by 1-5 years imprisonment and/or a fine of $5,000 - $10,000.

Possession of 20,000 - 40,000 grams is a second-degree felony punishable by between 5-8 years of imprisonment, and/or a maximum fine of $15,000.

Possession of more than 40,000 grams is a second-degree felony punishable by at least 8 years imprisonment and/or a maximum fine of $20,000.

See
- Ohio Rev. Code Ann. § 2925.11 (2015)

* A minor misdemeanor does not create a criminal record in Ohio.

Cultivation

Penalties for the cultivation of marijuana are identical to the penalties for possessing an equivalent amount, in weight, of marijuana. See the chart above for further guidance.

See
- Ohio Rev. Code Ann. §2925.04 (2015)

** Ohio provides an affirmative defense for this level of cultivation if the defendant can meet the burden to prove that the marijuana was intended solely for personal use by a preponderance of the evidence. If this defense is successful, the defendant can still be convicted of, or plead guilty to, a misdemeanor violation of illegal cultivation of marijuana.

Sale/Distribution/Trafficking

A gift of 20 grams or less is a minor misdemeanor punishable by a maximum fine of $150.

A second conviction for a gift of 20 grams or less is a misdemeanor punishable by a maximum sentence of 60 days imprisonment and a maximum fine of $500.

The sale of up to 200 grams is a felony, punishable by a maximum sentence of 12 months imprisonment and/or a maximum fine of $2,500.

The sale of 200 grams - 1,000 grams is a fourth degree felony, punishable by up to 18 months imprisonment and/or a maximum fine of $2,500.

The sale of 1,000 - 20,000 grams is a third degree felony punishable by a sentence of 1-5 years imprisonment and/or a maximum fine of $10,000.

The sale of 20,000 - 40,000 grams is a second-degree felony punishable by between 5-8 years imprisonment and/or a maximum fine of $15,000.

The sale of over 40,000 grams is a second-degree felony, punishable by a mandatory 8 years imprisonment and/or a maximum fine of $20,000.

The sale of marijuana to a minor, within 1,000 feet of a school, within 100 feet of a juvenile, or by one who has a previous drug conviction is a felony which will increase the length of the term of imprisonment and the fine.

See
- Ohio Rev. Code Ann. § 2925.03 (2015)
- Ohio Rev. Code Ann. § 2929.13 (2015)
- Ohio Rev. Code Ann. § 2929.18 (2015)
- Ohio Rev. Code Ann. § 2929.22 (2015)

Hash & Concentrates

Possession of up to 5 grams of solid hashish (1 gram of liquid hashish) is a minor misdemeanor punishable by a fine no greater than $150.

Possession of 5-10 grams of solid hashish (1-2 grams of liquid hashish) is a misdemeanor punishable by a fine no greater than $250 and/or a term of imprisonment no greater than 30 days.

Possession of 10-50 grams of solid hashish (2-10 grams of liquid hashish) is a felony punishable by a maximum fine of $2,500 and/or a maximum term of 1-year imprisonment.

Possession 50 -1,000 grams of solid hashish (10 - 200 grams of liquid hashish) is a felony punishable by a fine no greater than $10,000 and/or a term of imprisonment no less than 9 months and no greater than 3 years.

Possession of 1,000- 2,000 grams of solid hashish (200 - 400 grams of liquid hashish) is a felony in the second degree, punishable by up to 8 years imprisonment and/ or up to a $15,000 fine.

Possession of over 2,000 grams of solid hashish (400 grams of liquid hashish) is a felony in the second degree punishable by a fine no greater than $15,000 and/or a term of imprisonment of 8 years.

See
- Ohio Rev. Code Ann. §2925.11(C)(7) (2015)
- Ohio Rev. Code Ann. §2929.28 (2015)
- Ohio Rev. Code Ann. §2929.24 (2015)
- Ohio Rev. Code Ann. §2929.18 (2015)
- Ohio Rev. Code Ann. §2929.14 (2015)

Selling less than 10 grams of solid hashish (less than 2 grams of liquid hashish) is a felony punishable by a maximum fine of $2,500 and/or a term of imprisonment no less than 6 months and no greater than 1 year.

Selling 10 - 50 grams of solid hashish (2 -10 grams) of liquid hashish is a felony punishable by a fine no greater than $5,000 and/ or a term of imprisonment no less than 6 months and no greater than 18 months.

Selling between 50 - 250 grams of solid hashish (10-50 grams of liquid hashish) is a felony, punishable by a fine no greater than $10,000 and/or a term of imprisonment no less than 9 months and no greater than 3 years.

Selling between 250- 1,000 grams of solid hashish (50 -200 grams of liquid hashish) is a felony punishable by a fine no greater than $10,000 and/or a term of imprisonment no less than 9 months and no greater than 3 years.

Selling between 1,000 - 2,000 grams of solid hashish (200 - 400 grams of liquid hashish) is a felony punishable by a fine no greater than $15,000 and a term of imprisonment no less than 5 years and no greater than 8 years.

Selling over 2,000 grams of solid hashish (over 400 grams of liquid hashish) is a felony by a maximum fine of $15,000 and /or a term of imprisonment of 8 years.

See
- Ohio Rev. Code Ann., §2925.03(C)(7) (2015)
- Ohio Rev. Code Ann. §2929.18 (2015)
- Ohio Rev.Code Ann. §§2929.14 (2015)

Manufacturing hashish is a felony of the second degree punishable by a maximum fine of $15,000 and a maximum of 8 years imprisonment.

See
- Ohio Rev. Code Ann. §2925.04(C)(2) (2015)
- Ohio Rev. Code Ann. § 2929.18 (2015)
- Ohio Rev. Code Ann. §2929.14 (2015)

Paraphernalia

Possession of marijuana paraphernalia is a minor misdemeanor, punishable by a maximum fine of $150, possible community service, and suspension of the offender's driver's license for 6 months - five years.

See
- Ohio Rev. Code Ann. § 2925.141 (2015)

The sale of paraphernalia is a misdemeanor punishable by a maximum sentence of 90 days imprisonment and a maximum fine of $750.

See
- Ohio Rev. Code Ann. § 2925.14 (2015)
- Ohio Rev. Code Ann. § 2929.13 (2015)
- Ohio Rev. Code Ann. § 2929.22 (2015)

Any device or equipment used to create or manufacture hashish is considered drug paraphernalia. Possession of such equipment is a misdemeanor of the fourth degree punishable by a maximum fine of $250 and/or maximum 30-day jail sentence. Selling or manufacturing any such device or equipment is a misdemeanor of the second degree punishable by maximum fine of $750 and/or a maximum 90-day term of imprisonment. If any such device or equipment was sold to a minor, the offense is a misdemeanor in the first degree punishable by a fine no greater than $1,000 and/or a term of imprisonment no greater than 180 days. Advertising the sale of such equipment is a misdemeanor, punishable by a fine no greater than $750 and a term of imprisonment no greater than 90 days.

See
- Ohio Rev. Code Ann. §2925.14(2) (2015)
- Ohio Rev. Code Ann. §2929.18 (2015)
- Ohio Rev. Code Ann. §2929.14 (2015)

Miscellaneous

Any conviction for possession of a controlled substance is subject to driver's license revocation for no less than 6 months and no more than 5 years.

See
- Ohio Rev. Code Ann. § 2925.11(E)(2) (2015)
- Ohio Rev. Code Ann. § 2925. 14 (2015)

OKLAHOMA
LAWS & PENALTIES

Offense	Penalty	Incarceration	Max. Fine
POSSESSION			
Any amount (first offense)	N/A	1 year	$ 0
Any amount (subsequent offense)	Felony	2 - 10 years	$ 0
SALE OR DISTRIBUTION			
Less than 25 lbs	Felony	2 years - life	$ 20,000
25 - 1000 lbs	Felony	4 years - life	$ 100,000
1000 lbs or more	Felony	4 years - life	$ 500,000

To a minor carries a double period of incarceration and fine.

Within 2000 feet of schools, public parks, or public housing carries a double period of incarceration and fine, and a mandatory minimum sentence.

CULTIVATION			
See Possession and Sale sections for details.			
HASH & CONCENTRATES			
Possession	Misdemeanor	1 year	$ 1,000
Distributing, dispensing, transporting or possession with intent	Felony	2 years - life	$ 20,000
Converting marijuana into hashish or concentrates	Felony	2 years - life	$ 50,000
PARAPHERNALIA			
Possession of paraphernalia (first offense)	Misdemeanor	1 year	$ 1,000
Possession of paraphernalia (second offense)	Misdemeanor	1 year	$ 5,000
Possession of paraphernalia (third offense)	Misdemeanor	1 year	$ 10,000
MISCELLANEOUS			
Any conviction will lead to a driver's license suspension from 6 months - 3 years.			

Possession

Possession of any amount of marijuana is a crime, subject to up to one year of incarceration (conditional release may be granted).

A subsequent conviction for possession is a felony which carries the penalty of 2-10 years of incarceration.

See
• Okla. Stat. tit. 63, § 2-401 (2015)

Sale or Distribution

The sale of less than 25 pounds is a felony, punishable by incarceration for a period of 2 years-life, as well as a fine of $20,000.

Selling between 25 and 1,000 pounds. Penalties include a fine of between $25,000 and $100,000, between four years and life imprisonment, or both.

Selling 1,000 pounds or more is punishable with a maximum fine of $500,000, and/or between four years and life imprisonment.

The sale to minors is a felony, which is punishable by doubling the penalty for both the period of incarceration, as well as the fine to be paid.

The sale within 2,000 feet of schools, public parks, or public housing is a felony, punishable by a double penalty for both the period of incarceration as well as the fine to be paid. A conviction carries with it a mandatory minimum sentence of 50% of the imposed sentence.

See
• Okla. Stat. tit. 63 § 2-401 (2015)

Cultivation

Cultivating up to 1,000 plants is a felony, punishable by a maximum $25,000 fine and between 20 years and life imprisonment. Cultivation of more than 1,000 plants is punishable of a fine up to $50,0000 and between 20 years and life imprisonment.

See
• Okla. Stat. tit. 63 § 2-401 (2015)

Hash & Concentrates

Hashish or concentrates fall under Oklahoma's definition of marijuana and are Schedule I drugs.

See
• Okla. Stat. tit. 63 § 2-101 (2015)
• Okla. Stat. tit. 63 § 2-204(C)(12) (2015)

Converting or attempting to convert marijuana into hashish or concentrates is a felony punishable by a fine no greater than $50,000 and a term of imprisonment no less than 2 and up to remainder of the offender's life. Subsequent convictions are punishable by a fine no greater than $100,000 and a term of imprisonment greater than 4 years and up to the remainder of the offender's life.

See
• Okla. Stat. tit. 63 § 2-509 (2015)

Distributing, dispensing, transporting with intent to distribute, possessing with intent to manufacture, distribute, or dispense, hashish or concentrates is a felony punishable by a fine no greater than $20,000 and a term of imprisonment no less than 2 years and up to the remainder of the offender's life.

See
• Oklahoma Stat. tit. 63 § 2-401 (2015)

Possessing hashish or concentrates is a misdemeanor punishable by a fine no greater than $1,000 and/or a term of imprisonment no greater than 1 year. A second or subsequent conviction is punishable by a fine no greater than $5,000 and/or a term of imprisonment no less than 2 years and no greater than 10 years. If the offense occurred within 1,000 feet of a school, recreation center, public park, or in the presence of a child under 12 years of age, the offense becomes a felony punishable by a fine no greater than $2,000 and/or a term of imprisonment no greater than 2 years. A second or subsequent conviction for possession of hashish or concentrates within 1,000 feet of a school, recreation center, public park, or in the presence of a child under 12 years of age is punishable by a fine no greater than $10,000 and/or a term of imprisonment no less than 4 years and no greater than 20 years.

See
• Okla. Stat. tit. 63 § 2-402(B)(2) (2015)
• Okla. Stat. tit. 63 § 2-402 (C) (2015)

Any equipment or device used to create hashish or concentrates is considered paraphernalia. Possessing, transporting, using, or manufacturing any such equipment or device is a misdemeanor punishable by a fine no greater than $1,000 and/or a term of imprisonment no greater than 1 year. A second conviction is punishable by a fine no greater than $5,000 and/or a term of imprisonment no greater than 1 year. A third conviction is punishable by a fine no greater than $10,000 and/or a term of imprisonment no greater than 1 year.

See
• Okla. Stat. tit. 63 § 2-101(36) (2015)
• Okla. Stat. tit. 63 § 2-405 (2015)

Paraphernalia

A conviction for possession of paraphernalia is a misdemeanor that is punishable by up to one-year imprisonment as well as a $1,000 fine.

A second paraphernalia conviction is a misdemeanor that is punishable by up to one-year imprisonment as well as a $5,000 fine.

A third paraphernalia conviction is a misdemeanor that is punishable by up to one-year imprisonment and a $10,000 fine.

See
• Okla. Stat. tit. 63 § 2-405 (2015)

Miscellaneous

Any conviction will lead to a driver's license suspension from 6 months to 3 years. Immediately revoke for any conviction of misdemeanor or felony conviction for possessing, distributing, dispensing, manufacturing, trafficking, cultivating or selling a controlled substance.

See
• Okla. Stat. tit. 47 § 6-205(A)(6) (2015)

OREGON
LAWS & PENALTIES

Offense	Penalty	Incarceration	Max. Fine
POSSESSION			
In Public			
1 oz or less	No Penalty	None	$ 0
More than 1 – 2 oz	Violation	N/A	$ 650
More than 2 - 4 oz	Misdemeanor	6 months	$ 2,500
More than 4 oz	Misdemeanor	1 year	$ 6,250
At Home			
8 oz or less homegrown	No Penalty	None	$ 0
More than 1 – 2 lbs	Misdemeanor	6 months	$ 2,500
More than 2 lbs	Misdemeanor	1 year	$ 6,250
MANUFACTURE, DELIVERY, OR DISTRIBUTION			
Manufacture			
Any amount	Felony	5 years	$ 125,000
Within 1000 feet of school grounds	Felony	20 years	$ 375,000
Personal home gardens and licensed production sites exempted.			
Delivery			
1 oz or less homegrown without compensation	No Penalty	None	$ 0
More than 1 oz - 16 oz without compensation	Violation	None	$ 2,000
16 oz or more with compensation	Misdemeanor	1 year	$ 6,250
To a minor	Felony	5 years	$ 125,000
Within 1000 feet of school grounds	Felony	20 years	$ 375,000
Delivery with or without compensation of 150 g or more is punished more severely.			
CULTIVATION			
Up to 4 plants homegrown	No Penalty	None	$ 0
More than 4 - 8 plants	Misdemeanor	6 months	$ 2,500
More than 8 plants homegrown or any amount away from home (unlicensed)	Felony	5 years	$ 125,000
Within 1,000 feet of a school (except home-grown or licensed)	Felony	20 years	$ 375,000
HASH & CONCENTRATES			
16 oz or less solid infused at home	No Penalty	None	$ 0
72 oz or less liquid infused at home	No Penalty	None	$ 0
1 oz or less extract at home	No Penalty	None	$ 0
0.25 oz or less not purchased from retailer	Misdemeanor	6 months	$ 2,500
More than 0.25 oz not purchased from retailer	Felony	5 years	$ 125,000
Note that processing, or extracting is Manufacturing under Oregon law.			
PARAPHERNALIA			
Sale, delivery, possession with intent to sell or deliver, or manufacture with intent sell or deliver	Civil Penalty	N/A	$ 10,000
CIVIL ASSET FORFEITURE			
Vehicles and other property may be seized.			
MISCELLANEOUS			
Knowingly maintaining a structure used for drug offenses	Misdemeanor	1 year	$ 6,250
Commercial drug offenses are punished more severely.			

A conviction for possession of more than 1 oz, delivery, or Cultivation of marijuana can result in an automatic 6 months suspension of driving privileges.

Penalty Details

Marijuana is a Schedule II substance under the Oregon Uniform Controlled Substances Act as decided by rulemaking by the Oregon Board of Pharmacy.

See
- Oregon Rev. Stat. § 574.059
Oregon Admin. R. 855-080-022

Possession
In Public

There is no fine or penalty for possession of 1 ounce or less of marijuana in public. However, the use of any marijuana is a class B violation punishable by a maximum fine of $1,000.

Possession of more than 1 – 2 ounces of marijuana is a class B violation punishable by a fine of up to $1,000.

Possession of more than 2 – 4 ounces of marijuana is a class B misdemeanor punishable by up to 6 months in prison jail and a fine of up to $2,500.

Possession of more than 4 ounces of marijuana is a class A misdemeanor punishable by up to 1 year in prison and a fine of up to $6,250.

At Home

There is no fine or penalty for possession of 8 ounces or less of " homegrown" marijuana if at home.

Possession of more than 1 – 2 pounds of marijuana at home is a class B misdemeanor punishable by up to 6 months in prison and a fine of up to $2,500.

Possession more than 2 pounds of marijuana at home is a class A misdemeanor punishable by up to 1 year in prison and a fine of up to $6,250.

See
- Oregon Rev. Stat. §§ 153.005 - .021
- Oregon Rev. Stat. §§ 161.605 - .685
- Oregon Rev. Stat. § 161.615
- Oregon Rev. Stat. § 161.625
- Oregon Rev. Stat. § 161.635
- Oregon Rev. Stat. § 475.864
- Oregon Rev. Stat. § 475.900(2)(b)(E)
- Sentencing Grid of the Oregon Criminal Justice Commission
  http://www.oregon.gov/cjc/about/Documents/guidelinesgrid.pdf

Commercial Sale and Regulation

Retail sales of cannabis by state-licensed entities to those over the age of 21 are regulated in this state beginning in 2016. State-licensed medical dispensaries are permitted to begin sales to non-medical persons age 21 or older on October 1, 2015. Sales to adults will be limited to no more than one-quarter ounce per person, per visit, per day. Marijuana sales by unlicensed entities remain subject to criminal penalties as described above.

The Oregon Liquor Control Commission has until January 1, 2016, to implement regulations on production, processing, and commercial sale of marijuana. Applications to grow, process, or sell marijuana for personal use will be accepted by the state starting January 4, 2016. The state will start issuing licenses during the first half of 2016. Application and licensing fees be set by the OLCC during rulemaking.

Manufacture, Delivery, or Distribution
Manufacture

Manufacture of any amount of marijuana is a class C felony punishable by up to 5 years in prison and a fine of up to $1,250, except for home gardens of 4 plants and licensed production sites and medical marijuana growsites.

Manufacture of marijuana within 1,000 feet of school grounds is a class A felony punishable by up to 20 years in prison and a fine of up to $375,000, except for home gardens of 4 plants and licensed production sites and medical marijuana growsites.

Delivery

Delivery of 1 ounce or less of "homegrown" marijuana without compensation carries no fine or penalty.

Delivery of more than 1 ounce - 16 ounces of marijuana without compensation is a Class A violation punishable by a fine not to exceed $2,000. Delivery of 16 ounces or more of marijuana with compensation is a misdemeanor by up to 1 year imprisonment and/or a fine up to $6,250.

Delivery of any amount of marijuana to a minor is a class C felony punishable by up to 5 years in prison and a fine of up to $125,000.

Delivery of any amount marijuana within 1,000 feet of school grounds is a class A felony punishable by up to 20 years in prison and a fine of up to $375,000.

Any delivery (with or without compensation) of 150 grams or more is punished more severely with the term of imprisonment varying depending on the offender's prior record.

See
- Oregon Rev. Stat. § 153.005 - 025
- Oregon Rev. Stat. §§ 161.605 - .685
- Oregon Rev. Stat. § 161.615
- Oregon Rev. Stat. § 161.625
- Oregon Rev. Stat. § 161.635
- Oregon Rev. Stat. § 475.856
- Oregon Rev. Stat. § 475.900(1)(a)(E)
- Oregon Rev. Stat. § 475.862
- Sentencing Grid of the Oregon Criminal Justice Commission
  http://www.oregon.gov/cjc/about/Documents/guidelinesgrid.pdf

Cultivation

There is no fine or penalty for cultivation of up to 4 plants homgrown at home.

Cultivation of more than 4 - 8 plants is a Class B misdemeanor punishable by up to 6 months imprisonment and/or a fine up to $2,500.

See
- Oregon Rev. Stat. § 153.005 - 025
- Oregon Rev. Stat. § 161.605
- Oregon Rev. Stat. § 161.625
- Oregon Rev. Stat. § 475.856
- Oregon Rev. Stat. § 475.858
- Oregon Rev. Stat. § 475.900(1)(a)(E)
- Oregon Rev. Stat. § 475.900(1)(c)

- Sentencing Grid of the Oregon Criminal Justice Commission
  http://www.oregon.gov/cjc/about/Documents/guidelinesgrid.pdf

Hash & Concentrates
Possession

There is no fine or penalty for possession of 16 ounces or less of solid infused cannabinoid products, 72 ounces or less of liquid infused cannabinoid products and 1 ounce or less of cannabinoid extracts at home.

Possession of ¼ ounce or less of cannabinoid extract not purchased from retailer is a class B misdemeanor punishable by up to 6 months in prison and a fine of up to $2,500.

Possession of more than ¼ ounce of cannabinoid extract not purchased from retailer is a class C felony punishable by up to 5 years in prison and a fine of up to $125,000.

Note that processing, or extracting is Manufacturing under Oregon law.

See
- Oregon Rev. Stat. § 153.005 - 025
- Oregon Rev. Stat. § 161.605 - .685
- Oregon Rev. Stat. § 475.005(16)
- Oregon Rev. Stat. § 475.864
- Oregon Rev. Stat. § 475.900
- Oregon v. Ness, 635 P.2d 1025
- Or. Ct. App. 1981

Paraphernalia

Sale, delivery, possession with intent to sell or deliver, or manufacture with intent to sell paraphernalia is subject to a civil penalty of $2,000 to $10,000.

See
- Oregon Rev. Stat. § 475.525
- Oregon Rev. Stat. § 475.565

Sentencing

Oregon determines the length of sentence by using a sentence grid.

See
- Sentencing Grid of the Oregon Criminal Justice Commission
  http://www.oregon.gov/cjc/about/Documents/guidelinesgrid.pdf

Diversion: The courts may defer the proceedings for first time possession offenders and place them on probation. If the individual violates the terms of his/her probation, the courts will terminate the probation and find the defendant guilty. Upon successful completion of probation, courts will dismiss the case.

See
- Oregon Rev. Stat. § 475.245

Forfeiture
Criminal

Vehicles and other property may be seized for violations of the Oregon Uniform Controlled Substances Act. The seizing agency, in conjunction with the district attorney, has 30 days to determine if it will pursue a criminal forfeiture proceeding. Should the district attorney decide to pursue criminal forfeiture, it shall be brought in the same proceding as the underlying offense. When property has been seized, a person with an interest in it (other than the defendant) has 15 days from actual knowledge or notice, whichever is earlier, to file a motion to show cause.

See
- Oregon Rev. Stat. § 131.558
- Oregon Rev. Stat. §§ 131.564(2), (8)
- Oregon Rev. Stat. § 131.582(4)

Civil

Vehicles and other property may be seized for violations of the Oregon Uniform Controlled Substances Act. The seizing agency, in conjunction with the district attorney, has 30 days to determine if it will pursue a civil forfeiture proceeding. Forfeiture notice may be given by the police officer when seizing the property or within 15 days of the seizure by the seizing agency. Those claiming an interest in the property have 21 days after forfeiture notice to file a claim with the agency's forfeiture counsel. There can be no forfeiture without a criminal conviction.

See
- Oregon Rev. Stat. § 131A.020
- Oregon Rev. Stat. § 131A.105
- Oregon Rev. Stat. §§ 131A.150(2)-(3)
- Oregon Rev. Stat. § 131A.165

Miscellaneous
Commercial drug offense

Possession, delivery, or cultivation of marijuana can be considered a commercial drug offense if 3 factors out of a long list are satisfied, including the delivery was for compensation, the person was in possession of $300 or more in cash, they possessed materials for the packaging of controlled substances, among many others. Commercial drug offenses are punished more severely with the term of imprisonment varying depending on the offender's prior record.

See
- Oregon Rev. Stat. § 475.900(b)
- Sentencing Grid of the Oregon Criminal Justice Commission
  http://www.oregon.gov/cjc/about/Documents/guidelinesgrid.pdf

Knowingly maintaining a structure used for drug offenses

It is a Class A misdemeanor punishable by up to 1 year imprisonment and/or a fine up to $6,250 to maintain a structure (including houses and vehicles) that the owner knows is used for using, storing, or selling marijuana.

See
- Oregon Rev. Stat. § 161.615
- Oregon Rev. Stat. § 161.635
- Oregon Rev. Stat. § 475.914

Suspension of Driving Privileges

A conviction for possession of one ounce or more, delivery, or cultivation of marijuana results in an automatic 6 month suspension of driving privileges, unless the court finds compelling reasons not to suspend the driving privileges.

See
- Oregon Rev. Stat. § 809.265
- Oregon Rev. Stat. § 809.280(10)

PENNSYLVANIA
LAWS & PENALTIES

Offense	Penalty	Incarceration	Max. Fine
POSSESSION			
30g or less	Misdemeanor	30 days	$ 500
More than 30g	Misdemeanor	1 year	$ 5,000

First possession conviction is eligible for conditional release. Subsequent conviction can lead to a doubled penalty.

Offense	Penalty	Incarceration	Max. Fine
SALE OR DISTRIBUTION			
30g or less for no remuneration	Misdemeanor	30 days	$ 500
2 - 10 lbs	Felony	1 year	$ 5,000
10 - 50 lbs	Felony	3 years	$ 25,000
Less than 1000 lbs	Felony	3 years	$ 25,000
More than 1000 lbs	Felony	10 years	$ 100,000

Within 1000 ft of a school or within 250 ft of recreational playground punishable by 2-4 years in prison.

To a minor, or after a previous drug conviction, brings doubled penalties.

Courts are authorized to increase the maximum fine to exhaust all proceeds from drug sales.

Offense	Penalty	Incarceration	Max. Fine
CULTIVATION			
Any number of plants	Felony	1 - 5 years	$ 15,000
HASH & CONCENTRATES			
Possession of 8 g or less	Misdemeanor	30 days	$ 500
Possession of more than 8 g	Misdemeanor	1 year	$ 5,000
Manufacture	Felony	5 years	$ 15,000

Penalties for selling or Trafficking hashish or concentrates are the same as the Trafficking penalties for marijuana. Please see the marijuana penalties section for further details.

Offense	Penalty	Incarceration	Max. Fine
PARAPHERNALIA			
Possession or sale of paraphernalia	Misdemeanor	1 year	$ 2,500
To a minor at least 3 years younger	Misdemeanor	2 year	$ 5,000
MISCELLANEOUS			

Suspension of driving privileges upon receiving a conviction of any offense involving the possession, sale, and delivery of any controlled substance.

Penalty Details

Marijuana is a Schedule I controlled substance.

See
- Pennsylvania Consolidated Statutes

Possession

Possession of 30 grams or less is a misdemeanor punishable by 30 days in jail and/or a $500 fine.

Possession of more than 30 grams is a misdemeanor with a maximum penalty of one/or year in jail and a $5,000 fine.

First possession conviction is eligible for conditional release, wherein the offender gets probation for up to a year instead of jail time.

A second or subsequent conviction can lead to a doubled penalty.

See
- 35 PA. Cons. Stat § 780-113
- 35 P.S. §780-113(a)(16)

Sale or Distribution

Distribution of 30g or less of marijuana without compensation is a misdemeanor punishable by up to 30 days in jail and a fine of up to $500.

Sale of less than 1,000 pounds is a felony punishable by up to 3 years in jail and a $25,000 fine. If the offender has a prior drug conviction, then the sentence is 3 years and the fine will be $25,000. The court is authorized to increase the fines beyond the maximum to exhaust the proceeds of the crime.

Selling 2-10 pounds of marijuana carries a sentence of 1 year in jail and a $5,000 fine. These penalties are doubled if the conviction is a second or subsequent drug offense or if the sale is to a minor. The court is authorized to increase the fines beyond the maximum to exhaust the proceeds of the crime.

Sale of more than 1,000 pounds is a felony with a maximum penalty of 10 years in prison and a $100,000 fine. These penalties are doubled if the conviction is a second or subsequent drug offense or if the sale is to a minor. The court is authorized to increase the fines beyond the maximum to exhaust the proceeds of the crime.

Delivery of marijuana within 1,000 ft of a school or within 250 ft. of recreational playground is punishable by 2-4 years in prison.

Distribution to a minor by one over the age of 21 is a felony and brings doubled penalties upon conviction.

See
- 35 PA. Cons. Stat.§ 780-113
- 18 PA. Cons. Stat. § 106
- 18 PA. Cons. Stat. § 1101
- 18 PA. Cons. Stat. § 1103
- 18 PA. Cons. Stat.§ 1104

Cultivation

Growing marijuana, even with no intention of selling it, is a felony and is punishable up to five years in prison and $15,000 in fines. The Pennsylvania Sentencing Guidelines state that possession with intent to deliver less than 10 plants is felony.

See
- 35 PA. Cons. Stat. § 780-113
- 18 PA. Cons. Stat. § 106
- 18 PA. Cons. Stat. § 1101
- 18 PA. Cons. Stat. § 1103
- 18 PA. Cons. Stat. § 1104

Hash & Concentrates

Hashish and THC concentrates are Schedule I drugs.

See
- 35 PA. Cons. Stat. §780-102
- 35 PA. Cons. Stat. §780-104(i)(iii)(16)

Possessing less than 8 grams of hashish or concentrates is a misdemeanor punishable by a fine no greater than $500 and/or a term of imprisonment no greater than 30 days. Possessing more than 8 grams of hashish or concentrates is a misdemeanor punishable by a fine no greater than $5,000 or a term of imprisonment no greater than 1 year.

See
- 35 PA. Cons. Stat. §780-113(b)
- 35 PA. Cons. Stat. §780-113(g)

Manufacturing hashish or concentrates is a felony punishable by a fine no greater than $15,000 and/or a term of imprisonment no greater than 5 years. Subsequent convictions for manufacturing hashish are punishable by a fine no greater than $30,000 and/or a term of imprisonment no greater than 10 years.

See
- 35 PA. Cons. Stat. §780-113(a)(30)
- 35 PA. Cons. Stat. §780-113(f)(2)
- 35 PA. Cons. Stat. §780-115(a)

The offenses and penalties for selling or trafficking hashish or concentrates are the same as the trafficking penalties for marijuana. For more information see Pennsylvania's marijuana laws section of this website.

Any device or equipment used to manufacture or create hashish or concentrates is considered drug paraphernalia. Possession of any such device or equipment is a misdemeanor punishable by a fine no greater than $2,500 and/or imprisonment no greater than 1 year. Manufacturing or selling any such device or equipment is a misdemeanor punishable by a fine no greater than $2,500 and/or a term of imprisonment no greater than 1 year. If any such device or equipment was sold to a minor, the offense is a misdemeanor of the second degree punishable by a fine no greater than $5,000 and/or a term of imprisonment no greater than 2 years. Advertising the sale of any such device or equipment is a misdemeanor punishable by a fine no greater than $2,500 and/or a term of imprisonment no greater than 1 year.

See
- 35 PA. Cons. Stat. §780-102(b)
- 35 PA. Cons. Stat. §780-113(31)-(34)
- 35 PA. Cons. Stat. §780-113(i)

Paraphernalia

Possessing or selling paraphernalia is a misdemeanor punishable with up to 1 year in jail and a fine of not more than $2,500. Delivering paraphernalia to a minor who is 3 or more years his junior is a second-degree misdemeanor punishable by not more than 2 years and a fine not exceeding $5,000.

See
- 35 PA. Cons. Stat. § 780-113
- 18 PA. Cons. Stat. § 106
- 18 PA. Cons. Stat. § 1101
- 10 PA. Cons. Stat. § 1103
- 18 PA. Cons. Stat. § 1104

Sentencing

Sentencing for marijuana crimes in PA varies by the weight of the plant matter seized.

In PA, all first time drug convictions have the possibility for probation for a first offense.

A second or subsequent drug related conviction makes the offender eligible for double penalties.

See
- 35 PA. Cons. Stat. § 780-113
- 18 PA. Cons. Stat. § 106
- 18 PA. Cons. Stat. § 1101
- 18 PA. Cons. Stat. § 1103
- 18 PA. Cons. Stat. § 1104

Miscellaneous

The department shall suspend the operating privilege of any person upon receiving a certified record of the person's conviction of any offense involving the possession, sale, delivery, offering for sale, holding fr sale or giving away of any controlled substance under the laws of the US, this Commonwealth or any other state. (1st offense six months, 2nd one year, 3+ two years).

See
- PA. Cons. Stat. § 1532(c)

RHODE ISLAND
LAWS & PENALTIES

Offense	Penalty	Incarceration	Max. Fine
POSSESSION			
Personal Use			
Less than 1 oz	Civil Violation	None	$ 150
1 oz - 1 kg	Misdemeanor	1 year	$ 500
With Intent to Distribute			
1 - 5 kg	Felony	10* - 50 years	$ 500,000
More than 5 kg	Felony	25 years* - life	$ 100,000
Within 300 yards of a school may result in double penalty.			
1 kg is approximately 35 oz			
* Mandatory minimum sentence			
SALE OR CULTIVATION			
Less than 1 kg	Felony	30 years	$ 100,000
1 - 5 kg	Felony	10* - 50 years	$ 500,000
More than 5 kg	Felony	20 years* - life	$ 10,000
To a minor at least three years younger	Felony	2 - 5 years	$ 100,000
Within 300 yards of a school may result in double penalty.			
1 kg is approximately 35 oz			
* Mandatory minimum sentence			
HASH & CONCENTRATES			
Penalties for hashish are the same as for marijuana. Please see the marijuana penalties section for further details.			
PARAPHERNALIA			
Manufacture, sale, delivery, or possession with intent to sell or deliver	Not Classified	2 years	$ 5,000
Delivery to a person under 18 years	Not Classified	5 years	$ 5,000
MISCELLANEOUS			
Possession while driving will result in a driver's license suspension for a period of 6 months.			

Penalty Details

Possession for Personal Use

Possession of marijuana up to one ounce by an individual 18 years or older is a civil violation, punishable by a $150 fine, no jail time, and no criminal record.

Possession of 1 ounce to 1 kilogram is a misdemeanor that is punishable by a maximum of 1 year imprisonment and a maximum fine of $500.

See
- R.I. Gen. Laws § 21-28-4.01 (2015)
- R.I. Gen. Laws § 21-28-2.08 (2015)

Possession with Intent to Distribute

Possession of between 1-5 kilograms is a felony punishable by a mandatory minimum sentence of 10 years and a maximum of 50 years imprisonment and a maximum fine of $500,000.

Possession of more than 5 kilograms is a felony punishable by a mandatory minimum sentence of 25 years and a maximum sentence of life imprisonment as well as a maximum fine of $100,000.

Sale or possession within 300 yards of a school may result in a doubling of the penalties.

Possession while driving will result in a driver's license suspension for a period of 6 months.

See
- R.I. Gen. Laws § 21-28-4.01 (2015)
- R.I. Gen Laws § 21-28- 2.08 (2015)

Sale or Cultivation

Sale or cultivation of less than 1 kilogram is a felony punishable by a maximum sentence of 30 years imprisonment and a maximum fine of $100,000.

Sale or cultivation of between 1-5 kilograms is punishable by a mandatory minimum sentence of 10 years imprisonment and a maximum sentence of 50 years imprisonment as well as a maximum fine of $500,000.

Sale or cultivation of 5 kilograms or more is punishable by a mandatory minimum sentence of 20 years imprisonment and a maximum of life imprisonment as well as a maximum fine of $500,000.

Delivery to a minor at least three years younger than the offender carries with it the additional penalty of between 2-5 years imprisonment and a maximum fine of $10,000.

Sale or possession within 300 yards of a school, public park, or playground doubles the penalties.

See
- R.I. Gen. Laws § 21-28- 401.2 (2015)
- R.I. Gen. Laws § 21-28- 2.08 (2015)
- R.I. Gen. Laws § 21-28-4.07 (2015)

Hash & Concentrates

Hashish and concentrates fall under the definition of marijuana.

See
- R.I. Gen. Laws § 21-28-1.02 (26) (2015)

Paraphernalia

The manufacture, sale, delivery, or possession with the intent to sell or deliver, of paraphernalia is punishable by a fine not exceeding five thousand dollars ($5,000) and up to two (2) years imprisonment.

Any person eighteen (18) years of age or over who delivers drug paraphernalia to a person under eighteen (18) years of age shall be subject to a fine not to exceed five thousand dollars ($5,000) and imprisonment not to exceed five (5) years.

See
- R.I. Gen. Laws § 21-28.5-2 (2015)

Miscellaneous

Possession while driving will result in a driver's license suspension for a period of 6 months.

See
- R.I. Gen. Laws § 21-28- 2.08 (2015)
- R.I. Gen. Laws § 21-28-2.03 (2015)
- R.I. Gen. Laws § 21-28.4.01 (2015)

If the offense involves the use of any automobile to transport the substance or the substance is found within an automobile, then a person convicted or who pleads nolo contendere shall be subjected to a loss of license for a period of six months for a first offense and one year for each offense after this.

See
- R.I. Gen. Laws § 21- 28-4.01(4)(iv) (2015)

SOUTH CAROLINA
LAWS & PENALTIES

Offense	Penalty	Incarceration	Max. Fine
POSSESSION			
1 oz or less (first offense)	Misdemeanor	30 days	$ 200
1 oz or less (subsequent offense)	Misdemeanor	1 year	$ 2,000
SALE OR TRAFFICKING			
Less than 10 lbs	Felony	5 years	$ 5,000
10 - 100 lbs (first offense)	Felony	1* - 10 years	$ 10,000
10 - 100 lbs (second offense)	Felony	5* - 20 years	$ 25,000
10 - 100 lbs (third offense)	Felony	25 years*	$ 25,000
100 - 2000 lbs	Felony	25 years*	$ 25,000
2,000 - 10,000 lbs	Felony	25 years*	$ 50,000
More than 10,000 lbs	Felony	25 years*	$ 200,000
To a minor, or within a 1/2 mile of a school, playground, or public park	Felony	10 years	$ 10,000
* Mandatory minimum sentence			
CULTIVATION			
Less than 100 plants	Felony	5 years	$ 5,000
100 - 1000 plants	Felony	25 years*	$ 25,000
1000 - 10,000 plants	Felony	25 years*	$ 50,000
More than 10,000 plants	Felony	25 years*	$ 200,000
* Mandatory minimum sentence			
HASH & CONCENTRATES			
Possession of 10 g or less	Misdemeanor	30 days	$ 200
Possession of more than 10 g	Misdemeanor	5 years	$ 5,000
Subsequent offenses carry greater penalties			
PARAPHERNALIA			
Possession of paraphernalia	Civil Citation	N/A	$ 500

Penalty Details

Possession

Possession of 1 ounce or less is a misdemeanor punishable by a maximum sentence of 30 days imprisonment and a fine of $100-$200.*

* A conditional release based upon participation in the pretrial intervention program may be granted.

A subsequent conviction for possession of 1 ounce or less is a misdemeanor punishable by a maximum sentence of 1 year imprisonment and a maximum fine of $2,000.

See
- S.C. Code Ann. § 44-53-110 (2015)
- S.C. Code Ann. § 44-53-190(d), 44-53-370(a) (2015)
- S.C. Code Ann. § 44-53-370 (2015)

Sale or Trafficking

Sale of up to 10 pounds is a felony punishable by a maximum sentence of 5 years imprisonment and a maximum fine of $5,000.

Sale of between 10 pounds and 100 pounds is a felony punishable, for a first offense, by a mandatory minimum sentence of 1 year imprisonment and a maximum sentence of 10 years imprisonment, as well as a maximum fine of $10,000.

Sale of 10 pounds-100 pounds is a felony punishable, for a second offense, by a mandatory minimum sentence of 5 years imprisonment and a maximum sentence of 20 years imprisonment, as well as a fine of $25,000.

Sale of 10 pounds-100 pounds is a felony punishable, for a third or subsequent offense, by a mandatory sentence of 25 years imprisonment, as well as a fine of $25,000.

Sale of 100 pounds-2,000 pounds is a felony punishable by a mandatory minimum sentence of 25 years imprisonment and a maximum fine of $25,000.

Sale of 2,000 pounds-10,000 pounds is a felony punishable by a mandatory minimum sentence of 25 years imprisonment and a maximum fine of $50,000.

Sale of more than 10,000 pounds is a felony punishable by a mandatory minimum sentence of 25 years imprisonment and a maximum fine of $200,000.

Sale to a minor, or within a one-half mile radius of a school, playground, or public park is a felony punishable by a maximum sentence of 10 years imprisonment and a maximum fine of $10,000.

See
- S.C. Code Ann. § 44-53-110 (2015)
- S.C. Code Ann. § 44-53-370(e) (2015)

Cultivation

Cultivation of fewer than 100 plants is a felony punishable by a maximum sentence of 5 years imprisonment and a maximum fine of $5,000.

Cultivation of 100-1,000 plants is a felony punishable by a mandatory minimum sentence of 25 years imprisonment and a maximum fine of $25,000.

Cultivation of 1,000- 10,000 plants is a felony punishable by a mandatory minimum sentence of 25 years imprisonment and a maximum fine of $50,000.

Cultivation of more than 10,000 plants is a felony punishable by a mandatory minimum sentence of 25 years imprisonment and a maximum fine of $200,000.

See
- South Carolina Criminal Code, Section 44-53-110
- South Carolina Criminal Code, Section 44-53-370(e)

Hash & Concentrates

Simple possession of 10 grams or less of hashish or hashish concentrate is a misdemeanor, and upon conviction, is punishable by imprisonment of up to 30 days and a fine between $100-$200.

For a second or subsequent offense, the offender is guilty of a misdemeanor and, upon conviction, must be imprisoned not more than one year or fined not less than two hundred dollars nor more than one thousand dollars, or both. Pre-trial intervention and conditional release may be granted for first time offenders.

See
- S.C. Code Ann. § 44-53-370(d)(4)

Possession of more than 10 grams of hashish or hashish oil is per se possession with intent to distribute. A conviction for PUID is punishable, for a first offense, by imprisonment for not more than five years and a fine of not more than $5,000.

For a second offense, whether the conviction was in SC or in another state, the offender is guilty of a felony and, upon conviction, must be imprisoned not more than ten years nor fined more than $10,000.

For a third or subsequent offense, the offender is guilty of a felony and, upon conviction, must be imprisoned not less than five years nor more than twenty years, and/or fined not more than $20,000.

See
- S.C. Code Ann. § 44-53-370(b)(2) (2015)

Paraphernalia

It is illegal to manufacture or sell drug paraphernalia. Possession of paraphernalia is a "civil citation" punishable by a maximum fine of $500.

See
- S.C. Code Ann. § 44-53-110 (2015)
- S.C. Code Ann. § 44-53-391 (2015)

SOUTH DAKOTA
LAWS & PENALTIES

Offense	Penalty	Incarceration	Max. Fine
POSSESSION			
2 oz or less	Misdemeanor	1 year	$ 2,000
2 oz - 1/2 lb	Felony	1 years	$ 4,000
1/2 - 1 lb	Felony	5 years	$ 10,000
1 - 10 lbs	Felony	10 years	$ 20,000
More than 10 lbs	Felony	15 years	$ 30,000
SALE			
Less than 1/2 oz	Misdemeanor	15 days* - 1 year	$ 2,000
1/2 - 1 oz	Felony	2 years	$ 4,000
1 oz - 1/2 lb	Felony	5 years	$ 10,000
1/2 - 1 lb	Felony	10 years	$ 20,000
More than 1 lb	Felony	15 years	$ 30,000
Within 1000 ft of a school or 500 ft of other designated areas	N/A	5 years*	$ 10,000
To a minor is a felony that carries additional incarceration and fine.			
* Mandatory minimum sentence			
HASH & CONCENTRATES			
Possession	Felony	10 years	$ 20,000
Manufacturing, distributing, or dispensing	Felony	10 years	$ 20,000
Subsequent offenses carry greater penalties			
PARAPHERNALIA			
Possession of paraphernalia	Misdemeanor	30 days	$ 500
MISCELLANEOUS			
Inhabiting a room where marijuana is being used or stored	Misdemeanor	1 year	$ 2,000

Penalty Details

Possession

Possession of 2 ounce or less is a Class 1 misdemeanor, punishable by a maximum sentence of 1 year imprisonment and a maximum fine of $2,000.

Possession of more than 2 ounce - 0.5 lb is a Class 6 felony, punishable by a maximum sentence of 2 years imprisonment and a maximum fine of $4,000.

Possession of 0.5 pound - 1 pound is a Class 5 felony, punishable by a maximum sentence of 5 years imprisonment and a maximum fine of $10,000.

Possession of 1 pound -10 pounds is a Class 4 felony, punishable by a maximum sentence of 10 years imprisonment and a maximum fine of $20,000.

Possession of more than 10 pounds is a Class 3 felony, punishable by a maximum sentence of 15 years imprisonment and a maximum fine of $30,000.

A civil penalty may also be imposed following a conviction. This penalty cannot exceed $10,000.

See
- S.D. Codified Laws § 22-42-6 (2015)
- S.D. Codified Laws § 22-6-1 (2015)
- S.D. Codified Laws § 22-6-2 (2015)

Sale

The sale or distribution of less than 1/2 ounce is a Class 1 misdemeanor punishable by a mandatory minimum sentence of 15 days- 1 year imprisonment and a maximum fine of $2,000.

The sale or distribution of 1 ounce or less is a Class 6 felony punishable by a maximum sentence of 2 years imprisonment and a maximum fine of $4,000.

The sale or distribution of 1 ounce - 0.5 pound is a Class 5 felony which is punishable by a maximum sentence of 5 years imprisonment and a maximum fine of $10,000.

The sale or distribution of 0.5 pound - 1 pound is a Class 4 felony which is punishable by a maximum sentence of 10 years imprisonment and a maximum fine of $20,000.

The sale or distribution of more than 1 pound Is a Class 3 felony, punishable by a maximum sentence of 15 years imprisonment and a maximum fine of $30,000.

The sale or distribution of 1 ounce or less to a minor is a Class 5 felony, punishable by a maximum sentence of 5 years imprisonment and a maximum fine of $10,000.

The sale or distribution of 1 ounce - 0.5 pound to a minor is a Class 4 felony which is punishable by a maximum sentence of 10 years imprisonment and a maximum fine of $20,000.

The sale or distribution of 0.5 pound - 1 pound to a minor is a Class 3 felony which is punishable by a maximum sentence of 15 years imprisonment and a maximum fine of $30,000.

The sale or distribution of more than 1 pound to a minor is a Class 2 felony which is punishable by a maximum sentence of 25 years imprisonment and a maximum fine of $50,000.

* The first felony conviction is punishable by a mandatory minimum sentence of 30 days imprisonment. A second or subsequent felony conviction is punishable by a mandatory minimum sentence of 1 year imprisonment.

The sale within 1,000 feet of a school or within 500 feet of other designated areas is a penalty that is punishable by a mandatory minimum sentence of 5 years imprisonment and a maximum fine of $10,000.

See
- S.D. Codified Laws § 22-42-7 (2015)
- S.D. Codified Laws § 22-6-1 (2015)
- S.D. Codified Laws § 22-6-2 (2015)

Cultivation

Cultivation in South Dakota will be punished based upon the aggregate weight of the plants found as either simple possession or as possession with the intent to distribute. See the "Possession" and "Sale" sections for further penalty details.

Hash & Concentrates

South Dakota defines hashish as the resin extracted from any part of the cannabis plant. Hashish and concentrates constitute a Schedule I controlled substance.

See
- S.D. Codified Laws § 34-20B-1(9) (2015)
- S.D. Codified Laws § 34-20B-14 (10) (2015)

Manufacturing, distributing, dispensing or possessing with intent to manufacture, distribute, or dispense, hashish or concentrates is a Class 4 felony punishable by a term of imprisonment of 10 years and a fine no greater than $20,000. A first time conviction carries a minimum term of imprisonment of 1 year, with subsequent conviction carrying a minimum term of imprisonment of 10 years. If the hashish or concentrates were distributed or dispensed to a minor, then the offense is a Class 2 felony punishable by a term of imprisonment of 25 years and a fine no greater than $50,000. A first conviction involving a minor carries a minimum term of imprisonment of 5 years, with subsequent convictions carrying a minimum term of imprisonment of 15 years.

See
- S.D. Codified Laws § 22-42-2 (2015)
- S.D. Codified Laws § 22-6-1 (2015)

Possession of hashish or concentrates is a Class 4 felony punishable by a term of imprisonment of 10 years and a maximum fine of $20,000.

See
- S.D. Codified Laws § 22-42-5 (2015)
- S.D. Codified Laws § 22-6-1 (2015)

If hashish or concentrates were manufactured, distributed, dispensed, or possessed with intent to distribute or dispense within 1,000 feet of a school or playground or 500 feet of a youth center, public swimming pool, or arcade the offense is a Class 4 felony punishable by a minimum term no less than 5 years and no greater than 10 years and a fine no greater than $20,000.

See
- S.D. Codified Laws § 22-42-19 (2015)

Any equipment or device that is used to create or manufacture hashish or concentrates is considered drug paraphernalia. Possessing any such device is a Class 2 misdemeanor punishable by a term of imprisonment of 30 days and/or a fine of $500. Manufacturing or delivering any such device is Class 6 felony punishable by term of imprisonment of 2 years and/or a fine no greater than $4,000.

See
- S.D. Codified Laws § 22-42A-1(2) (2015)
- S.D. Codified Laws § 22-6-2 (2015)
- S.D. Codified Laws § 22-6-1(9) (2015)

Paraphernalia

The possession of paraphernalia is a Class 2 misdemeanor, punishable by a maximum sentence of 30 days imprisonment and a maximum fine of $500.

See
- S.D. Codified Laws § 22-42A-3 (2015)

Miscellaneous

Inhabiting a room where marijuana is being used or stored is a misdemeanor which is punishable by a maximum sentence of 1 year imprisonment and a maximum fine of $2,000.

TENNESSEE
LAWS & PENALTIES

Offense	Penalty	Incarceration	Max. Fine
POSSESSION			
1/2 oz or less (first offense)	Misdemeanor	1 year	$ 250
1/2 oz or less (second offense)	Misdemeanor	1 year	$ 500
1/2 oz or less (third offense)	Felony	1 - 6 years	$ 1,000
Fines for possession are mandatory.			
SALE			
1/2 oz - 10 lbs	Felony	1 - 6 years	$ 5,000
10 - 70 lbs	Felony	2 - 12 years	$ 50,000
70 - 300 lbs	Felony	8 - 30 years	$ 10,000
More than 300 lbs	Felony	15 - 60 years	$ 200,000
Includes possession With Intent to Distribute.			
Subsequent offense carries higher penalty.			
CULTIVATION			
10 plants or less	Felony	1 - 6 years	$ 5,000
10 - 19 plants	Felony	2 - 12 years	$ 50,000
20 - 99 plants	Felony	3 - 15 years	$ 100,000
100 - 499 plants	Felony	8 - 30 years	$ 200,000
More than 500 plants	Felony	15 - 60 years	$ 500,000
Subsequent offense carries higher penalty.			
HASH & CONCENTRATES			
Possession	Misdemeanor	11 months	$ 2,500
Manufacture, deliver, or sell less than 2 lbs	Felony	6 years	$ 5,000
Manufacture, deliver, or sell 2 - 4 lbs	Felony	12 years	$ 50,000
Manufacture, deliver, or sell 4 - 8 lbs	Felony	15 years	$ 100,000
Manufacture, deliver, or sell 8 - 15 lbs	Felony	30 years	$ 200,000
Manufacture, deliver, or sell more than 15 lbs	Felony	60 years	$ 500,000
PARAPHERNALIA			
Possession of paraphernalia	Misdemeanor	1 year	$ 2,500
Sale of paraphernalia	Felony	1 - 6 years	$ 3,000
MISCELLANEOUS			
Falsification of drug tests	Misdemeanor	1 year	$ 2,500

Penalty Details

Marijuana is a Schedule VI drug in TN.500,000200,000

See
- Tenn. Code Ann. § 39-17-415 (2015)

Possession

Possession of a half ounce of marijuana or less is a misdemeanor punishable by up to one year in jail and maximum fine of $2,500. A $250 fine is required for all first time convictions. A second offense brings a $500 mandatory minimum fine. Third time offenders are charged with a Class E felony, punishable by between 1 and 6 years in prison and a mandatory minimum fine of $1,000.

See
- Tenn. Code Ann. §39-17-418 (2015)
- Tenn. Code Ann. §39-17-428 (2015)

Sale

The sale or possession with the intent to distribute between a half ounce of marijuana and 10 pounds is a Class E felony punishable with between 1-6 years of incarceration and a fine of no more than $5,000.

The sale or possession with the intent to distribute between 10 pounds -70 pounds of marijuana is a Class D felony punishable with between 2-12 years of incarceration and a fine of no more than $50,000.

The sale or possession with the intent to distribute between 70-300 pounds of marijuana is a Class B felony punishable with between 8-30 years of incarceration and a fine of no more than $100,000.

The sale or possession with the intent to distribute more than 300 pounds of marijuana is a Class A felony punishable with between 15-60 years of incarceration and a fine of no more than $500,000.

A first-time felony conviction will receive a minimum fine of at least $2,000.

A second felony conviction will bring a minimum fine of at least $3,000. The third and all subsequent felony convictions will bring a fine of at least $5,000, and will be punished at one grade higher.

See
- Tenn. Code Ann. § 39-17-417
- Tenn. Code Ann. § 40-35-111

Sale to a minor is a felony, which results in an increased penalty (determined by amount of marijuana present) by one sentencing grade.

See
- Tenn. Code Ann §39-17-417(k)

Sale to a minor within 1,000 ft. of a school is an unclassified felony which results in a increase in the grade of the offense (determined by amount of marijuana present) by one sentencing grade.

See
- Tenn. Code Ann. §39-17-432(b)

Cultivation

Cultivation of 10 plants or less is a Class E felony and can lead to incarceration of between 1 and 6 years, and will bring a maximum fine of $3,000.

Cultivation of between 10 and 19 plants is a Class D felony and can lead to incarceration of between 2 and 12 years, and will bring a maximum fine of $50,000.

Cultivation of between 20 and 99 plants is a Class C felony and can lead to incarceration of between 3 and 15 years, and will bring a maximum fine of $100,000.

Cultivation of between 100 and 499 plants is a Class B felony and can lead to incarceration of between 8 and 30 years, and will bring a maximum fine of $200,000.

Cultivation of 500 or more plants is a Class A felony and can lead to incarceration of between 15 and 60 years, and will bring a maximum fine of $500,000.

First-time felony convictions will receive a mandatory minimum fine of at least $2,000.

Second-time felony convictions will receive a mandatory minimum fine of at least $3,000.

Any repeat felony conviction after the second will receive a mandatory minimum fine of at least $5,000.

See
- Tenn. Code Ann. §39-17-417

Hash & Concentrates

Possession of hashish or concentrates is a crime. If the amount of hashish or concentrates is less than 14.75 grams the offense is a Class A misdemeanor punishable by a fine no greater than $2,500 and a term of imprisonment no greater than 11 months and 29 days. A second or subsequent conviction is punishable as a Class E felony punishable by a fine no greater than $3,000 and a term of imprisonment no less than 1 year and no greater than 6 years.

See
- Tenn. Code Ann. § 39-17-418
- Tenn. Code Ann. § 40-35-111

It is a crime to manufacture, deliver, sell, or possess hashish or concentrates. If the amount of hashish or concentrates is less than 2 pounds, the offense is a Class E felony punishable by a fine no greater than $5,000 and a term of imprisonment between 1-6 years.

If the amount of hashish or concentrates is greater than 2 pounds but less than 4 pounds, the offense is a Class D felony punishable by a fine no greater than $50,000 and a term of imprisonment between 1-12 years.

If the amount of hashish or concentrates is greater than 4 pounds but less than 8 pounds, the offense is a Class C felony punishable by a fine no greater than $100,000 and a term of imprisonment between 3-15 years.

If the amount of hashish or concentrates is greater than 8 pounds but less than 15 pounds, the offense is a Class B felony punishable by a fine no greater than $200,000 and a term of imprisonment between 8- 30 years.

If the amount of hashish or concentrates is greater than 15 pounds, the offense is a Class A felony punishable by a fine no greater than $500,000 and a term of imprisonment between 15-60 years.

If the offense occurred within 1,000 feet of a school, recreation center, public library, child day care facility, or park , the penalty is increased by one class, i.e. a Class D felony becomes a Class C felony, a Class B felony becomes a Class A felony, etc.

See
- Tenn. Code Ann. § 39-17-417(g),(h),(i)
- Tenn. Code Ann. § 40-35-111(b)
- Tenn. Code Ann. § 39-17-432

Any device or equipment used to make or create hashish is considered drug paraphernalia. Using paraphernalia or possessing paraphernalia with the intent to use is a Class A misdemeanor punishable by a fine no greater than $2,500 and a term of imprisonment no greater than 11 months and 29 days. Possessing or manufacturing with intent to deliver drug paraphernalia is a Class E felony punishable by a fine no greater than $3,000 and a term of imprisonment no less than 1 year and no greater than 6 years.

See
- Tenn. Code Ann. § 39-17-402(12)
- Tenn. Code Ann. § 39-17-425
- Tenn. Code Ann. § 40-35-111

Paraphernalia

Possession of paraphernalia is a Class A misdemeanor and is punishable with up to 1 year of incarceration and a fine of between $150 and $2,500. For a second or subsequent violation, the mandatory minimum fine increases to $250.

See
- Tenn. Code Ann. §39-17-424
- Tenn. Code Ann. §39-17-428

Sale of paraphernalia is a Class E felony, punishable with 1-6 years of incarceration and a maximum fine of $5,000.

See
- Tenn. Code Ann. §39-17-425

Miscellaneous

Falsification of Drug Tests

Falsifying a dug test is a Class A misdemeanor and is punishable with up to 1 year of incarceration and a fine not to exceed $2,500.

See
- Tenn. Code Ann. §39-17-425

TEXAS
LAWS & PENALTIES

Offense	Penalty	Incarceration	Max. Fine
POSSESSION			
2 oz or less	Misdemeanor	180 days	$ 2,000
2 - 4 oz	Misdemeanor	1 year	$ 4,000
4 oz to 5 lbs	Felony	180 days* - 2 years	$ 10,000
5 - 50 lbs	Felony	2* - 10 years	$ 10,000
50 - 2000 lbs	Felony	2* - 20 years	$ 10,000
More than 2000 lbs	Felony	5* - 99 years	$ 50,000
* Mandatory minimum sentence			
SALE			
7 g or less for no remuneration	Misdemeanor	180 days	$ 2,000
7 g or less	Misdemeanor	1 year	$ 4,000
7 g to 5 lbs	Felony	180 days* - 2 years	$ 10,000
5 - 50 lbs	Felony	2* - 20 years	$ 10,000
50 - 2000 lbs	Felony	5* - 99 years	$ 10,000
More than 2000 lbs	Felony	10* - 99 years	$ 100,000
To a minor	Felony	2* - 20 years	$ 10,000
* Mandatory minimum sentence			
CULTIVATION			
See Possession section for penalty details.			
HASH & CONCENTRATES			
Possession of less than 1 g	Felony	180 days - 2 years	$ 10,000
Possession of 1 - 4 g	Felony	2 - 10 years	$ 10,000
Possession of 4 - 400 g	Felony	2 - 20 years	$ 10,000
Possession of more than 400 g	Felony	10 years - life	$ 50,000
Manufacture or delivery of less than 1 g	Felony	180 days - 2 years	$ 10,000
Manufacture or delivery of 1 - 4 g	Felony	2 - 20 years	$ 10,000
Manufacture or delivery of 4 - 400 g	Felony	5 - 99 years	$ 10,000
Manufacture or delivery of more than 400 g	Felony	10 years - life	$ 10,000
PARAPHERNALIA			
Possession of paraphernalia	Misdemeanor	N/A	$ 500
Sale of paraphernalia (first offense)	Misdemeanor	1 year	$ 4,000
Sale of paraphernalia (subsequent offense)	Felony	90 days* - 1 year	$ 4,000
To a minor	Felony	180 days* - 2 years	$ 10,000
* Mandatory minimum sentence			
MISCELLANEOUS			
Falsifying a drug test	Misdemeanor	180 days	$ 2,000
A person's driver's license is automatically suspended on final conviction of a drug offense.			

Penalty Details

Possession

Possession of 2 ounces or less of marijuana is a Class B misdemeanor, punishable by up to 180 days imprisonment and a fine not to exceed $2,000.

Possession of between 2 and 4 ounces of marijuana is a Class A misdemeanor, punishable by imprisonment of up to 1 year and a fine not to exceed $4,000.

Possession of between 4 ounces and 5 pounds of marijuana is a felony, punishable by a mandatory minimum sentence of 180 days imprisonment, a maximum of 2 years imprisonment, and a fine not to exceed $10,000.

Possession of between 5 pounds and 50 pounds of marijuana is a felony, punishable by a mandatory minimum sentence of no less than 2 years imprisonment, a maximum sentence of 10 years imprisonment, and a fine not to exceed $10,000.

Possession of between 50 pounds and 2,000 lbs of marijuana is a Second Degree felony, punishable by a mandatory minimum sentence of 2 years imprisonment, a maximum sentence of 20 years imprisonment, and a fine not to exceed $10,000.

Possession of more than 2,000 pounds of marijuana is a felony, punishable by a mandatory minimum sentence of 5 years, a maximum sentence of 99 years, and a fine of no more than $50,000.

See
- Texas Stat. Code § 481.121
- Texas Stat. Code § 12.33
- Texas Stat.Code § 12.34
- Texas Stat.Code § 12.35
- Texas Stat. Code § 12.21
- Texas Stat. Code § 12.22

Sale

The sale or delivery of 7 grams of marijuana or less, as a gift, is a misdemeanor, punishable by up to 180 days imprisonment and a fine not to exceed $2,000.

The sale or delivery of 7 grams of marijuana or less, is a misdemeanor, punishable by imprisonment of up to 1 year and a fine not to exceed $4,000.

The sale or delivery of between 7 grams and 5 pounds is a felony, punishable by a mandatory minimum sentence of 180 days imprisonment, a maximum of 2 years imprisonment, and a fine not to exceed $10,000.

The sale or delivery of between 5 pounds and 50 pounds of marijuana is a second degree felony, punishable by a mandatory minimum sentence of 2 years imprisonment, a maximum sentence of 20 years imprisonment, and a fine not to exceed $10,000.

The sale or delivery of between 50 pounds and 2,000 pounds of marijuana is a first degree felony, punishable by a mandatory minimum sentence of 5 years imprisonment, a maximum sentence of life imprisonment, and a fine not to exceed $10,000.

The sale or delivery of more than 2,000 pounds of marijuana is a felony, punishable by a mandatory minimum sentence of 10 years in prison, a maximum sentence of life imprisonment, and a fine not to exceed $100,000.

Selling marijuana to a child is a Second Degree felony, punishable by a mandatory minimum sentence of 2 years imprisonment, a maximum sentence of 20 years imprisonment, and a fine not to exceed $10,000.

See
- Texas Stat.Code § A481.120
- Texas Stat. Code § A481.122
- Texas Stat. Code § 12.32
- Texas Stat. Code §12.33
- Texas Stat. Code § 12.35
- Texas Stat. Code § 12.21
- Texas Stat. Code § 12.22

Cultivation

Cultivation in Texas will be punished based upon the aggregate weight of the plants found. See the "Possession" section for further penalty details.

Hash & Concentrates

Hashish and concentrates are not considered marijuana.

See
- Texas Stat, Code § 481.002(26)(A)

Possession of hashish or concentrates is a crime. If hashish or concentrates is less than one gram, the offense is considered a state jail felony punishable by term of imprisonment no less than 180 days and no greater than 2 years and a fine no greater than $10,000.

If the amount of hashish or concentrates is more than 1 gram but less than 4 grams, the offense is considered a felony of the third degree punishable by a term of imprisonment no less than 2 years and no greater than 10 years and a fine no greater than $10,000.

If the amount of hashish or concentrates is greater than 4 grams but less than 400 grams, the offense is considered a felony in the second degree punishable by a term of imprisonment no less than 2 years and no greater than 20 years and a fine no greater than $10,000.

If the amount of hashish or concentrates is more than 400 grams, the offense is punishable by lifetime imprisonment or a term of imprisonment no less than 10 years and no greater 99 years and a fine no greater than $50,000.

See
- Texas Stat. Code § 481.116
- Texas Stat. Code § 481.35
- Texas Stat. Code § 12.34
- Texas Stat. Code § 12.33

Manufacturing and selling hashish or concentrates also is a crime. If the amount of hashish or concentrates is less than 1 gram, the offense is considered a state jail felony punishable by a term of imprisonment no less than 180 days and no greater than 2 years and a fine no greater than $10,000.

If the amount of hashish or concentrates is more than 1 gram but less than four grams, the offense is considered a felony of the second degree punishable by a term of imprisonment no less than 2 years and no greater than 20 years and a fine no greater than $10,000.

If the amount of hashish or concentrates is more than 4 grams but less than 400 grams, the offense is considered a felony of the first degree punishable by a term of imprisonment no less than 5 years and no greater than 99 years and a fine no greater than $10,000.

If the amount of hashish or concentrates is greater than 400 grams, the offense is punishable by lifetime imprisonment or a term of imprisonment no less than 10 years and no greater than 99 years and a fine no greater than $100,000.

See
- Texas Stat. Code § 481.113
- Texas Stat. Code § 12.35
- Texas Stat. Code § 12.33
- Texas Stat. Code § 12.32

The sale of hashish or concentrates to a person under 18 years of age or a person enrolled in primary or secondary school is a felony, punishable by a term of imprisonment no less than 2 years and no greater than 20 years and a fine no greater than $10,000. This is only applicable if the offender is older than 18 years of age.

See
- Texas Stat. Code § 481.122
- Texas Stat. Code §12.33

Any device used for the purpose of creating hashish or concentrates is considered drug paraphernalia. Possession of any such device is a Class C misdemeanor punishable by a fine no greater than $500. Manufacturing, delivering, or possessing with intent to deliver any such device is a Class A Misdemeanor punishable by a term of imprisonment no greater than 1 year and/or a fine no greater than $4,000.

See
- Texas Stat. Code § 481.002(17)
- Texas Stat. Code § 481.125
- Texas Stat. Code § 12.23
- Texas Stat. Code § 12.21

If any of the previously listed offenses occurred within 1,000 feet of a school, youth center or playground, or within 300 feet of a public swimming pool or video arcade, the degree of the offense is increased by one level: i.e. if the offense was a felony of the third degree is now a felony of the second degree and if the offense was a felony of the second degree it is now a felony of the first degree, etc.

See
- Texas Stat. Code § 481.134(b)

If the perpetrator of any of the previously listed offenses was found to have involved a person under the age of 18, the degree of the offense is increased one level; i.e. if the offense was a felony in the third degree it is now a felony of the second degree, and if the offense was a felony of the second degree it is now a felony of the first degree, etc.

See
- Texas Stat. Code § 481.140

Paraphernalia

Possession of paraphernalia is a Class C misdemeanor, punishable by a fine not to exceed $500.

Selling, or possessing with intent to sell or deliver, paraphernalia is a Class A misdemeanor, punishable by imprisonment of up to 1 year and a fine not to exceed $4,000, unless the offender has previously been convicted of this offense, in which case the offense is a felony, punishable by a mandatory minimum sentence of 90 days imprisonment and a maximum sentence of 1 year imprisonment.

Selling paraphernalia to a minor is a state jail felony, punishable by a mandatory minimum sentence of 180 days imprisonment, a maximum of 2 years imprisonment, and a fine not to exceed $10,000.

See
- Texas Stat. Code § 481.125
- Texas Stat. Code § 12.35
- Texas Stat. Code § 12.21
- Texas Stat. Code § 12.23

Miscellaneous

Falsifying a drug test, or possessing with intent to use any material for the falsification of a drug test, is a Class B misdemeanor, punishable by up to 180 days imprisonment and a fine not to exceed $2,000.

See
- Texas Stat. Code § A481.133
- Texas Stat. Code § 12.22

A person's driver's license is automatically suspended on final conviction of: (1) an offense under the Controlled Substances Act or (2) a drug offense.

See
- Texas Stat. Code § 521.372

UTAH
LAWS & PENALTIES

Offense	Penalty	Incarceration	Max. Fine
POSSESSION			
Less than 1 oz	Misdemeanor	6 months	$ 1,000
1 oz - 1 lb	Misdemeanor	1 year	$ 2,500
1 - 100 lbs	Felony	5 years	$ 5,000
More than 100 lbs	Felony	1 - 15 years	$ 10,000
SALE			
Any amount	Felony	5 years	$ 5,000

In the presence of a minor or within 1000 ft of a school and other designated public areas is subject to increased penalties.

CULTIVATION			

See Possession section for details.

HASH & CONCENTRATES			

Penalties for hashish are the same as for marijuana. Please see the Penalty Details section for further information.

Offense	Penalty	Incarceration	Max. Fine
PARAPHERNALIA			
Possession of paraphernalia	Misdemeanor	6 months	$ 1,000
Sale of paraphernalia	Misdemeanor	1 year	$ 2,500
To a minor	Felony	5 years	$ 5,000
MISCELLANEOUS			

Any conviction will result in a driver's license suspension for 6 months.

Penalty Details

Possession

Possession of less than 1 ounce is a class B misdemeanor punishable by a maximum sentence of 6 months imprisonment and a maximum fine of $1,000. Upon a second conviction the person is guilty of a class A misdemeanor, and upon a third or subsequent conviction the person is guilty of a third degree felony

See
- Utah Code Ann. § 58-7-8 (2015)
- Utah Code Ann. § 76-3-204 (2015)

Possession of 1 ounce - 1 pound is a class A misdemeanor punishable by a maximum sentence of 1 year imprisonment and a maximum fine of $2,500.

Possession of 1 pound -100 pounds is a third degree felony punishable by a maximum sentence of 5 years imprisonment and a maximum fine of $5,000.

See
- Utah Code Ann. § 76-3-203 (2015)
- Utah Code Ann. § 76-3-301 (2015)

Possession of 100 pounds or more is a second degree felony punishable by 1-15 years imprisonment and a maximum fine of $10,000.

See
- Utah Code Ann. § 58-7-8 (2015)
- Utah Code Ann. §76-3-301 (2015)

Sale

The sale of any amount is a second degree felony punishable by a maximum sentence of 5 years imprisonment and a maximum fine of $5,000.

See
- Utah Code Ann. § 58-37-8 (2015)
- Utah Code Ann. §§ 76-3-203-301 (2015)

The sale in the presence of a minor or within 1,000 feet of a school and other designated public areas is subject to increased penalties.

See
- Utah Code Ann. § 58-37-8 (2015)

Cultivation

Cultivation in Utah will be punished based upon the aggregate weight of the plants found. See the "Possession" section for further penalty details.

Hash & Concentrates

Hashish and concentrates are schedule 1 controlled substances and fall under the definition of marijuana.

See
- Utah Code Ann. §§ 58-37-2-8 (2015)
- Utah Code Ann. §§ 76-3-203-301 (2015)

Paraphernalia

Possession of paraphernalia is a class B misdemeanor punishable by a maximum sentence of 6 months imprisonment and a maximum fine of $1,000.

See
- Utah Code Ann. §§ 58-37a-3-5 (2015)
- Utah Code Ann. §§ 76-3-203-301 (2015)

The sale of paraphernalia is a class A misdemeanor punishable by a maximum sentence of 1 year imprisonment and a maximum fine of $2,500.

The sale of paraphernalia to a minor is a third degree felony which is punishable by a maximum sentence of 5 years imprisonment and a maximum fine of $5,000.

See
- Utah Code Ann. §§ 76-3-203-204 (2015)
- Utah Code Ann. § 76-3-301 (2015)

Miscellaneous

Any conviction will result in a driver's license suspension for 6 months.

See
- Utah Code Ann. § 53-3-2201(1)(c)(i)(A) (2015)

VERMONT
LAWS & PENALTIES

Offense	Penalty	Incarceration	Max. Fine
POSSESSION			
1 oz or less (first offense)*	Civil Violation	None	$ 200
1 oz or less (second offense)*	Civil Violation	None	$ 300
1 oz or less (subsequent offense)*	Civil Violation	None	$ 500
1 - 2 oz (first offense)	Misdemeanor	6 months	$ 500
1 - 2 oz (subsequent offense)	Misdemeanor	2 years	$ 2,000
2 oz - 1 lb	Felony	3 years	$ 10,000
1 - 10 lbs	Felony	5 years	$ 100,000
10 lbs or more	Felony	15 years	$ 500,000
* By persons 21 years of age or older.			
SALE			
Less than 1/2 oz	Misdemeanor	2 years	$ 10,000
1/2 oz - 1 lb	Felony	5 years	$ 100,000
1 - 50 lbs	Felony	15 years	$ 500,000
More than 50 lbs	Felony	30 years	$ 1,000,000
To a minor	Felony	5 years	$ 25,000
CULTIVATION			
1 - 2 plants (first offense)	Misdemeanor	6 months	$ 500
1 - 2 plants (subsequent offense)	Misdemeanor	2 years	$ 2,000
3 - 10 plants	Felony	3 years	$ 10,000
11 - 25 plants	Felony	5 years	$ 100,000
More than 25 plants	Felony	15 years	$ 500,000
HASH & CONCENTRATES			
5 grams or less (first offense)*	Civil Violation	None	$ 200
5 grams or less (subsequent offense)*	Civil Violation	None	$ 500
more than 5 grams (first offense)	Misdemeanor	6 months	$ 500
more than 5 grams (subsequent offense)	Misdemeanor	2 years	$ 2,000
* By persons 21 years of age or older.			

Penalties for hashish are similar to marijuana penalties. Please see the marijuana penalties section for further details.

Offense	Penalty	Incarceration	Max. Fine
PARAPHERNALIA			
Possession of paraphernalia*	Civil Violation	None	$ 200
Sale of paraphernalia	Misdemeanor	1 year	$ 1,000
To a minor	Misdemeanor	2 years	$ 2,000
* By persons 21 years of age or older.			

Penalty Details

Possession

Possession of one ounce or less of marijuana by a person 21 years of age older, is punishable with a civil violation not a criminal offense.

Possession of 1 - 2 ounce is a misdemeanor punishable by a maximum sentence of 6 months imprisonment and a maximum fine of $500.*

* There is a possible deferred sentence for first-time offenders.

A subsequent conviction for possession of 1 - 2 ounce is a misdemeanor punishable by a maximum sentence of 2 years imprisonment and a maximum fine of $2,000.

Possession of 2 ounce-1 pound is a felony punishable by a maximum sentence of 3 years imprisonment and a maximum fine of $3,000.

Possession of 1 pound-10 pounds is a felony punishable by a maximum sentence of 5 years imprisonment and a maximum fine of $100,000.

Possession of more than 10 pounds is a felony punishable by a maximum sentence of 15 years imprisonment and a maximum fine of $500,000.

See
• Vt. Stat. Ann. tit. 18 § 4230 (2015)

Sale

The sale or delivery of less than 1/2 ounce is a misdemeanor punishable by a maximum sentence of 2 years imprisonment and a maximum fine of $10,000, or both.

The sale or delivery of 1/2 ounce - 1 pound is a felony punishable by a maximum sentence of 5 years imprisonment and a maximum fine of $100,000, or both.

The sale or delivery of 1 pound - 50 pounds is a felony punishable by a maximum sentence of 15 years imprisonment and a maximum fine of $500,000.

The sale or delivery of more than 50 pounds is presumed to be trafficking and is punishable by a maximum sentence of 30 years imprisonment and a maximum fine of $1,000,000.

The sale or delivery to a minor is a felony punishable by a maximum sentence of 5 years imprisonment and a maximum fine of $25,000.

See
• Vt. Stat. Ann. tit. 18 § 4230 (2015)

Cultivation

Cultivation of 1-2 plants is a misdemeanor punishable by a maximum sentence of 6 months imprisonment and a maximum fine of $500 for the first offense. A subsequent offense increases incarceration to a maximum sentence of 2 years and a maximum fine of $2000.

Cultivation of 3-10 plants is a felony punishable by a maximum sentence of 3 years imprisonment and a maximum fine of $10,000.

Cultivation of 11-25 plants is a felony punishable by a maximum sentence of 5 years imprisonment and a maximum fine of $100,000.

Cultivation of more than 25 plants is a felony punishable by a maximum sentence of 15 years imprisonment and a maximum fine of $500,000.

See
• Vt. Stat. Ann. tit. 18 § 4230 (2015)

Hash & Concentrates

The law decriminalizes possession of 5 grams or less of hashish by a person 21 years of age or older. Civil fines are no more than $200 first offense, no more than $300 second offense, no more than $500 third or subsequent offense. Possession of more than 5 grams of hashish is a misdemeanor punishable by 6 months imprisonment and a maximum fine of $500 for a first offense. A subsequent offense increases incarceration to a maximum sentence of 2 years and a maximum fine of $2000.

Vermont classifies hashish and concentrates as marijuana. For more information regarding penalties associated with hashish or concentrates see the section for Vermont laws on marijuana.

See
• Vt. Stat. Ann. tit. 18 § 4201 (2015)

Paraphernalia

The possession of marijuana paraphernalia by a person 21 years of age or older is punishable by a civil fine only -- no arrest, no jail time, and no criminal record. Civil fines are no more than $200 first offense, no more than $300 second offense, no more than $500 third or subsequent offense.

The sale of paraphernalia is a misdemeanor punishable by a maximum sentence of 1 year imprisonment and a maximum fine of $1,000.

The sale of paraphernalia to a minor is punishable by a maximum sentence of 2 years imprisonment and a maximum fine of $2,000.

See
• Vt. Stat. Ann. tit. 18 § 4476 (2015)

VIRGINIA
LAWS & PENALTIES

Offense	Penalty	Incarceration	Max. Fine
POSSESSION			
Less than 1/2 oz (first offense)	Misdemeanor	30 days	$ 500
Less than 1/2 oz (subsequent offense)	Misdemeanor	1 year	$ 2,500
SALE/MANUFACTURE/TRAFFICKING			
1/2 oz - 5 lbs	Felony	1* - 10 years	$ 2,500
5 lbs - 100 kg	Felony	5* - 30 years	$ 1,000
More than 100 kg	Felony	20 years* - life	$ 100,000
To a minor who is at least 3 years younger	Felony	2* - 50 years	$ 100,000
Within 1000 ft of a school or school bus stop	Felony	1* - 5 years	$ 100,000
Manufacture of marijuana	Felony	5* - 30 years	$ 10,000
Transporting more than 5 lbs into the state	Felony	5* - 40 years	$ 1,000,000
Includes possession With Intent to Distribute			
* Mandatory minimum sentence			
HASH & CONCENTRATES			
Possessing hashish oil	Felony	1 - 10 years	$ 2,500
Manufacturing, selling, giving, distributing, or possessing with intent	Felony	5 - 40 years	$ 500,000
Bringing more than 1 oz of hashish oil into the state	Felony	5 - 40 years	$ 1,000,000
Subsequent offenses carry greater penalties			
PARAPHERNALIA			
Sale or possession with intent to sell paraphernalia	Misdemeanor	1 year	$ 2,500
To a minor who is at least 3 years younger	Felony	1 year	$ 2,500
CIVIL ASSET FORFEITURE			
Vehicles and other assets can be seized in a civil proceeding, regardless of whether criminal charges are brought.			
MISCELLANEOUS			
Maintaining a fortified drug house	Felony	1* - 10 years	$ 0
A convicted person shall be deprived of driving privileges for 6 months.			
* Mandatory minimum sentence			

Penalty Details

Possession
Possession of marijuana is a Class I misdemeanor punishable by no more than 30 days in jail and/or a find of up to $500 for a first offense. A second or subsequent offense is punishable with up to 12 months in jail and/or a up to $2,500 fine. Possession of less than a one half ounce of marijuana is simple possession (possession for personal use).

See
• Va. Code Ann. §§ 182.248-250

Conditional Release
First time offenders may be placed on probation instead of receiving jail time, if the offender agrees to undergo and pay for a series of drug tests during probation and a drug treatment program. Probation terms may also require up to 24 community service hours for a misdemeanor conviction and up to 100 hours for a felony conviction. The conviction still shows up on the offender's record as a conviction and applicable driver's license revocation proceedings are not waived. Violations of the terms of probation can lead to the full penalty as otherwise applicable.

See
• Va. Code Ann. §18.2- 251 (2015)

Sale/Delivery
In VA, having a large quantity of marijuana is not proof of intent to distribute alone. Distributing more than a half-ounce of marijuana, but less than 5 pounds, is a Class 5 felony, punishable by at least one year but not more than 10 years in jail. For a first offense, the judge may use his discretion to sentence the offender to a term in jail for not more than 12 months and a fine of not more than $2,500.

See
• Va. Code. Ann. § 18.2-248.1 (2015)

Distributing more than 5 pounds, but less than 100kg., of marijuana is a felony punishable by no less than 5 and no more than 30, years in prison.

See
• Va. Code. Ann. § 18.2-248.1 (2015)

Distributing more than 100kg of marijuana is punishable with an automatic 20 years to life sentence, with 20 years being the mandatory minimum sentence. This mandatory minimum may be reduced by the judge if:

1. the person does not have a prior conviction for an drug-related offense;
2. the person did not use violence or credible threats of violence or possess a firearm or other dangerous weapon in committing the offense and did not convince another participant in the offense to do so;
3. the offense did not result in death or serious bodily injury to any person;
4. the person was not an organizer, leader, manager, or supervisor of others in the offense, and was not engaged in a continuing criminal enterprise; and
5. the offender cooperates with police and judicial officials by providing to the State all information and evidence the person has concerning the offense, but the fact that the person has no relevant or useful other information to provide or that the Commonwealth already is aware of the information shall not preclude a determination by the court that the defendant has complied with this requirement.

A third sale or intent to distribute conviction brings a mandatory minimum sentence of 5 years.

See
• Va. Code Ann. §18.2-248 (H) (2015)

Distributing more than 1 ounce of marijuana to any person under 18 years of age who is at least 3 years younger than the offender, or using such a minor to distribute more than 1 ounce of marijuana, is a felony and will be punished with a mandatory minimum jail sentence of 5 years, a maximum sentence of 50 years, and a fine of no more than $100,000.

See
• Va. Code Ann. § 18.2-255 (2015).

Distributing 1 ounce of marijuana or less to any person under 18 years of age who is at least 3 years younger than the offender, or using such a minor to distribute less than 1 ounce of marijuana, is a felony and will be punished with a mandatory minimum jail sentence of 2 years, a maximum sentence of 50 years, and a fine of no more than $100,000.

See
• Va. Code Ann. § 18.2-255 (2015)

Distributing more than a half-ounce of marijuana within 1,000 ft. of a school or school bus stop is a felony, punishable with a mandatory minimum sentence of 1 year and a maximum sentence of 5 years, plus a fine not to exceed $100,000. However, if such person proves that he sold such controlled substance or marijuana only as an accommodation to another individual and not with intent to profit thereby, he shall be guilty of a Class 1 misdemeanor, punishable by confinement in jail for not longer than 12 months and a fine not to exceed $2,500.

See
• Va. Code Ann. § 18.2-255.2 (2015)
• Va. Code Ann. § 63.2-100 (2015)

Manufacture
Any person who manufactures marijuana, or possesses marijuana with the intent to manufacture such substance, not for his own use is guilty of a felony punishable by mandatory imprisonment of not less than five, nor more than 30, years and a fine not to exceed $10,000.

See
• Va. Code Ann. § 18,2-248.1 (2015)

Trafficking
Transporting 5lbs or more of marijuana into Virginia with the intent to distribute it is a felony, punishable with a mandatory minimum sentence of 5 years, a maximum sentence of 40 years, and a fine not to exceed $1,000,000. A second or subsequent conviction for the same crime raises the mandatory minimum sentence to 10 years.

See
• Va. Code Ann. § 18.2-248.01 (2015)

Hash & Concentrates
In Virginia, hashish and concentrates fall under the definition of marijuana as long as they contain less than 12 percent of THC by weight, meaning that the restrictions and penalties associated with marijuana also apply to hashish and concentrates. Hashish oil, falls outside the definition of marijuana and is Schedule I substance. Possessing hashish oil is a Class 5 felony punishable by a term of imprisonment no less than 1 year and no greater than 10 years. For a first offense, the judge or jury may reduce the sentence to a term of imprisonment no greater than 5 years and/or a fine of $2,500.

See
• Va. Code Ann. § 18.2-247(D)

Manufacturing, distributing, or possessing with intent to manufacture, sell, or give hashish oil is punishable by no less than 5 years and no greater than 40 years imprisonment and a fine no greater than $500,000. A second conviction carries a term of imprisonment no less than 5 years, the mandatory minimum, and up to the remainder of the offender's life. A third conviction carries a mandatory minimum term of imprisonment for no less than five years and up to the remainder of the offender's life.

See
• Va. Code Ann. §18.2-248 (C) (2015)

More than 1 ounce of hashish oil into Virginia is a felony, punishable by a no less than 5 years imprisonment and no greater than 40 years, with a minimum term of 3 years and a fine no greater than $1,000,000. A second conviction increases the minimum term of imprisonment to 10 years.

See
• Va. Code Ann. §18.2-248.01 (2015)

Distributing hashish oil to a person under 18 years of age, or using a person under the age of 18 in the distribution of hashish oil is a crime if the minor is 3 years the offenders junior. The crime is punishable by a fine of $100,000 and a term of imprisonment no less than 10 years and no greater than 50 years, with a minimum term of imprisonment of 5 years.

See
• Va. Code Ann. §18.2-255(a) (2015)

Manufacturing, distributing, or possessing hashish oil with intent to sell, give, or distribute hashish oil near certain designated areas is a felony punishable by a term of imprisonment no less than 1 year and no greater than 5 years and/or a fine no greater than $100,000. A second conviction is punishable by a mandatory minimum term of imprisonment no less than 1 year and no greater than 5 years and/or a fine no greater than $100,000.

The designated areas include:

• all areas open to the public within 1,000 feet of any school or marked child day care facility or school buses; all areas open to the public within 1,000 feet of a school bus stop during hours where the bus stop is in use; public community or recreation centers; public libraries; all areas open to the public within 1,000 feet of a hospital or, out-patient center; or any other state operated medical facility.

See
• Va Code Ann. §18.2-255.2 (2015)
• Va Code Ann §37.2-100 (2015)

Paraphernalia
Any person who sells or possesses with intent to sell drug paraphernalia, knowing that it is either designed for use or intended by such person for use to illegally plant, propagate, cultivate, grow, harvest, manufacture, inhale, or otherwise introduce into the human body marijuana is guilty of a Class 1 misdemeanor, punishable by no more than 12 months in jail and a fine of no more than $2,500.

See
• Va. Code Ann. §§ 18.2-11- 18.2-265.3 (2015)

Any person eighteen years of age or older who sells drug paraphernalia to a minor who is at least three years junior to the accused is guilty of an additional Class 6 felony, which is punishable by not more than 12 months in jail and a fine of not more than $2,500.

See
• Va. Code. Ann § 18.2-265.3 (2015)

Advertising for the sale of drug paraphernalia is a Class I misdemeanor with a punishment of confinement for not more than 12 months in jail and a fine of not more than $2,500.

See
• Va. Code Ann. §18.2-265.5 (2015)

Knowingly distributing any printed material the distributor knows contains advertisements for drug paraphernalia is a Class 1 misdemeanor, punishable by confinement in jail for not more than 12 months and a fine of not more than $2,500.

See
• Va. Code Ann. §18.2-265.5 (2015)

Miscellaneous

Fortified drug house
Maintaining a fortified drug house is a Class 5 felony, punishable with a mandatory minimum sentence of 1 year, and a maximum sentence of 10 years.

See
• Va. Code Ann. §18.2-258.02 (2015)

Driver's license suspension
In addition to any other sanction or penalty imposed for a violation of this article, the (i) judgment of conviction under this article or (ii) placement on probation following deferral of further proceedings is enough to deprive the person convicted or placed on probation of their privilege to drive or operate a motor vehicle for six months.

See
• Va. Code Ann. 18.2-259.1(A) (2015)

125

WASHINGTON
LAWS & PENALTIES

Offense	Penalty	Incarceration	Max. Fine
POSSESSION			
Personal Use			
1 oz or less (private possession/ consumption)	No Criminal Penalty	None	$ 0
1 oz or less (public consumption)	Civil Penalty	None	$ 100
1 oz - 40 g	Misdemeanor	24 hours* - 90 days	$ 1,000
More than 40 g	Felony	5 years	$ 10,000
* Mandatory minimum sentence			
With Intent to Distribute			
Any amount	Felony	5 years	$ 10,000
SALE OR DISTRIBUTION			
Any amount	Felony	5 years	$ 10,000
To a minor at least 3 years younger	Felony	10 years	$ 10,000
Within 1000 ft of a school, school bus stop or in a public park, in a public housing project designated as a drug-free zone, in public transportation, and other locations is punishable by double fines and imprisonment.			
CULTIVATION			
Any amount	Felony	5 years	$ 10,000
Within 1000 ft of a school, school bus stop or in a public park, in a public housing project designated as a drug-free zone, in public transportation, and other locations is punishable by double fines and imprisonment.			
HASH & CONCENTRATES			
16 oz or less marijuana-infused product solid form	No Criminal Penalty	None	$ 0
72 oz or less marijuana-infused product liquid form	No Criminal Penalty	None	$ 0
7 g marijuana concentrate	No Criminal Penalty	None	$ 0
Possession of more than 40 g	Felony	5 years	$ 10,000
Manufacture, sale, delivery or possession with intent	Felony	5 years	$ 10,000
Subsequent offenses carry greater penalties.			
Patients may possess hash and concentrates for medical use. See details section.			
PARAPHERNALIA			
Advertisement	Misdemeanor	24 hours* - 90 days	$ 1,000
* Mandatory minimum sentence			
CIVIL ASSET FORFEITURE			
Vehicles and other property may be seized.			
MISCELLANEOUS			
Knowingly maintaining a structure used for drug offenses	Felony	5 years	$ 10,000
Controlled substances homicide	Felony	10 years	$ 20,000
Parents of a minor to whom a controlled substance was sold or transferred have a cause of action against the seller.			
Juveniles will have their driving privileges revoked.			

Penalty Details

Marijuana is a Schedule I hallucinogenic substance under the Washington Uniform Controlled Substances Act.

See
- Wash. Rev. Code §69.50.204

Possession for Personal Use

The adult possession, in private, of up to one ounce of cannabis for Personal Use (as well as the possession of up to 16 ounces of marijuana-infused product in solid form, and 72 ounces of marijuana-infused product in liquid form) is not subject to criminal or civil penalty. The public consumption of marijuana is subject to a civil violation and fine. Any consumption of cannabis while one is in a moving vehicle is defined as a traffic infraction. Traffic safety laws further require that ANY CANNABIS POSSESSED in a moving vehicle must be located in a sealed container in either the trunk, glove compartment, or some other area that is inaccessible to the driver or passengers.

Possession of one ounce to 40 grams is a misdemeanor, punishable by a mandatory minimum of 24 hours and maximum of 90 days in jail. A mandatory fine of $250 is imposed for the first offense, and a mandatory fine of $500 is imposed for the second or subsequent violations. This is in addition to a possible fine up to $1,000. The imprisonment will not be suspended or deferred unless it is determined that it "will pose a substantial risk to the defendant's physical or mental well-being or that local jail facilities are in an overcrowded condition." The mandatory fine may not be suspended or deferred unless the defendant is found to be indigent.

Possession of more than 40 grams is a class C felony punishable by up to 5 years imprisonment and/or a fine up to $10,000. An additional mandatory $1,000 fine applies to first time offenses and a $2,000 fine to second or subsequent offenses.

See
- Wash. Rev. Code §9A.20.021
- Wash. Rev. Code §69.50.4014
- Wash. Rev. Code §69.50.4013
- Wash. Rev. Code §69.50.425
- Wash. Rev. Code §69.50.430

Possession with Intent to Distribute

Possession with intent to distribute any amount of marijuana is a class C felony punishable by up to 5 years imprisonment and/or a fine up to $10,000. There is an additional mandatory fine of $1,000 for the first offense and $2,000 for a second or subsequent offense.

See
- Wash. Rev. Code §9A.20.021
- Wash. Rev. Code §69.50.401
- Wash. Rev. Code §69.50.430

Sale or Distribution

Retail sales of cannabis by state-licensed entities to those over the age of 21 are regulated in this state. Marijuana sales by unlicensed entities remain subject to criminal penalties.

Sale or distribution of any amount of marijuana is a C felony punishable by up to 5 years imprisonment and/or a fine up to $10,000. An additional mandatory fine of $1,000 applies to first offenses and $2,000 fine to second or subsequent offenses.

See
- Wash. Rev. Code §9A.20.021
- Wash. Rev. Code §69.50.401
- Wash. Rev. Code §69.50.430

Distribution by a person aged 18 years or older to a person less than 18 years who is 3 years the distributor's junior is a class B felony punishable by an imprisonment term double that for sale (10 years total) and/or a fine of up to $10,000.

See
- Wash. Rev. Code §69.50.406(2)

Cultivation

Cultivation for either personal use or distribution is a class C felony punishable by up to 5 years imprisonment and/or a fine up to $10,000. An additional mandatory fine of $1,000 applies to first offenses and $2,000 to second or subsequent offenses.

See
- Wash. Rev. Code §9A.20.021
- Wash. Rev. Code §69.50.401
- Wash. Rev. Code §69.50.430

Hash & Concentrates

Washington's definition of marijuana includes "all parts of the plant Cannabis," including "the resin extracted from any part of the plant; and every compound, manufacture, salt, derivative, mixture, or preparation of the plant, its seeds or resin." Under this definition hashish or concentrates, which are compounds made from the resin of the plant, would be considered marijuana.

See
- Wash. Rev. Code §69.50.101(q)

Possession of 16 ounces of marijuana-infused product in solid form; 72 ounces of marijuana-infused product in liquid form; or 7 grams of marijuana concentrate is not subject to criminal or civil penalty.

Possession of more than 40 grams of hashish or concentrates is a class C felony punishable by a term of imprisonment no greater than 5 years and/or a fine no greater than $10,000.

See
- Wash. Rev. Code §69.50.4014
- Wash. Rev. Code §69.50.425
- Wash. Rev. Code §69.50.4013
- Wash. Rev. Code §9A.20.021(1)(c)

Manufacture, delivery or possession with intent to manufacture or deliver, hashish or concentrates is a class C felony punishable by a term of imprisonment no greater than 5 years and/or a fine no greater than $10,000.

See
- Wash. Rev. Code §69.50.401(c)
- Wash. Rev. Code §9A.20.021(1)(c)

Selling hashish or concentrates is a crime punishable by a term of imprisonment no greater than 5 years and a fine no greater than twice the value of the hashish or concentrates. Subsequent offenses for selling hashish or concentrates is a crime punishable by a mandatory term of imprisonment for 5 years and a fine no greater than twice the value of the hashish or concentrates.

See
- Wash. Rev. Code §69.50.410

Hashish and concentrates can be used medically in Washington since hashish and concentrates are considered a marijuana product.

See
- Wash. Rev. Code §69.51A.040

Selling, manufacturing, transferring, or possessing with intent to manufacture, sell, or transport hashish or concentrates within designated areas is a crime punishable by a term of imprisonment no greater than 10 years and/or a fine no greater than $20,000 or four times the value of the hashish or concentrates. There is an affirmative defense available allowing the accused to prove that the offense was entirely within a private residence. The designated areas are:

- within schools;
- within 1,000 feet of school grounds
- within school buses;
- within 1000 feet of a school bus stop;
- within public parks;
- within public housing projects designated drug free zones;
- within -public transit vehicles
- at a public transit stop center;
- within civic centers designated drug free zones;
- within 1,000ft of any civic center designated a drug free zone.

See
- Wash. Rev. Code §69.50.435
- Wash. Rev. Code §69.50.410
- Wash. Rev. Code §69.50.412
- Wash. Rev. Code §9A.20.021(c)

Paraphernalia

Advertisement of paraphernalia is a misdemeanor punishable by a mandatory minimum of 24 hours and maximum of 90 days in jail and a fine of not more than $1,000.

See
- Wash. Rev. Code §69.50.412
- Wash. Rev. Code §69.50.425

Sale or giving of drug paraphernalia is also a class I civil infraction punishable by a $250 fine.

See
- Wash. Rev. Code §7.80.120
- Wash. Rev. Code §69.50.4121

Sentencing

Drug offenses are sentenced according to drug offense seriousness level and a drug offense sentencing grid.

See
- Wash. Rev. Code § 9.94A517
- Wash. Rev. Code § 9.94A518

First time marijuana offenders may have the imposition of the standard sentence waived with conditions. For violations which involve a small amount of drugs (as determined by the judge), the offender may have the standard sentence waived in lieu treatment or a prison-based alternative.

See
- Wash. Rev. Code §9.94A.517
- Wash. Rev. Code §9.94A.660
- Wash. Rev. Code §9.94A.662
- Wash. Rev. Code §9.94A.664

Suspension of sentencing is available for all drug offenses, at the discretion of the court. Conditions to this probation may include paying fines and reporting to a probation officer.

See
- Wash. Rev. Code §9.92.060

Any person convicted of a second or subsequent offense is subject to double the term of imprisonment authorized for the offense and double the fine authorized for the offense. However, this does not apply to certain possession offenses. A second or subsequent offense is any offense of this statute committed by a person with a prior conviction under this statute or any statute of the United States or any state relating to narcotics, marijuana, depressants, hallucinogens, or stimulants.

See
- Wash. Rev. Code §69.50.408

Forfeiture

Criminal

Vehicles and other property may be seized for violations of the Washington Uniform Controlled Substances Act if certain conditions are met. A seizure of property commences a forfeiture proceeding in which the law enforcement agency must give notice to the owner and others with an interest in the property within 15 days. After notice has been served, those with an interest in the property have 45 days in the case of personal property and 90 days in the case of real property to respond, or else the items will be deemed forfeited.

See
- Wash. Rev. Code §69.50.505

Civil

Private or state actors may file an action for damages and forfeiture of property involved in delivery, cultivation, or possession with intent to deliver or cultivate marijuana.

See
- Wash. Rev. Code §9A.82.100

Miscellaneous

Involving a person under the age of 18 in a drug offense

Involving a person under the age of 18 (compensating, soliciting, or threatening) in a transaction to cultivate, sell, or deliver marijuana is a class C felony punishable by up to 5 years imprisonment and/or a fine up to $10,000. An additional mandatory fine of $1,000 applies to first offenses and $2,000 to second or subsequent offenses.

See
- Wash. Rev. Code §9A.20.021
- Wash. Rev. Code §69.50.4015
- Wash. Rev. Code §69.50.430

Knowingly maintaining a structure used for drug offenses

It is a class C felony punishable by up to 5 years imprisonment and/or a fine up to $10,000 to knowingly maintain a structure (including homes and vehicles) that is resorted to by persons using controlled substances in violation of the law for that purpose, or which is used to sell or store substances. An additional mandatory fine of $1,000 applies to first offenses and $2,000 to second or subsequent offenses.

See
- Wash. Rev. Code §9A.20.021
- Wash. Rev. Code §69.50.402(f)
- Wash. Rev. Code §69.50.430

Civil damages

Parents or legal guardians of a minor to whom a controlled substance was sold or transferred have a cause of action against the person who sold or transferred the substances. Damages may include costs of rehabilitation services for the minor, forfeiture of any money made in the transaction, and attorney's fees.

See
- Wash. Rev. Code §69.50.414

Controlled substances homicide

A person who delivers a controlled substance, which is subsequently used by the person delivered to and results in their death, is guilty of a class B felony punishable by up to 10 years imprisonment and/or a fine up to $20,000. An additional mandatory fine of $1,000 applies to first offenses and $2,000 to second or subsequent offenses.

See
- Wash. Rev. Code §9A.20.021
- Wash. Rev. Code §69.50.415
- Wash. Rev. Code §69.50.430

Revocation of juvenile's driving privileges

Juveniles (age 13-21) will have their driving privileges revoked for any offense under this statute. For the first offense, the privileges will be revoked for 1 year or until the person reaches 17 years old, whichever is longer. A second or subsequent offense will result in the revocation of privileges for 2 years or until the individual is 18 years old, whichever is longer.

See
- Wash. Rev. Code §46.20.265
- Wash. Rev. Code §69.50.420

Violations committed on or in certain public places or facilities

Cultivation, sale, delivery, or possession with intent to cultivate, sell, or deliver marijuana in a school, on a school bus, within 1,000 feet of a school bus stop or school grounds, in a public park, in a public housing project designated as a drug-free zone, in public transportation, and other locations is punishable by a fine that is twice that authorized for the offense and/or imprisonment for a term that is twice the amount authorized for the offense. It is an affirmative defense that the conduct took place exclusively within the confines of a private residence and the transaction did not involve profit.

See
- Wash. Rev. Code §69.50.435

Chemical dependency

If the court finds that the offender is chemically dependent and this has contributed to their offense, the court may order the offender take part in rehabilitation.

See
- Wash. Rev. Code §9.94A.607

Mandatory Fee

Any individual convicted, sentenced to a lesser charge, or given deferred prosecution under WA's DUID statute must pay a $200 fee to compensate the State for the drug test, in addition to any fine imposed by the Court. This fee applies to each individual conviction but may be waived for poverty.

See
- RCW § 46.61.5054(1).

WEST VIRGINIA
LAWS & PENALTIES

Offense	Penalty	Incarceration	Max. Fine
POSSESSION			
Any amount	Misdemeanor	90 days - 6 months	$ 1,000
SALE OR DISTRIBUTION			
Any amount	Felony	1* - 5 years	$ 15,000
Trafficking marijuana into WV	Felony	1* - 5 years	$ 15,000
To a minor or within 1000 ft of a school	Felony	2 years*	$ 0
Includes possession With Intent to Distribute			
* Mandatory minimum sentence			
CULTIVATION			
See Possession and Sale sections for details.			
HASH & CONCENTRATES			
Penalties for hashish are the same as for marijuana. Please see the marijuana penalties section for further details.			
PARAPHERNALIA			
Involving all or part of an illegal drug paraphernalia business	Misdemeanor	6 months* - 1 year	$ 5,000
* Mandatory minimum sentence			
CIVIL ASSET FORFEITURE			
Everything involved in the production and transportation processes of controlled substances are liable to be forfeited.			
MISCELLANEOUS			
Attempts to adulterate drug screening test	Misdemeanor	0 - 1 year	$ 10,000
Mandatory driver's license revocation for any felony offense when a motor vehicle is used in its commission.			

Penalty Details

Marijuana is a Schedule I drug.

See
• W. Va. Code § 60A-2-204 (2015)

Possession

Possession of marijuana in any amount is a misdemeanor punishable by not less than 90 days, nor more than 6 months and not fined more than $1,000.

Conditional discharge for first offense of possession of less than 15 grams of marijuana: For a first drug related possession charge, the court can give the offender probation with the traditional array of drug testing and supervision traditionally part of the probation process. Discharge is not a legal conviction.

See
• W. Va. Code §§ 60A-4-401(c) -407 (2015)

Sale or Distribution

Includes possession with the intent to distribute marijuana.

Felony punishable by no less than 1 year, and no more than 5 years, imprisonment and a fine of not more than $15,000.

Trafficking marijuana into West Virginia is punishable by no less than 1 year and no more than 5 years imprisonment and fined up to $15,000.

West Virginia has a two-year mandatory minimum sentence for sale/distribution to a minor or if sale/delivery occurs within 1,000 feet of a school.

See
• W. Va. Code §§ 60A-4-401-409 (2015)

Cultivation

Cultivation in West Virginia will be punished based upon the aggregate weight of the plants found as either simple possession or as possession with the intent to distribute. See the "Possession" and "Sale or Distribution" sections for further penalty details.

Hash & Concentrates

Hashish and concentrates are considered a compound or preparation of marijuana and constitute a Schedule I controlled substance.

See
Hubbard v. Spillers, 202 S.E.2d 180 (W.Va 1974)
• W. Va. Code §§ 60A- 2-204(d) (19) (2015)

Paraphernalia

Any person who conducts, finances, manages, supervises, directs or owns all or part of an illegal drug paraphernalia business is guilty of a misdemeanor, and is subject to no more than a $5,000 fine, or no less than six months and no more than 1 year imprisonment.

See
• W. Va. Code §§ 60A-4-403 (2015)

Sentencing

Second or subsequent convictions for both possession and distribution are eligible for double the penalty set out in law.

See
• W. Va. Code §60A-4-408 (2015)

Conditional discharge for first offense of possession: For a first drug related possession charge, the court can give the offender probation with the traditional array of drug testing and supervision traditionally part of the probation process. Discharge is not a legal conviction.

See
W. Va. Code §60A-4-407 (2015)

Misdemeanor or Felony

Possession is a misdemeanor, while distribution and manufacture are felonies.

Mandatory Minimum

Mandatory two year minimum sentence (doubling WV's regular one year minimum for marijuana felonies) if the offender is:

Twenty-one years of age or older at the time of the distribution upon which the conviction is based, and the person to whom the controlled substance was distributed was under the age of eighteen years at the time of the distribution; or

Eighteen years of age or older and the distribution upon which the conviction is based occurred in or on, or within one thousand feet of a public or private elementary, vocational or secondary school or a public or private college, junior college or university in this state.

See
W. Va. Code §60A-4-406 (b) (2015)

Trafficking marijuana into West Virginia carries a mandatory minimum sentence of not less than 1 year.

See
• W. Va. Code §60A-4-409(b)(2) (2015)

Forfeiture

Everything involved in the production and transportation processes of controlled substances, including cars, houses, and monetary funds, are liable to be forfeited to the State after a successful prosecution of a drug distribution or manufacturing case.

Paraphernalia: Any property, including money, used in violation of the provisions of this section may be seized and forfeited to the state.

See
• W. Va. Code §§ 60A-7-703-705 (2015)

Miscellaneous

Drug Screening Adulteration

Attempts to adulterate drug screening test or selling or knowingly possessing products for that purpose is punishable:

For a first offense is guilty of a misdemeanor and, upon conviction, shall be fined not more than one thousand dollars;

For a second offense is guilty of a misdemeanor and, upon conviction, be fined not more than five thousand dollars; and

For a third or subsequent offense is guilty of a misdemeanor and, upon conviction, be fined not more than ten thousand dollars or confined in the regional jail for not more than one year, or both.

See
• W. Va. Code §§ 60A- 4-412 (2015)

Driver's License Revocation

Any person convicted of driving under the influence of marijuana or any felony in the commission of which a motor vehicle is used, is subject to mandatory driver's license revocation.

Mandatory license revocation for any felony offense when a motor vehicle is used in its commission. This would include conviction for manufacturing or delivering pot, but simple possession would not qualify as a felony.

See
• W. Va. Code § 17B-3-5 (2015)
• W. Va. Code §60A-4-401 (2015)

WISCONSIN
LAWS & PENALTIES

Offense	Penalty	Incarceration	Max. Fine
POSSESSION			
Any amount (first offense)	Misdemeanor	6 months	$ 1,000
Any amount (subsequent offense)	Felony	3.5 years	$ 10,000
SALE OR DELIVERY			
200 g or less	Felony	3.5 years	$ 10,000
200 - 1000 g	Felony	6 years	$ 10,000
1000 - 2500 g	Felony	10 years	$ 25,000
2500 - 10,000 g	Felony	12.5 years	$ 25,000
More than 10,000 g	Felony	15 years	$ 50,000
Includes possession With Intent to Distribute			
Subsequent offense is subject to additional penalties			
CULTIVATION			
4 plants or fewer	Felony	3.5 years	$ 10,000
4 - 20 plants	Felony	6 years	$ 10,000
20 - 50 plants	Felony	10 years	$ 25,000
50 - 200 plants	Felony	12.5 years	$ 25,000
More than 200 plants	Felony	15 years	$ 50,000
Subsequent offense is subject to additional penalties			
HASH & CONCENTRATES			
Penalties for hashish and marijuana are generally treated equally under the law.			
PARAPHERNALIA			
Use or possession with intent to use paraphernalia	Misdemeanor	30 days	$ 500
Sale or Distribution of paraphernalia	Misdemeanor	90 days	$ 1,000
Selling to a minor	Misdemeanor	9 months	$ 10,000
CIVIL ASSET FORFEITURE			
All controlled substances and items used to distribute, including vehicles, are subject to forfeiture.			
MISCELLANEOUS			
Driving privileges may be suspended for 6 months - 5 years.			

Penalty Details

Marijuana is a Schedule I hallucinogenic substance under the Wisconsin Uniform Controlled Substances Act.

See
• Wis. Stat § 961 14 (2014)

Possession

A first offense for possession of marijuana is a misdemeanor punishable by a fine of up to $1,000 and/or imprisonment of up to 6 months. A second offense is a Class I felony and is punishable by a fine of up to $10,000 and/or imprisonment for up to 3.5 years.

See
• Wis. Stat. §§ 961.41(3g)& 961.495

The penalty for marijuana possession will vary according to number of convictions, with 100 hours of community service, in addition to the standard penalty for possession within 1,000 ft. of a school, youth center, public park, poo, housing project, jail or drug treatment facility. See
• Wis. Stat. §§ 961.41(3g)& 961.495

Sale or Cultivation

The sale or cultivation of 200 grams or less (4 plants or fewer) is a Class I felony, punishable by up to $10,000 in fines and/or imprisonment for up to 3.5 years.

The sale or cultivation of between 200 and 1,000 grams (5-12 plants) is a felony, punishable by up to $10,000 fine and/ or 6 years in prison.

The sale or cultivation of between 1,000 and 2,500 grams (21-50 plants) is punishable by up to $25,000 fines and/ or a maximum 10 years imprisonment.

The sale or cultivation of between 2,500 and 10,000 grams (51-200 plants) is punishable by up to $25,000 fine and/or 12 years and 6 months imprisonment.

The sale or cultivation of over 10,000 grams (more than 200 plants) is punishable with a maximum of 15 years imprisonment and/or a $25,000 fine.

See
• Wis. Stat. § 961.41(1)

Hash & Concentrates

Any compound containing THC is a Schedule I drug. While the definition of marijuana does not include hashish or concentrates, the penalties and offenses associated with marijuana are the same for hashish or concentrates. Please see the marijuana penalties section for further details.

See
• Wis. Stat. § 961.41(1)

Paraphernalia

It is illegal to use paraphernalia or possess paraphernalia with the intent to use it. Paraphernalia includes any item that will assist in the cultivation, distribution, ingestion, or inhalation of marijuana. This offense is a misdemeanor punishable by a fine of up to $500 or up to 30 days of imprisonment.

See
• Wis. Stat. § 961.573(1)

The sale of paraphernalia it is a misdemeanor and is punishable by a fine of up to $1,000 and/or 90 days of imprisonment.

See
• Wis. Stat. § 961.574(1)

Selling paraphernalia to a minor is a misdemeanor punishable by a fine of up to $10,000 an/or up to 9 months of imprisonment.

See
• Wis. Stat. § 961.573

Forfeiture

All controlled substances and items used to distribute them, including vehicles, are subject to forfeiture under Wisconsin law.

See
Wis. Stat. § 961.55

Miscellaneous

If a person is convicted of any violation the Uniform Controlled Substances Act, the court may, in addition to any other penalties that may apply to the crime, suspend the person's operating privilege for not less than 6 months nor more than 5 years. The person may be able to apply for an occupational license depending on the number of prior convictions.

See
• Wis. Stat. §061.50

WYOMING
LAWS & PENALTIES

Offense	Penalty	Incarceration	Max. Fine
POSSESSION			
Persons under the influence	Misdemeanor	6 months	$ 750
3 oz or less	Misdemeanor	12 months	$ 1,000
More than 3 oz	Felony	5 years	$ 10,000
Within 500 feet of a school is punishable by an additional $500 fine.			
SALE OR DISTRIBUTION			
Any amount	Felony	10 years	$ 10,000
CULTIVATION			
Any amount	Misdemeanor	6 months	$ 1,000
HASH & CONCENTRATES			
0.3 g liquid or less	Misdemeanor	12 months	$ 1,000
More than 0.3 g liquid	Felony	5 years	$ 10,000
PARAPHERNALIA			
Possession of paraphernalia	not classified	6 months	$ 750

Penalty Details

See
- Wyoming Controlled Substances Act, Wyo. Stat. Ann. § 35-7-1001 through 1057 (2014)

Possession

Any person using or under the influences marijuana is subject to a misdemeanor punishable by a maximum of 6 months imprisonment and a maximum fine of $750, or both.

See
- Wyo. Stat. Ann. § 35-7-1039

Possession of three ounces or less is a misdemeanor punishable by no more than 12 months imprisonment and a maximum fine of $1,000, or both.

See
- Wyo. Stat. Ann. § 35-7-1031 (2014)

Possession of more than 3 ounces is a felony punishable by a maximum of 5 years imprisonment and a maximum $10,000 fine, or both.

See
- Wyo. Stat. Ann. § 35-7-1031 (2014)

Sale or Distribution

Sale of any amount is a felony punishable by a maximum of 10 years imprisonment and a maximum fine of $10,000 or both.

See
- Wyo. Stat. Ann. § 35-7-1040 (2014)

Cultivation

Cultivating any amount of marijuana is misdemeanor, punishable by a maximum of 6 months imprisonment and a maximum fine of $1,000.

See
- Wyo. Stat. Ann. § 35-7-1002 (2014)

Hash & Concentrates

Any equipment, device, or material used to make hashish or extracts is considered paraphernalia.

See
- Wyo. Stat. Ann. § 35-7-1002(xxvii) (2014)

Possession of 0.3 grams or less of a liquid concentrate, such as hashish oil, is a misdemeanor, punishable by a maximum term of imprisonment of up to 12 months and/or a maximum fine of $1,000.

Possession of more than .3 grams of a liquid concentrate is a felony punishable by a maximum term of imprisonment up to 5 years and/or a fine of no more than $10,000.

See
- Wyo. Stat. Ann. § 35-7-1031 (2014)

Paraphernalia

Possession of paraphernalia is a crime which is punishable by a maximum of 6 months imprisonment and a maximum fine of $750.

See
- Wyo. Stat. Ann. § 35-7-1002 (2014)

Miscellaneous

A third or subsequent offense for possession of more than 3 ounces is punishable by a maximum of 5 years imprisonment, a maximum fine of $5,000, or both.

See
- Wyo. Stat. Ann. § 35-7-1031 (2014)

Anyone adult who distributes marijuana to someone under the age of 18 who is more than 3 years his junior is subject to felony charge, with a maximum penalty of 20 years imprisonment and/or a $10,000 fine. A conviction within 500 feet from a school is subject to an additional $500 fine.

See
- Wyo. Stat. Ann. § 35-7-1036(a) (2014)

STATE MEDICAL
MARIJUANA
LAWS

ALASKA
MEDICAL MARIJUANA LAW

Status: Operational • Law Signed: 1998

QUALIFYING CONDITIONS

- Cachexia
- Cancer
- Chronic Pain
- Glaucoma

- HIV or AIDS
- Multiple Sclerosis
- Nausea
- Seizures

PATIENT POSSESSION LIMITS

One ounce of usable marijuana

HOME CULTIVATION

Yes, six plants allowed, no more than three may be mature.

STATE-LICENSED DISPENSARIES ALLOWED

No

MEDICAL MARIJUANA STATUTES

Alaska Stat. §§17.37.10 - 17.37.80 (2007)
Alaska Stat. §17.37.010& (2007)

CAREGIVERS

Yes, the caregiver must be 21 years of age or older. The caregiver can never have been convicted of a felony controlled substances offense. The caregiver must be listed by the patient as either the primary caregiver or an alternate caregiver. Only one primary caregiver and one alternate caregiver may be listed in the registry for a patient. A person may be a primary caregiver or alternate caregiver for only one patient at a time, unless the primary caregiver or alternate caregiver is simultaneously caring for two or more patients who are related to the caregiver by at least the fourth degree of kinship by blood or marriage.

RECIPROCITY

No

CONTACT INFORMATION

Alaska Department of Health and Social Services, Division of Public Health: Marijuana Registry
http://dhss.alaska.gov/dph/VitalStats/Pages/marijuana.aspx

ARIZONA
MEDICAL MARIJUANA LAW

Status: Operational • Law Signed: 2011

QUALIFYING CONDITIONS

- Alzheimer's Disease
- Amyotrophic Lateral Sclerosis (Lou Gehrig's disease)
- Cachexia or wasting syndrome
- Cancer
- Chronic pain
- Crohn's Disease

- Glaucoma
- Hepatitis C
- HIV or AIDS
- Nausea
- Persistent Muscle Spasms
- PTSD
- Seizures

PATIENT POSSESSION LIMITS

Two and one-half ounces of usable marijuana

HOME CULTIVATION

Yes, if residence is further than 25 miles from a state-licensed dispensary facility. No more than twelve marijuana plants in an "enclosed, locked facility."

STATE-LICENSED DISPENSARIES ALLOWED

Yes, state-licensed nonprofit dispensaries may produce and dispense marijuana to authorized patients on a not-for-profit basis.

STATE-LICENSED DISPENSARIES OPERATIONAL

Yes

CAREGIVERS

Yes

RECIPROCITY

Yes, the act defines a 'visiting qualifying patient' as a person 'who has been diagnosed with a debilitating medical condition by a person who is licensed with authority to prescribe drugs to humans in the state of the person's residence.'

CONTACT INFORMATION

Final rules for the program, physician certification forms, and a frequently asked questions (FAQs) are all available online at the Arizona Medical Marijuana Program, www.azdhs.gov/licensing/medical-marijuana.

CALIFORNIA
MEDICAL MARIJUANA LAW

Status: Operational • Law Signed: 1996

QUALIFYING CONDITIONS

- Anorexia
- Arthritis
- Cachexia
- Cancer
- Chronic Pain
- HIV or AIDS
- Glaucoma

- Migraine
- Persistent Muscle Spasms
- Severe Nausea
- Seizures
- Any debilitating illness where the medical use of marijuana has been "deemed appropriate and has been recommended by a physician"

PATIENT POSSESSION LIMITS

No possession limits specified

HOME CULTIVATION

Yes, but no cultivation limits are specified.

STATE-LICENSED DISPENSARIES ALLOWED

Statewide regulations governing dispensaries are anticipated to take effect in 2017. Until that time, dispensaries are subject to local regulation.

MEDICAL MARIJUANA STATUTES

Cal. Health & Saf. Code, §11362.7 (2003)
Cal. Health & Saf. Code, §§ 11362.7 - 11362.83 (2003)
California Compassionate Use Act 1996, Cal. Health & Saf. Code, § 11362.5 (1996)

CAREGIVERS

Yes, primary caregiver is the individual, designated by a qualified patient or by a person with an identification card, who has consistently assumed responsibility for the housing, health, or safety of that patient or person. The caregiver must be 18 years of age or older (unless the primary caregiver is the parent of a minor child who is a qualified patient or a person with an identification card).

RECIPROCITY

No

CONTACT INFORMATION

For more information on California's medical marijuana law, please contact:
California NORML
2261 Market Street #278A
San Francisco, CA 94144
(415) 563-5858
http://www.canorml.org/

For detailed information on county or municipal medical marijuana guidelines, please visit:
http://www.canorml.org/medical-marijuana/local-growing-limits-in-California

For a list of California doctors who recommend medical cannabis, please visit:
http://listings.canorml.org/medical-marijuana-doctors-in-California/list.lasso

For a list of California medical cannabis providers, please visit:
http://canorml.org/medical-marijuana/California-collectives-and-dispensaries-guide

COLORADO
MEDICAL MARIJUANA LAW

Status: Operational • Law Signed: 2001

QUALIFYING CONDITIONS

- Cachexia
- Cancer
- Chronic pain
- Chronic nervous system disorders
- Glaucoma

- HIV or AIDS
- Nausea
- Persistent Muscle Spasms
- Seizures

PATIENT POSSESSION LIMITS

Two ounces of usable marijuana.

HOME CULTIVATION

Yes, patients (or their primary caregivers) may cultivate no more than six marijuana plants, with three or fewer being mature, flowering plants that are producing a usable form of marijuana.

STATE-LICENSED DISPENSARIES ALLOWED

Yes

STATE-LICENSED DISPENSARIES OPERATIONAL

Yes

MEDICAL MARIJUANA STATUTES

Colo. Rev. Stat. § 25-1.5-106 (2003) (originally enacted as § 25-1-107(1)(jj) (2001))
C.O. Const. art. XVIII, §14 (2001)
Colo. Rev. Stat. § 18-18-406.3 (2001)
Colo. Rev. Stat. §25-1.5-106 (2), (10) (2001)

CAREGIVERS

Yes, primary caregiver is a person other than the patient or the patient's physician. The caregiver must be 18 years of age or older. A patient can only have one primary caregiver at a time. A patient who has designated a primary caregiver for himself or herself may not be designated as a primary caregiver for another patient. A primary caregiver may be listed on the medical marijuana registry for no more than 5 patients.

RECIPROCITY

No

CONTACT INFORMATION

Colorado Department of Public Health and Environment
(www.colorado.gov/pacific/cdphe/medicalmarijuana)
HSVR-ADM2-A1
4300 Cherry Creek Drive South
Denver, CO 80246-1530
Phone: 303-692-2184

CONNECTICUT
MEDICAL MARIJUANA LAW

Status: Operational • Law Signed: 2012

QUALIFYING CONDITIONS

- Amyotrophic lateral sclerosis*
- Cachexia
- Cancer
- Crohn's disease
- Epilepsy
- Fabry disease*
- Glaucoma
- HIV or AIDS
- Intractable spasticity
- Multiple Sclerosis

- Parkinson's Disease
- Post-surgical back pain with a condition called chronic radiculopathy*
- Post-laminectomy syndrome*
- Post-traumatic Stress Disorder (PTSD)
- Severe psoriasis and psoriatic arthritis*
- Sickle cell disease*
- Ulcerative colitis*
- Other medical conditions may be approved by the Department of Consumer Protection

* approved by the programs physicians' board but awaiting regulatory approval

PATIENT POSSESSION LIMITS

One-month supply

HOME CULTIVATION

No

STATE-LICENSED DISPENSARIES

Yes

STATE-LICENSED DISPENSARIES OPERATIONAL

Yes

CAREGIVERS

Yes, a qualifying patient shall have not more than one primary caregiver at any time.

RECIPROCITY

No

CONTACT INFORMATION

Additional information for Connecticut patients and physicians regarding Public Act 12-55, An Act Concerning the Palliative Use of Marijuana is available online from the state Department of Consumer Protection, www.ct.gov/dcp.

DELAWARE
MEDICAL MARIJUANA LAW

QUALIFYING CONDITIONS

- Alzheimer's disease
- Amyotrophic Lateral Sclerosis
- Cachexia
- Cancer
- Chronic pain
- HIV/AIDS

- Intractable epilepsy*
- Nausea
- Post-traumatic Stress Disorder (PTSD)
- Seizures
- Severe and persistent muscle spasms

* If the qualifying patient is younger than 18 years of age, the recommending physician must be a pediatric neurologist, pediatric gastroenterologist, pediatric oncologist or pediatric palliative care specialist. Adolescent patients are only permitted to possess oils containing at least 15 percent CBD (and no more than 7 percent THC) and/or oils containing 15 percent THC acid (and no more than 7 percent THC).

PATIENT POSSESSION LIMITS

Six ounces

HOME CULTIVATION

No

STATE-LICENSED DISPENSARIES

Yes

STATE-LICENSED DISPENSARIES OPERATIONAL

Yes

CAREGIVERS

No

RECIPROCITY

No

CONTACT INFORMATION

Delaware Health and Social Services
Division of Public Health
http://dhss.delaware.gov/dph/hsp/medmarhome.html

DISTRICT OF COLUMBIA
MEDICAL MARIJUANA LAW

Status: Operational • Law Signed: 2010

QUALIFYING CONDITIONS

Any debilitating condition as recommended by a D.C.-licensed doctor

PATIENT POSSESSION LIMITS

Two ounces

HOME CULTIVATION

No

STATE-LICENSED DISPENSARIES ALLOWED

Yes, medical dispensaries may grow up to 500 plants on site at any one time. Both non-profit and for-profit organizations are eligible to operate the dispensaries.

STATE-LICENSED DISPENSARIES OPERATIONAL

Yes

MEDICAL MARIJUANA STATUTES

D.C. Act 13-138 §2 (3) (2010)

CAREGIVERS

Yes, a caregiver is a person designated by a qualifying patient as the person authorized to possess, obtain from a dispensary, dispense, and assist in the administration of medical marijuana. The caregiver must be 18 years of age or older. The caregiver must be registered with the Department as the qualifying patient's caregiver. A caregiver may only serve one qualifying patient at a time.

RECIPROCITY

No

CONTACT INFORMATION

D.C. City Council Committee on Health, http://dccouncil.us
D.C. Department of Health, http://doh.dc.gov/service/medical-marijuana-program.

HAWAII
MEDICAL MARIJUANA LAW

Status: Operational • Law Signed: 2000

QUALIFYING CONDITIONS

- Cachexia
- Cancer
- Chronic pain
- Crohn's disease
- Glaucoma

- HIV or AIDS
- Nausea
- Post-traumatic stress
- Persistent muscle spasms
- Seizures

PATIENT POSSESSION LIMITS

Four ounces of usable marijuana at any given time, jointly possessed between the qualifying patient and the primary caregiver. "Usable marijuana" does not include the seeds, stalks, and roots of the plant.

HOME CULTIVATION

Yes, no more than seven marijuana plants, whether immature or mature

STATE-LICENSED DISPENSARIES ALLOWED

Yes. The state Department of Health has until January 4, 2016 to finalize rules governing the dispensary program. Licensed dispensaries are anticipated to be operational by July 15, 2016. Once operational, qualified patients will be able to obtain up to four ounces of cannabis or cannabis-infused products, such as oils, tinctures, or lozenges, from a licensed provider every 15 days.

MEDICAL MARIJUANA STATUTES

Haw. Rev. Stat. §§ 329-121 to 329-128 (2008)
Haw. Rev. Stat. §§329-121; 329-123 (b),(c) (2008)

CAREGIVERS

Yes, primary caregiver is a person who has the responsibility for managing the well-being of the qualifying patient with respect to the medical use of marijuana. Primary caregiver is a person other than the qualifying patient, or the patient's physician. The caregiver must be 18 years of age or older. Qualifying patients shall have only one primary caregiver an any given time. Primary caregiver shall be responsible for the care of only one qualifying patient at any given time.

RECIPROCITY

No

CONTACT INFORMATION

Hawaii Department of Health, Medical Marijuana Registry:
http://health.hawaii.gov/medicalmarijuana

ILLINOIS
MEDICAL MARIJUANA LAW

Status: Not Yet Operational • Law Signed: 2013

QUALIFYING CONDITIONS

- Alzheimer's disease
- Amyotrophic Lateral Sclerosis (ALS)
- Arnold Chiari malformation
- Cachexia/wasting syndrome
- Cancer
- Causalgia
- Chronic Inflammatory Demyelinating Polyneuropathy
- Complex regional pain syndrome type 2
- Crohn's Disease
- Dystonia
- Fibromyalgia
- Fibrous dysplasia
- Glaucoma
- Hepatitis C
- HIV/AIDS
- Hydrocephalus
- Hydromyelia
- Interstitial Cystitis
- Lupus
- Multiple Sclerosis
- Muscular Dystrophy
- Myasthenia Gravis
- Myoclonus
- Nail patella syndrome
- Neurofibromatosis
- Parkinson's disease
- Reflex Sympathetic Dystrophy (RSD)
- Rheumatoid Arthritis
- Sjogren's syndrome
- Spinal cord disease
- Spinocerebellar Ataxia (SCA)
- Syringomyelia
- Tarlov cysts
- Tourette's syndrome
- Traumatic brain injury and post-concussion syndrome

PATIENT POSSESSION LIMITS

Two and a half ounces of cannabis per 14-day period

HOME CULTIVATION

No

STATE-LICENSED DISPENSARIES

Yes

STATE-LICENSED DISPENSARIES OPERATIONAL

Not yet

CAREGIVERS

Yes, caregivers, who may serve only one patient, are permitted to pick up medicine for very ill, homebound patients and are also subject to possession limit.

RECIPROCITY

No

CONTACT INFORMATION

Illinois Department of Public Health:
www.dph.illinois.gov/topics-services/prevention-wellness/medical-cannabis.

MAINE
MEDICAL MARIJUANA LAW

Status: Operational • Law Signed: 1999

QUALIFYING CONDITIONS

- Alzheimer's disease
- Amyotrophic Lateral Sclerosis
- Cachexia or wasting syndrome
- Cancer
- Chronic pain
- Crohn's disease
- Epilepsy
- Glaucoma
- Hepatitis C

- HIV or AIDS
- Huntington's disease
- Inflammatory bowel disease
- Multiple Sclerosis
- Nausea
- Nail-patella syndrome
- Parkinson's disease
- Post-traumatic stress disorder (PTSD)

PATIENT POSSESSION LIMITS

Two and one-half ounces

HOME CULTIVATION

Yes, patients (or their primary caregivers) may possess no more than six mature marijuana plants

STATE-LICENSED DISPENSARIES ALLOWED

Yes, a minimum of eight

STATE-LICENSED DISPENSARIES OPERATIONAL

Yes

MEDICAL MARIJUANA STATUTES

Me. Rev. Stat. Tit. 22, §2423-D (2010)
Me. Rev. Stat. Tit. 22, §§2422; 2425 (2010)
Me. Rev. Stat. tit. 22, § 2383-B(5), (6) (1999) (amended 2001)
Me. Rev. Stat. tit. 22, § 2383-B(3)(e) (amended 2001)

CAREGIVERS

Yes, primary caregiver is a person providing care for the registered patient. The caregiver must be 21 years of age or older. The caregiver can never have been convicted of a disqualifying drug offense. Patients can name one or two primary caregivers. (Only one person may be allowed to cultivate marijuana for a registered patient).

RECIPROCITY

Yes, authorizes visiting qualifying patient with valid registry identification card (or its equivalent), to engage in conduct authorized for the registered patient (the medical use of marijuana) for 30 days after entering the State, without having to obtain a Maine registry identification card. Visiting qualifying patients are not authorized to obtain in Maine marijuana for medical use.

CONTACT INFORMATION

Statement of Maine's Medicinal Marijuana Law:
http://norml.org/pdf_files/ME_Medicinal_Marijuana_Regulations_Summary.pdf

MARYLAND
MEDICAL MARIJUANA LAW

Status: Not Yet Operational • Law Signed: 2014

QUALIFYING CONDITIONS

- Cachexia, Anorexia, or Wasting Syndrome
- Chronic Pain
- Nausea

- Seizures
- Severe or persisitent muscle spasms

PATIENT POSSESSION LIMITS

30-day supply. Edible forms of cannabis are not permitted.

HOME CULTIVATION

No

STATE-LICENSED DISPENSARIES

Yes

STATE-LICENSED DISPENSARIES OPERATIONAL

Not yet

CAREGIVERS

No

RECIPROCITY

No

CONTACT INFORMATION

Natalie M. LaPrade Medical Cannabis Commission:
http://mmc.maryland.gov.

MASSACHUSETTS
MEDICAL MARIJUANA LAW

Status: Operational • Law Signed: 2013

QUALIFYING CONDITIONS

- Amyotrophic Lateral Sclerosis (ALS)
- Cancer
- Crohn's disease
- Glaucoma
- HIV or AIDS

- Hepatitis C
- Multiple Sclerosis
- Parkinson's disease
- Other conditions as determined in writing by a qualifying patient's physician

PATIENT POSSESSION LIMITS

Sixty-day supply

HOME CULTIVATION

Yes, limited amounts.

STATE-LICENSED DISPENSARIES ALLOWED

Yes, no more than 35 state-licensed dispensaries allowed.

STATE-LICENSED DISPENSARIES OPERATIONAL

Yes

MEDICAL MARIJUANA STATUTES

105 CMR 725.000

CAREGIVERS

Yes, individual patients will be permitted to designate a "personal caregiver" at least 21 years old to cultivate for them if they are unable to access a state-authorized dispensary or if they can verify "financial hardship."

RECIPROCITY

No

CONTACT INFORMATION

Massachusetts Patient Advocacy Alliance, www.compassionforpatients.com

MICHIGAN
MEDICAL MARIJUANA LAW

Status: Operational • Law Signed: 2008

QUALIFYING CONDITIONS

- Alzheimer's disease
- Amyotrophic Lateral Sclerosis
- Cachexia or wasting syndrome
- Cancer
- Chronic pain
- Crohn's disease
- Glaucoma

- HIV or AIDS
- Hepatitis C
- Nail patella
- Nausea
- Post-traumatic stress disorder (PTSD)
- Seizures
- Severe and persistent muscle spasms

PATIENT POSSESSION LIMITS

Two and one-half ounces of usable marijuana.

HOME CULTIVATION

Yes, no more than 12 marijuana plants kept in an enclosed, locked facility. OR, outdoor plants must not be "visible to the unaided eye from an adjacent property when viewed by an individual at ground level or from a permanent structure" and must be "grown within a stationary structure that is enclosed on all sides, except the base, by chain-link fencing, wooden slats, or a similar material that prevents access by the general public and that is anchored, attached or affixed to the ground, located on land that is owned, leased, or rented" by the registered grower and restricted to that grower's access.

STATE-LICENSED DISPENSARIES ALLOWED

No

MEDICAL MARIJUANA STATUTES

Mich. Comp. Law § 333.26424(j) (2008)
Mich. Comp. Law §§ 333.26423; 333.26426(d) (2008)

CAREGIVERS

Yes, primary caregiver is a person who has agreed to assist with a patient's medical use of marijuana. The caregiver must be 21 years of age or older. The caregiver can never have been convicted of a felony involving illegal drugs, or must not have been convicted of any felony within the last ten years, or any violent felony ever. Each patient can only have one primary caregiver. The primary caregiver may assist no more than 5 qualifying patients with their medical use of marijuana. State-qualified caregivers must not have been convicted of any felony within the last ten years, or any violent felony ever.

RECIPROCITY

Yes, other state, district, territory, commonwealth, or insular possession of the U.S. must offer reciprocity to have reciprocity in Michigan.

CONTACT INFORMATION

Michigan Medical Marijuana Program (MMMP):
Michigan.gov/mmp

Michigan Medical Marijuana Association:
http://michiganmedicalmarijuana.org/

MINNESOTA
MEDICAL MARIJUANA LAW

Status: Operational • Law Signed: 2014

QUALIFYING CONDITIONS

- Amyotrophic Lateral Sclerosis
- Cancer/cachexia
- Crohn's disease
- Glaucoma
- HIV/AIDS

- Seizures
- Severe and persistent muscle spasms
- Terminal illness
- Tourette's Syndrome

PATIENT POSSESSION LIMITS

30-day supply but only non-smokable preparations allowed

HOME CULTIVATION

No

STATE-LICENSED DISPENSARIES

Yes

STATE-LICENSED DISPENSARIES OPERATIONAL

Yes

CAREGIVERS

No

RECIPROCITY

No

CONTACT INFORMATION

Minnesota Department of Health, www.health.state.mn.us/topics/cannabis.

MONTANA
MEDICAL MARIJUANA LAW

Status: Operational • Law Signed: 2004

QUALIFYING CONDITIONS

- Cachexia or wasting syndrome
- Cancer
- Chronic pain
- Crohn's disease
- Glaucoma

- HIV/AIDS
- Nausea
- Seizures
- Severe or persistent muscle spasms

PATIENT POSSESSION LIMITS

One ounce

HOME CULTIVATION

Yes, four mature plants, up to 12 seedlings

STATE-LICENSED DISPENSARIES ALLOWED

No

MEDICAL MARIJUANA STATUTES

Montana Medical Marijuana Act, Mont. Code Ann. §§ 50-46-1 to 50-46-2 (2007)

CAREGIVERS

Yes, caregivers may accept no monetary compensation for providing cannabis to qualified patients.

RECIPROCITY

No

CONTACT INFORMATION

Montana Department of Public Health and Human Services, http://dphhs.mt.gov/marijuana.

NEVADA
MEDICAL MARIJUANA LAW

Status: Operational • Law Signed: 2001

QUALIFYING CONDITIONS

- AIDS
- Cachexia
- Cancer
- Glaucoma

- Post-traumatic stress disorder (PTSD)
- Persistent muscle spasms or seizures
- Severe nausea or pain
- Other conditions are subject to approval

PATIENT POSSESSION LIMITS

Two and one-half ounces and/or a maximum allowable quantity of edible marijuana products and marijuana-infused products as established by regulation of the Division.

HOME CULTIVATION

Yes, 12 mature plants. Limits on home cultivation if patients reside within 25 miles of an operating dispensary. However, patients who are cultivating specific strains of cannabis not provided by a local dispensary may continue to engage in the home cultivation of such strains. Patients who have an established history of cultivating medical cannabis prior to July 1, 2013, also may continue to do so until March 31, 2016.

STATE-LICENSED DISPENSARIES ALLOWED

Yes

STATE-LICENSED DISPENSARIES OPERATIONAL

Yes

MEDICAL MARIJUANA STATUTES

Nev. Rev. Stat. §§ 453A.010 - 453A.240 (2008)
Nev. Rev. Stat. Ann. §§435A.080(1)(a), (2); 435A.250(2) (2008)

CAREGIVERS

Yes, designated primary caregiver is a person who has significant responsibility for managing the well-being of a person diagnosed with a chronic or debilitating medical condition. Caregiver does not include the attending physician. The caregiver must be 18 years of age or older. Patients may only have one designated primary caregiver.

RECIPROCITY

Yes

CONTACT INFORMATION

Application information for the Nevada medical marijuana registry is available by writing or calling:
Nevada Department of Health and Human Services, Nevada State Health Division
4150 Technology Way, Suite 104
Carson City, Nevada 89706
Phone: 775-687-7594
Fax: 775-684-4156
http://dpbh.nv.gov.

NEW HAMPSHIRE
MEDICAL MARIJUANA LAW

Status: Not Yet Operational • Law Signed: 2013

QUALIFYING CONDITIONS

- ALS
- Alzheimer's disease
- Cachexia
- Cancer
- Chemotherapy induced anorexia
- Chronic pancreatitis
- Crohn's disease
- Elevated intraocular pressure
- Epilepsy
- Glaucoma
- Hepatitis C (currently receiving antiviral treatment)
- HIV/AIDS

- Lupus
- Moderate to severe vomiting
- Multiple Sclerosis
- Muscular Dystrophy
- Nausea
- Parkinson's disease
- Persistent muscle spasms
- Seizures
- Severe pain (that has not responded to previously prescribed medication)
- Spinal cord injury or disease
- Traumatic brain injury
- Wasting syndrome

PATIENT POSSESSION LIMITS

Two ounces

HOME CULTIVATION

No

STATE-LICENSED DISPENSARIES

Yes, no more than four

STATE-LICENSED DISPENSARIES OPERATIONAL

Not yet

CAREGIVERS

No

RECIPROCITY

Yes, for patients with conditions that are also classified as qualifying conditions in New Hampshire. Out-of-state patients may not service New Hampshire dispensaries, but may legally possess medical marijuana if they have entered the state with it.

CONTACT INFORMATION

New Hampshire Department of Health and Human Services, http://dhhs.state.nh.us/oos/tcp.

NEW JERSEY
MEDICAL MARIJUANA LAW

Status: Operational • Law Signed: 2010

QUALIFYING CONDITIONS

- Amyotrophic Lateral Sclerosis (ALS)
- Cancer (includes associated chronic pain and/or severe nausea)
- Crohn's disease
- Glaucoma
- HIV/AIDS (includes associated chronic pain and/or severe nausea)
- Inflammatory bowel disease (IBD)
- Multiple Sclerosis
- Muscular Dystrophy
- Seizure and/or spasticity disorders
- Any terminal illness if a doctor has determined the patient will die within a year

PATIENT POSSESSION LIMITS

Two ounces per month

HOME CULTIVATION

No

STATE-LICENSED DISPENSARIES

Yes, no more than six

STATE-LICENSED DISPENSARIES OPERATIONAL

Yes

MEDICAL MARIJUANA STATUTES

N.J. Stat. Ann. §§ 24-61-1-10 (2015)
N.J. Stat. Ann. §24:6I-3 (2010)

CAREGIVERS

Yes, primary caregiver is a person who has agreed to assist with a registered qualifying patient's medical use of marijuana. Primary caregiver cannot be the patient's physician. Primary caregiver must be a resident of New Jersey. The primary caregiver can never have been convicted of a felony drug offense. The caregiver must be 18 years of age or older. The caregiver may only have one qualifying patient at any one time.

RECIPROCITY

No

CONTACT INFORMATION

Medical Marijuana Program – Patient Registration Information:
http://www.state.nj.us/health/medicalmarijuana/pat_reg.shtml

New Jersey NORML:
http://www.normlnj.org

Coalition for Medical Marijuana – New Jersey:
http://www.cmmnj.org/

NEW MEXICO
MEDICAL MARIJUANA LAW

Status: Operational • Law Signed: 2007

QUALIFYING CONDITIONS

- Amyotrophic Lateral Sclerosis (Lou Gehrig's disease)
- Anorexia/cachexia
- Arthritis
- Cancer
- Cervical dystonia
- Chronic pain
- Crohn's disease
- Epilepsy
- Glaucoma
- Hepatitis C
- HIV/AIDS
- Hospice patients
- Huntington's disease
- Intractable nausea/vomiting
- Multiple sclerosis
- Painful peripheral neuropathy
- Parkinson's disease
- Post-traumatic Stress Disorder
- Spinal cord damage

PATIENT POSSESSION LIMITS

Six ounces of medical cannabis (or more if authorized by their physician)

HOME CULTIVATION

Yes, 16 plants (four mature, 12 immature)

STATE-LICENSED DISPENSARIES ALLOWED

Yes

STATE-LICENSED DISPENSARIES OPERATIONAL

Yes

MEDICAL MARIJUANA STATUTES

Lynn and Erin Compassionate Use Act, N.M. Stat. Ann. § 30-31C-1 (2007)
N.M. Stat. Ann. §26-2B-3(F) (2007)

CAREGIVERS

Yes, primary caregiver is designated by patient's practitioner as necessary to take responsibility for managing the well-being of a qualified patient with respect to the medical use of cannabis. Primary caregiver must be a resident of New Mexico. The caregiver must be 18 years of age or older.

RECIPROCITY

No

CONTACT INFORMATION

New Mexico Department of Health, http://nmhealth.org/about/mcp/svcs.

NEW YORK
MEDICAL MARIJUANA LAW

Status: Not Yet Operational • Law Signed: 2014

QUALIFYING CONDITIONS

- Amyotrophic Lateral Sclerosis (ALS)
- Cancer
- Epilepsy
- HIV/AIDS
- Huntington's Disease

- Inflammatory bowel disease
- Parkinson's Disease
- Multiple Sclerosis
- Neuropathies
- Spinal cord damage

PATIENT POSSESSION LIMITS

30-day supply but only non-smokable preparations allowed

HOME CULTIVATION

No

STATE-LICENSED DISPENSARIES

Yes, five producers of cannabis-based preparations and up to 20 dispensing centers to be licensed by the state.

STATE-LICENSED DISPENSARIES OPERATIONAL

Not yet

CAREGIVERS

No

RECIPROCITY

No

CONTACT INFORMATION

New York State Department of Health, www.health.ny.gov/regulations/medical_marijuana.

OREGON
MEDICAL MARIJUANA LAW

Status: Operational • Law Signed: 1998

QUALIFYING CONDITIONS

- Alzheimer's disease
- Cachexia
- Cancer
- Chronic pain
- Glaucoma
- HIV or AIDS

- Nausea
- Persistent muscle spasms
- Post-traumatic stress
- Seizures
- Other conditions are subject to approval

PATIENT POSSESSION LIMITS

Twenty-four ounces of usable cannabis

HOME CULTIVATION

Yes, six mature cannabis plants, 18 immature seedlings

STATE-LICENSED DISPENSARIES ALLOWED

Yes, a directory of state-licensed dispensaries is available online from Oregon.gov.

STATE-LICENSED DISPENSARIES OPERATIONAL

Yes

MEDICAL MARIJUANA STATUTES

Oregon Medical Marijuana Act, Or. Rev. Stat. § 475.300 (2007)
Or. Rev. Stat. §§ 475.302(5); 475.312(2) (2007)

CAREGIVERS

Yes, designated primary caregiver is the person that has significant responsibility for managing the well-being of a person who has been diagnosed with a debilitating medical condition. Primary caregiver does not include the patient's physician. The caregiver must be 18 years of age or older. A patient may only have one primary caregiver.

RECIPROCITY

No

CONTACT INFORMATION

Application information for the Oregon medical marijuana registry is available online at: https://public.health.oregon.gov/DiseasesConditions/ChronicDisease/MedicalMarijuanaProgram

RHODE ISLAND
MEDICAL MARIJUANA LAW

Status: Operational • Law Signed: 2006

QUALIFYING CONDITIONS

- Alzheimer's Disease
- Cachexia
- Cancer
- Chronic pain
- Crohn's disease
- Glaucoma

- Hepatitis C
- HIV/AIDS
- Nausea
- Persistent muscle spasms
- Seizures
- Other conditions are subject to approval

PATIENT POSSESSION LIMITS

Two and one-half ounces

HOME CULTIVATION

Yes, up to 12 plants and 12 seedlings. Must be stored in an indoor facility.

Two or more cardholders may cooperatively cultivate marijuana in residential or non-residential locations subject to the following restrictions:

Non-residential - no more than 10 ounces of usable marijuana, 48 mature marijuana plants, and 24 seedlings.

Residential - no more than 10 ounces of useable marijuana, 24 mature marijuana plants, and 12 seedlings.

STATE-LICENSED DISPENSARIES ALLOWED

Yes, no more than three

STATE-LICENSED DISPENSARIES OPERATIONAL

Yes

MEDICAL MARIJUANA STATUTES

R.I. Gen. Laws § 21-28.6-4(k) (2006)
R.I. Gen. Laws § 21-28.6 (2006)
R.I. Gen. Laws 1956, §21-28.6-3 (9) (2006)

CAREGIVERS

Yes, the caregiver must be 21 years of age or older. Primary caregiver may assist no more than 5 qualifying patients with their medical use of marijuana.

RECIPROCITY

Yes, authorizes a patient with a debilitating medical condition, with a registry identification card (or its equivalent), to engage in the medical use of marijuana. Also authorizes a person to assist with the medical use of marijuana by a patient with a debilitating medical condition.

CONTACT INFORMATION

State of Rhode Island Department of Health: www.health.ri.gov/healthcare/medicalmarijuana.
More helpful information can be found here: http://ripatients.org/.

VERMONT
MEDICAL MARIJUANA LAW

Status: Operational • Law Signed: 2004

QUALIFYING CONDITIONS

- Cachexia or wasting syndrome
- Cancer
- HIV or AIDS
- Multiple Sclerosis

- Seizures
- Severe pain
- Severe nausea

PATIENT POSSESSION LIMITS

Two ounces of usable marijuana

HOME CULTIVATION

Yes, no more than nine marijuana plants, of which no more than two may be mature.

STATE-LICENSED DISPENSARIES ALLOWED

Yes, no more than four. Dispensaries may lawfully engage in home delivery.

STATE-LICENSED DISPENSARIES OPERATIONAL

Yes

MEDICAL MARIJUANA STATUTES

Vt. Stat. Ann. tit. 18, §§ 4471- 4474d (2003)
Vt. Stat. Ann. Tit. 18, §4472(6); 4474(1),(2)(c) (2003)

CAREGIVERS

Yes, registered caregiver is a person who has agreed to undertake responsibility for managing the well-being of a registered patient with respect to the use of marijuana for symptom relief. The registered caregiver can never have been convicted of a drug-related crime. The caregiver must be 21 years of age or older. Patients may only have one registered caregiver at a time. Registered caregiver may serve only one registered patient at a time.

RECIPROCITY

No

CONTACT INFORMATION

Marijuana Registry
Department of Public Safety
103 South Main Street
Waterbury, Vermont 05671
802-241-5115
http://www.safeaccessnow.org/becoming_a_patient_in_vermont

WASHINGTON
MEDICAL MARIJUANA LAW

Status: Operational • Law Signed: 1998

QUALIFYING CONDITIONS

- Cachexia
- Cancer
- Crohn's disease
- Glaucoma
- Hepatitis C
- HIV or AIDS
- Intractable pain

- Persistent muscle spasms, and/or spasticity
- Nausea
- Post-Traumatic Stress Disorder
- Seizures
- Traumatic Brain Injury
- Any "terminal or debilitating condition"

PATIENT POSSESSION LIMITS

Those entered in the state's voluntary patient database may possess: 48 ounces of marijuana-infused product in solid form; 3 ounces of useable marijuana; 216 ounces of marijuana-infused product in liquid form; or 21 grams of marijuana concentrates.

HOME CULTIVATION

Those entered in the state's voluntary patient database may cultivate, in his or her domicile, up to six plants for the personal medical use and possess up to 8 ounces of useable marijuana produced from his or her plants. If the health care professional determines that the medical needs of a qualifying patient exceed the amounts provided, the health care professional may specify on the authorization that it is recommended that the patient be allowed to grow, in his or her domicile, up to 15 plants, yielding up to 16 ounces, of usable marijuana for the personal medical use of the patient.

If a qualifying patient has not been entered into the medical marijuana authorization database, he/she may grow, in his or her domicile, up to four plants for the personal medical use of the qualifying patient and possess up to 6 ounces of useable marijuana in his or her domicile.

STATE-LICENSED DISPENSARIES ALLOWED

No, but retail providers may also engage in the sale of medical cannabis.

MEDICAL MARIJUANA STATUTES

Wash. Rev. Code §§ 69.51A - 69.51A.901 (2007)
Wash. Rev. Code §§69.51A.010, 69.51A.040 (2007)

CAREGIVERS

Yes, a person who has been designated in writing by a patient to serve as a designated provider. The caregiver must be 21 years of age or older. The provider must also possess either authorization from the qualifying patient's health care professional or has been entered into an authorized database. The provider must only provide cannabis to the expressed patient.

RECIPROCITY

No

CONTACT INFORMATION

Washington State Department of Health, www.doh.wa.gov.

USING MARIJUANA IS A CIVIL LIBERTY

It's so easy to jump on a political-cause bandwagon regarding a simple issue that people readily applaud. For me, the great joy is finding an important cause that the general public doesn't readily understand or applaud, and then raising awareness so that they realize it is an evil in our society and its importance and correctness become simple.

That for me is the crusade to legalize marijuana. Perhaps because I've spent a third of my adult life traveling through Europe where laws are more pragmatic and less riddled with fear, I picked up the notion that a society needs to make a choice: tolerate alternative lifestyles or build more prisons. As I learned more about the reality of America's war on drugs, I saw a big evil and found my calling. That's when I stopped just stewing over it, joined NORML, and went public.

I am not pro-pot. I just believe that the responsible recreational use of marijuana among adults is a civil liberty. For me, speaking out on drug policy reform has been as patriotic as waving a flag. It's good citizenship.

In the last decade I've ramped my activism up, becoming a board member of NORML, working drug policy reform into my lectures around the country, going to conventions that grapple with the theme of not *should* we legalize but *how* do we legalize (something no political entity has actually done). Sure, a joint in the Netherlands is about as exciting as a can of beer, and they haven't arrested a pot smoker for decades. But smoking pot in Amsterdam is not legal and the entire back end (wholesale, production, distribution) remains murky, outside the law, and what they call "the grey area."

In the United States, I've advocated not just decriminalizing (and living with that "grey area") but finding a way to legalize, tax, and regulate the recreational sale of marijuana in a way that is pragmatic harm reduction. The goal: design a system that undercuts the black market by creating legal, taxable, and regulated businesses. And for these businesses to provide safe and reliable marijuana to recreational users, employment for people in that new industry, and taxes for state government (much of which is allocated to education and drug programs).

We're living in an age where drug policy is changing rapidly. To help advocates of drug policy reform as well as cannabis consumers' need to stay up to date, NORML has authorized this helpful new book. *The Citizen's Guide To State-By-State Marijuana Laws* is an essential companion for today's cannabis cultivators, sellers, and consumers in America. Hopefully, in the near future, a legal compendium such as this will be less necessary, but — especially during this period of rapid change — it is a timely and practical information source.

In my lectures I always acknowledge that marijuana is a drug, and it can be abused. But I also stress that it is a civil liberty. I like to say, "I'm a hard-working, church-going, kid-raising, tax-paying American citizen. If I work hard all day long and want to go home to light up a joint and just stare at the fireplace for three hours, that's my civil liberty. — *Rick Steves*

Rick Steves is a best-selling travel writer, TV host, and guide who serves on NORML's board of directors and was the co-petitioner in Washington State's successful political campaign to legalize marijuana in 2012.

ABOUT THE AUTHOR

Paul Armentano is the Deputy Director of NORML, the National Organization for the Reform of Marijuana Laws, and a Senior Policy Advisor for Freedom Leaf, Inc: The Marijuana Legalization Company. He also serves on the faculty of Oaksterdam University, where he lectures on the science in regard the the relative safety and therapeutic efficacy of cannabis.

Mr. Armentano's writing and research on marijuana policy have appeared in over 750 publications, scholarly and/or peer-reviewed journals, as well as in more than a dozen textbooks and anthologies. He is the co-author of the book *Marijuana is Safer: So Why Are We Driving People to Drink?* (2009, Chelsea Green), which has been licensed and translated internationally. Mr. Armentano is the 2013 Freedom Law School Health Freedom Champion of the Year and the 2013 Alfred R. Lindesmith Award recipient in the achievement in the field of scholarship.

He lives in California with his wife and son.

ACKNOWLEDGMENTS

The state-specific information contained in this book is the result of many hours of research and review by various members of the NORML staff. In particular, I wish to acknowledge the tireless efforts of Jennifer Goldstein, Laura Judy, and Jena Smith in compiling and updating these state-by-state charts and summaries. I would also like to thank NORML Founder Keith Stroup and NORML Executive Director Allen St. Pierre for their professional guidance and direction. — *Paul Armentano.*

Shutterstock/aastock